New Negro, Old Left

•

New Negro, Old Left
•

African-American Writing and Communism Between the Wars

William J. Maxwell

Columbia University Press
New York

Columbia University Press
PUBLISHERS SINCE 1893
New York   Chichester, West Sussex

Copyright © 1999 Columbia University Press
All rights reserved

An earlier version of chapter 3 originally appeared in *Radical Revisions: Rethinking* 1930s *Culture*, ed. Bill Mullen and Sherry Lee Linkon (Urbana: University of Illinois Press, 1996). Reprinted by permission of the publisher and the Board of Trustees of the University of Illinois. An earlier version of chapter 5 originally appeared in *Knowing Your Place: Rural Identity and Cultural Hierarchy*, ed. Barbara Ching and Gerald R. Creed (New York: Routledge, 1996). Copyright © 1996. Reproduced by permission of Routledge, Inc.

Credits continued on page 255

Library of Congress Cataloging-in-Publication Data

Maxwell, William J.
New Negro, old left : African-American writing and Communism
between the wars / William J. Maxwell.
p.   cm.
Includes bibliographical references and index.
ISBN 0–231–11424–9 (alk. paper).
ISBN 0–231–11425–7 (pbk. : alk. paper).
1. American literature—Afro-American authors—History and criticism.
2. Communism and literature—United States—History—20th century.
3. American literature—20th century—History and criticism.
4. Political fiction, American—History and criticism.
5. Right and left (Political science) in literature.
6. Afro-Americans—Intellectual life—20th century.
7. Afro-Americans—Politics and government.
8. Afro-Americans in literature. I. Title.
PS153.N5M269   1999
810.9´896073—dc21   98-52487

Printed in the United States of America
Designed by Ben Farber

c 10 9 8 7 6 5 4 3 2 1
p 10 9 8 7 6 5 4 3 2 1

In memory of my mother, Angela Giardina Maxwell (1937–1990)

Contents

Acknowledgments

My father, William J. Maxwell, Sr., the integrated schools of Jersey City and Teaneck, New Jersey, and two distinguished teachers—Amiri Baraka and J. Lee Greene—are responsible for my scholarly interest in African-American culture. To them I owe a deep thanks rivaled only by my gratefulness to those historians of American literary radicalism who embraced my work when it was even more obscure. Barbara Foley, Cary Nelson, and Alan Wald saw the wheat in the chaff and showed that the idea of a critical community was not oxymoronic. The generosity, intelligence, and commitment of all those above inform the good parts of what follows.

I have also had luck enough to live in three different academic settlements, located in two states and one canton, that forced me to think or sink. At Duke University in Durham, North Carolina, my dissertation committee was searching and encouraging. Tom Ferraro suggested something close to this book's title; Karla F. C. Holloway inspired me by sharing my words with her father; Susan Willis demonstrated the arts of specifying and staying true; and Jane Tompkins and my formidable director, Frank Lentricchia, offered friendship and needed tips on how to write outside the persona of a nervous classicist. Rick Roderick and Jane ought to know how much I continue to draw on their contrary but equally emphatic pedagogies. My shadow committee, composed of some of the sharpest graduate students in Blue Devil history, was headed by Martine De Vos, Paul Gripp, Marty Hipsky, Angela Hubler, Caren Irr, Carolyn Lesjak, and Joe McGeary. Tim Dayton, Dana Phillips, and Terry Whalen often eclipsed our official instructors in critical theory.

At the University of Geneva in Switzerland, Jay Blair provided an idyllic locale in which to teach and write, all the while introducing me to Swiss customs and the professional folkways of American Studies. Saba Bahar, Niall Bond, Wlad Godzich, Marie-Geneviève Iselin, André Kaenel, Roy Kay, Simone Oettli, Valeria Wagner, and Rick Waswo usefully commented on my works and days. Barbara Will, fellow *assistant* in American Literature and Civilization, allowed me to become a hanger-on and intellectual sibling. My students in classes on Ralph Ellison, modernism, and literary theory, perhaps still speaking English with New Jersey accents, alerted me to more than the high quality of Geneva's secondary schools.

Rarely have so many done so much for a new professor as at the University of Illinois in Urbana-Champaign. Nina Baym, Leon Chai, and Bob Parker carefully and perceptively read and reformed the manuscript; Michael Bérubé, Chester Fontenot, Stephanie Foote, Simon Joyce, and Cary Nelson sparked renovations of individual chapters and approaches. August Gering and Rochelle Rives, graduate students extraordinaire, saved me from errors of fact and expression, while their peers in seminars on the Harlem Renaissance and American modernisms sharpened and expanded my overall vision. Amanda Anderson and bad citizen Joe Valente donated especially keen advice about the wilds of publishing. Karen Hewitt of the University of Illinois Press shared french fries and beneficial responses to an early book précis. Along with all these benefactors, Dennis Baron, Alice Deck, Jan Hinely, Jim Hurt, David Kay, Janet Lyon, Bruce Michelson, Carol Neely, Lori Newcomb, Rick Powers, Jack Stillinger, Zohreh Sullivan, and Dick Wheeler went out of their way to people the wide-open spaces.

This book would still be floating in ether without the aid of the University of Illinois Research Board and a Mellon Fellowship from the Harry Ransom Center at the University of Texas, Austin, where John Ratliff played host and interlocutor, as always. The Ransom Center staff was an instructive combination of enterprising and calming, as were the librarians of the Duke University Rare Book Room, the Library of Congress, the Schomburg Center for Research in Black Culture, and the Tamiment Institute at New York University. Scholars I met at these collections and other academic crossroads also helped the book mature. David Anderson, James D. Bloom, Barbara Ching, Gerald Creed, Gerald Early, Bob Gross, Gary Holcomb, Arthur Knight, Sherry Linkon, Bill Mullen, Larry Rodgers, Jim Smethurst, Werner Sollors, Tyrone Tillery, Kathleen Wallace, Craig Werner, Jeff Williams, and the late Franklin Folsom answered inquiries, evaluated pages and proposals, and swapped cautionary tales.

Ann Miller, my editor at the Columbia University Press, drove matters from convention-floor spiel to bound volume with amazing speed and sureness; her assistant, Alexander Thorp, made phoning Manhattan a counterintuitive experience of cordiality. Columbia's reviewers turned the manuscript into an appreciably better place to live and work; copyeditor Sarah St. Onge led a crash course in fine points that matter; and Do Mi Stauber skillfully constructed the index.

Above, beyond, and beneath these acknowledgments, however, is my love for Julia Walker, in whose house on Capitol Landing Road the majority of this book was written and in whose eyes alone I will know its quality. In her is the soul of courage, the best of philosophical minds, and all the kindness of the Walkers. To the Moores, Maxwells, Binders, Riegers, and Giardinas, mazel tov.

William J. Maxwell
Champaign, Illinois
October 1998

New Negro, Old Left

•

Introduction: Black and Red All Over?

Howard "Stretch" Johnson, a charismatic Harlemite who graduated from Cotton Club dancer to Communist youth leader, once claimed that in late-1930s New York "75% of black cultural figures had [Communist] Party membership or maintained a regular meaningful contact with the Party" (qtd. in Naison 193). He stretched the truth, but barely. Between the world wars, Harlem salons increasingly rang with talk of Communist drives against lynch law, "white chauvinism," and less immediate, imperial enemies of black freedom. Especially during the Great Depression, it was not always easy to distinguish Communist Party rolls from lists of prominent Harlem artists, the recurring names on the cultural pages of *The Daily Worker* from those in the black-owned *Amsterdam News*. This book examines why so many interwar African-American writers in particular moved to the "Old," Soviet-allied Communist left and what they created once there, in and beyond black Manhattan. Unlike most previous takes on the subject, it assumes that these questions cannot be pursued without acknowledging both modern black literature's debt to Communism and Communism's debt to modern black literature. The Old Left, normally sketched as a dire scene of white connivance and black self-cancellation, in truth promoted a spectrum of exchanges between black and white authors, genres, theories, and cultural institutions. Red interracialisms of word and deed, I argue, opened two-way channels between radical Harlem and Soviet Moscow, between the New Negro renaissance and proletarian literature. Without conjuring up an Edenic red past for happy-family multiculturalism, I propose that Communism's rare sustenance for African-American initiative and crossracial adventure was an urgent reason why scores of literary "New Negroes" became Old Leftists—and the major reason why the disillusion of a canonical handful would be so outspoken. Ultimately, I suggest that recognizing black volition and interracial education on the Old Left is crucial to understanding weighty developments in the history of U.S. racial and radical cultures, from the stumbles and small victories of American anticapitalism, to the mapping of African-American writing onto modernity, to the intimate contact between black and white American modernisms.[1]

Minus the glaring absence of Nella Larsen, Zora Neale Hurston, and several other Harlem Renaissance principals, the gallery of black literary intellectuals variously affiliated with Communism in the 1920s and 1930s makes a fair who's who of African-American writing from the same decades. Richard Wright, once classed as the exemplary black author of the period, joined the party with gusto. So did Harlem Renaissance instigator Claude McKay, whom federal intelligence agencies imagined as "President of the Negro Section of the Executive Committee of the 3rd International" (United States, 19 January 1923).[2] Unlikely party member Countee Cullen endorsed the Communists' 1932 national election ticket (James W. Ford, the party's choice for vice president, was the first African-American candidate for the office in U.S. history). Longstanding fellow traveler Langston Hughes, compelled to disclaim party membership before Senator Joseph McCarthy's investigating committee in 1953, could not deny having served as president of the Communist League of Struggle for Negro Rights. Like McKay, Louise Thompson, Dorothy West, and sometime essayist Paul Robeson, Hughes had in fact toured the Soviet home of Communism in action. William Attaway, Arna Bontemps, Gwendolyn Brooks, Sterling Brown, Frank Marshall Davis, Owen Dodson, Ralph Ellison, Robert Hayden, Chester Himes, Melvin Tolson, Margaret Walker, and Theodore Ward all wrote or edited or apprenticed within the Old Left's literary networks. By the late 1930s Alain Locke, the preeminent entrepreneur of black modernism, had become a regular at party-sponsored gatherings, praising Soviet answers to the race problem and linking the Harlem Renaissance he had touted to "the class proletarian art creed of today's younger generation" ("Resume"). W. E. B. Du Bois, predictor of the century's "problem of the color line" (*The Souls* xi), closed out the decade defending the Hitler-Stalin pact along with the value of Marxist historiography. Given the sheer extent of this involvement with Communism, it is neither ironic nor incidental that the most celebrated single text in the African-American canon, Ralph Ellison's *Invisible Man*, lavishes hundreds of pages on its hero's career as a Communist word slinger. The history of African-American letters cannot be unraveled from the history of American Communism without damage to both.

New Negro, Old Left is motivated by the belief that the inseparability of these two histories qualifies among the least understood features of modern black writing. Well after 1989's lyric revolutions sparked arguments over the end of class history, Communism haunts African-American literary studies more as a dusty specter than as a vital, reopened controversy. Admittedly, those versed in the scholarship on black writers' excursions into the Old Left may not find this too regrettable. Otherwise dissimilar postwar critical generations agreed that Communism proved hazardous to the health of African-American writing. All found that the party's dedication to some combination of Stalin, white power, and socialist realism impinged on the black tradition's autonomous unfolding and indigenous sources of vernacular nourishment. An entry in the index to James O. Young's *Black Writers of the Thirties* (1973) puts the chronic judgment succinctly: "Communist party: stultifying influence of" (253). The steady discovery of red obstacles in the path of black literary evolution suggested tragic literary-historical emplotments. Mark Naison observes that "manipulation, disillusionment, and betrayal" are the three dynamics through which political historians have typically viewed the black encounter with Communism (xv). In literary history per se, this trio provided a beginning, middle, and end to narratives of black writers suffering near-death experiences in party clutches.

Manipulation, disillusionment, and betrayal are spotlit, of course, throughout the discourses that sustained the second American red scare, ignited in the wake of World War II. The prevalence of tragic plot points in postwar scholarship on black literature and the Old Left partially reflects the long intellectual reach of cold war anti-Communism. For special reasons, African-Americanist criticism was not specially resistant to this reach: performance bans and passport denials made Robeson and Du Bois striking, precautionary examples of the costs of resisting the crackdown; adversaries of the civil rights movement, J. Edgar Hoover at their head, maddeningly saw Soviet agents behind every sit-in.[3] Meanwhile, some of the biggest symbols and brokers of the engagement between African-American writing and the Old Left had metamorphosed into vocal advocates of divorce. The first wave of disaffection reached bookstores in 1940, delivering McKay's party-bashing Baedeker *Harlem: Negro Metropolis*. In 1950 Wright's "I Tried to Be a Communist," drawn from a repressed section of his autobiography, appeared in the English-language bible of Communist apostasy, *The God That Failed*. The year 1953 brought Wright's existential novel *The Outsider*, with its export of anti-Communist themes to the European shores of the Black Atlantic. Of more lasting influence were the cases for black-Communist separation detected in what became benchmark African-American fictions of midcentury and pervasive classroom primers in blackness: Wright's *Native Son* (1940) and Ellison's *Invisible Man* (1952). Despite Ellison's oedipal striving with Wright's tome and Wright's comparatively fraternal admonition of the party, both these explosive novels were read to license cautionary histories of African-

American contacts with Communism. Both, imprinted by the battle lines of the 1930s, wound up boosting the mistaken impression that the Depression's passing signaled a mass return of black writers from the left fringe. Both helped to conflate red crimes and misdemeanors with America's white problem. In *Invisible Man*, Ellison distinctly figures the party as another pale patron holding puppet strings, one more shortsighted white projector onto the screen of blackness.[4]

The blooming institutional power of *Native Son* and *Invisible Man* fostered the stultification line on black party writing as the cold war warmed and ended. If proponents of black nationalist aesthetics in the late 1960s and 1970s borrowed anything outright from anti-Communist liberalism, it was just this line, now wielded against the integrationism of earlier black radicals and a crop of younger white leftists calling themselves new. Harold Cruse's *The Crisis of the Negro Intellectual* (1967), the unignorable nationalist survey of the black intellectual past, tracked the faults of forty years of black writing to a program of white Communist discipline born in the 1920s.[5] Indispensable challenges to black nationalist criticism issued by African-American feminism and black vernacular theory in the 1980s and early 1990s refrained from questioning this criticism's wisdom on black writers under red management. In their common project of reversing the midcentury victory of Wright's example over Hurston's, feminist and vernacular critics often banked on Communism's supposed hostility to black folk materials and their textualization.[6] For more recent studies reenvisioning a literary modernism jointly authored by blacks and whites, the written record of then-unrivaled integration on the Old Left shows little trace of either interracial mutuality or admiring white investments in the racial Other. Vintage truths about the party's manhandling of black writers here illuminate a modern nadir of crossracial contact, one in which white writers honor only the criminal element in their love and theft of blackness. Ironically, that pocket of twentieth-century U.S. literature that adopted interracialism most earnestly in its texts—and rather literally in its institutions—is unveiled as an exception to the rule of "mulatto modernism."[7] Even after the Soviet Union has sunk into memory and academic Marxisms have become old school, the cold war–derived verdict on blacks and Reds thus still polarizes Communism and African-American literary achievement. To this day, semester after semester, thousands of U.S. high school and college students are taught the justice of Wright's and Ellison's profiles in Communist racial hypocrisy. *Invisible Man* indeed remains one of a diminishing few must-read inscriptions of U.S. anti-Communism, an ideology that English majors may now know most vividly as a black intellectual response to false "Brotherhood."

What is troubling about the persistent verdict against black-Communist association is not its aversion to Stalinism, no less a valid sign of the Old Left's blindness without insight than what Vivian Gornick calls an "armor-plated word . . . deny[ing] the teeming, contradictory life behind it" (19). U.S. literary Communism took scant dictation from Moscow,[8] but it did pledge itself to what became a Stalin-devoted national party, one whose zest for the dictator's Soviet and international policies was second to none from the 1930s through the 1956 Khrushchev revelations.[9] As I will show, African-American Communists receiving Soviet support for race-radical initiatives were as likely as nonblack peers to trust Stalin's benevolence. No more objectionable is the detection of vestiges of political calculation and white intransigence within the Communist approach to the "Negro Question." The party hoped to transform U.S. realpolitik and to hurry racial capitalism to its grave but failed to transcend either. What is inadequate about the verdict, however, is the supposition that the meeting of black and white Reds remade only the black. With its appetite for evidence of white seduction and betrayal of black mouthpieces, the cautionary history joins fifty years of red squads in assuming that black intellectuals were incapable of transforming their party or their white radical counterparts, save through denunciations issued after escape. Such history thus begins by denying African-American literary Communists what it would seem finally to prize: a historically consequential self-direction. Postessentialist accounts of racial identity, post–cold war revisions of U.S. radical culture, and postsegregationist studies of America's literatures make the present high time to rethink this debilitating premise.[10]

New Negro, Old Left accordingly reviews the bonds between black writing and Communism with eyes open for African-American agency, understood in this case as a fully historical ability to affect Old Left history, not an ever-ready, subjective power to decree it. Along with the *posts* just mentioned, this agenda obviously takes cues from what Arthur A. Schomburg, writing in 1925, could already describe as a fundamental conclusion of black historical research: "that the Negro has been . . . an active collaborator, and often a pioneer, in the struggle for his own freedom and advancement" (232). My attention to black Communist initiative is comparably informed by the findings of presently active scholars of U.S. radicalism. Innovative critics of U.S. radical literature such as Barbara Foley, James A. Miller, and Alan Wald have begun to reconsider the purported abuse of black writers by the Old Left, underscoring the wide range and post-

Depression life of African-American involvements with Communism, the surprising literary utility of selected party guidelines, and the prefiguration of Black Arts movement methods.[11] Leading new historians of U.S. Communism such as Robin D. G. Kelley and Mark Naison have minimized neither the party's intermittent successes in organizing African-American communities nor the power of these communities to rescript party lines and languages.[12]

This book could not have been written without these influences, whose specific impacts are discussed in individual chapters. Yet it also departs from them in several respects. Most important, it enlarges the historical frame to encompass the 1920s.[13] Instead of fixing on the Old Left's Depression heyday, the book's first half explores the encounter between black and white, U.S.- and Soviet-based radicals during the Harlem Renaissance, a moment when the definition of a modern New Negro and the direction of the young Soviet Union were still up for grabs and still perceived as related matters. Working-class Harlem internationalists impressed by both the Russian Revolution and a local pro-Soviet left forged links between African-American writing and the Old Left while angling to jump-start Harlem's rebirth. The red decades in black literature began in a rocky, sometimes mostly rhetorical Harlem-proposed alliance, not in a Depression-fed enlistment of literary innocents. I offer this alternative tale of origins in the interest of more than novelty or the measured long view. The pressure African-American writers brought to bear on Communism throughout the interwar period was rooted in the thought, aura, and sociology of the 1920s renaissance of the New Negro, if not wholly dependent on them. In this renaissance's blazing of black routes into international modernity, together with the contemporaneous Great Migration of African Americans into the northern, urban proletariat, interwar black intellectuals found firm ground from which to budge U.S. radicalism.

My identification of a black working-class protagonist at the commencement of the New Negro–Old Left union also clarifies overlooked efforts by renaissance intellectuals to "blacken" anticapitalist tactics and rhetorics. From the late teens into the twenties, black Old Leftists such as Claude McKay cross-examined the customary socialist contention that racism was a doomed by-product of class domination and pleaded the centrality of black workers to U.S. class struggle, class consciousness, and class representation. These leftists anticipated present-day whiteness studies in revisiting the history of militant white identifications to detach them from the engines of U.S. working-class insurgency. They first conceived of the contradictory unity between left integrationism and black nationalism lately detected in Depression-era proletarian fictions of race.[14] At their most ambitious, they envisioned joint ventures between two of modernity's immanent counterlogics: Marxism, whose materialist criticism and dialectical vision dissect the advantages as well as the impoverishments of modern capitalism, urbanization, and industrialization; and the vernacular culture of the descendants of African slaves, whose utopias target the toll on body and soul of modernity's racial oppression.[15]

Such efforts were pursued with varying degrees of energy and rarely received instant praise from mainstream intellectual organs or the U.S. Communist Party. Their successes can be discerned, however, by scanning the negotiations of African-American literary intellectuals with official Communist versions of "white" Marxist theory and with white literary peers who likewise depicted changing equations among blackness, labor, and modernity. My emphasis on these two underexamined types of interracial exchange further differentiates this study from its predecessors; more crucially, it discloses the shaping black presence within two of the Old Left's distinctive products: proletarian literature and a controversial nation-centered program for African America. Black pilgrims to the Soviet Union helped the Communist International decide on 1928's Black Belt Nation thesis, which projected an African-American southern nation, subject to special oppression but boasting a distinct, oppositional culture. The impracticality and inconsistent application of this thesis notwithstanding, its seductive promise to weld Marxism and black nationalism, black folk and proletarian cultures, pointed hundreds of African Americans to Communism during the 1930s. Black intellectuals such as Richard Wright thus had good reason to read the party as both a relative haven of integration and a reracializing institution offering privileged reconnection with the racy vernacular earth of the Black Belt. For their part, more than a few white (and particularly Jewish) writers, such as Mike Gold, embraced the party with assistance from their own affective relations to blackness and the hunch that Communist interracialism could solve the American dilemma. Proletarian literature, the Soviet-minded genre cast as the creature of these writers, fittingly evinces real and imaginary intimacies with African-American expression. The allure of Harlem's renaissance filtered into proletarianism's fictional and critical registers. And more: New Negro and proletarian literatures, the major, self-conscious movements of black and left-wing modernism in the United States, shared textual strategies and well-placed staff in both interwar decades. Protesting the imposition of an alien Communism on black writers shell-shocked by the Depression thus means ignoring the black provocation within salient party enterprises beginning in the 1920s. Without discounting limits and tensions set by a demanding, largely white party leadership, this book proposes that when African-American literature drew from 1930s Communism, it tapped a partial product of its own legacy. Among the typical Americanisms of the Old Left—whatever its allegiance to the Soviet Union—was an erratically conceded debt to blackness.

To African-American activist and essayist Louise Thompson, a onetime protégée of notorious Harlem Renaissance patron Charlotte Osgood Mason, the party at its Depression height represented an antidote to "white philanthropy" and the black "distaste and hatred" it incited (qtd. in Naison 43). For her, as throughout this study, the Old Left was no synonym for snow-white, no second coming of the altruistic "Negrotarianism" Hurston saw in renaissance infrastructures. All the same, Thompson's continuing low profile is an enduring index of the barriers erected by an Old Left culture that usually cultivated racial integration by imaging it as manly proletarian exercise. One concern cutting across this book's second half is how gender differences and engendered representations affected black writers' regard for Communism and their access to literary authority and interracial intimacy when aligned with it. Restrictive party visions of interracialism between men sharpened the anti-Communism of some African-American women writers. For other such writers moved by party struggles around race and poverty, however, these visions appear to have been troubling yet enabling literary problems; Thompson herself, for example, creatively disturbed the homosocial vocabulary of early Scottsboro protest literature with devices adopted from African-American women's discourses and alternate party-applauded forms. Less expectable is the book's conclusion that the limitations of homosocial interracial rhetoric were marked by Wright, the foremost black male voice of the Depression-era party.

New Negro, Old Left thus aims to offer a broad-ranging, multidimensional revisionary account of the intersection of African-American literature and Communism over two decades. As the hefty catalog of authors at the start of this introduction testifies, however, comprehensive reexamination of the Old Left as a primary site for modern black writing can only be a collective endeavor; if I manage to suggest something of the scale and reciprocity of the transactions this site hosted during a crucial slice of its life, I will rest easy. To this end, the book's six chapters address a variety of cruxes in literary history and cultural and political theory within an overarching narrative chronicle that mixes the archival and the interpretive.

Two eminent names—Claude McKay and Richard Wright—make repeat appearances amid a procession of well- and less-known black and white authors. Andy Razaf, Mike Gold, Langston Hughes, Louise Thompson, Zora Neale Hurston, and Nelson Algren each briefly take center stage. Similarly numerous are the genres in which I trace these figures' converse with Communism and with each other. Widely anthologized and newly rediscovered poems, plays, stories, novels, essays, and memoirs appear alongside less reputable song lyrics, personal correspondence, and political pamphlets. The book's multiform, interdisciplinary subject not just permits but requires such a large cast of texts, characters, and approaches.

The first three chapters address the Harlem Renaissance and the era between the end of World War I and the coming of the Great Depression. Chapter 1 joins the question of Communism's presence in the cultural field of this renaissance by scouting the early work of Andy Razaf. Best recalled—if at all—as the lyricist of the songs "Ain't Misbehavin' " and "Black and Blue," Razaf began his writing life at *The Crusader*, perhaps the first Harlem-based journal to summon "a renaissance of Negro power and culture" ("Aims of *The Crusader*" 1) and the first anywhere to bridge black nationalism and Soviet Marxism. Examining both careful poems and throwaway floor-show lyrics by Razaf, this chapter argues that white bolsheviks were desired company at Harlem's rebirth, that the *Crusader* group's black bolshevism sponsored expressive culture with a strategic impact on high and low renaissance art, and that Communism's conviction for the death of the renaissance is something of a frame-up. The New Negro's entrance onto the Old Left, I hold, was early, voluntary, and key to the formative modern instant in African-American intellectual life.

Chapter 2 recounts *Crusader* favorite Claude McKay's pilgrimage to the Soviet Union in 1922–23 and closely reads the treatise he wrote there, *The Negroes in America* (1923). It contends that McKay's revamping of classical Marxist ideas of self-realizing history, the naturalness of class consciousness, and the immateriality of race, culture, and desire penetrated the Comintern's Black Belt Nation thesis, the centerpiece of party policy on African America in the 1930s. By salvaging McKay's donation to Comintern thinking on race and the Negro Question, this chapter questions the assumption that black writers acquainted themselves with "official" Marxist theory without reshaping it.

Chapter 3 shifts attention from McKay's own work to his shadow in the literary labors of white party writer Mike Gold, early memorialist of the Jewish ghetto and long-expectant father of U.S. proletarian literature. The focus here is the determined response of Gold's criticism and fiction to

McKay and the greater Harlem Renaissance, a movement Gold first encountered while he and McKay coedited the Marxist *Liberator* in the early 1920s. With aid from *Hoboken Blues* (1927), Gold's forgotten antiminstrel show, the chapter disputes the precept that proletarian literature and the Harlem Renaissance were wholly discrete, antagonistic schools.

Chapter 4, the study's chronological pivot, leaves Gold and McKay behind to approach Communism's tendency to masculinize the very prospect of interracial radicalism during the early 1930s. In particular, I investigate how the party's admirable campaign to dismantle the triangular lynch myth of the black male rapist, the white female victim, and the white male protector initially installed another interracial-homosocial triangle. This antilynch triangle posed common distaste for white female accusers as the medium of affiliation between black and white male proletarians. By means of Langston Hughes's and Louise Thompson's writings on the Scottsboro case, I pursue a number of questions raised by these dueling, parallel triangles: Did Communist attacks on the rape myth paradoxically embolden anti-Communist myths of the party's dangling of white female bait, one more example of triangular-homosocial logic? Did triangular-homosocial representations of Communist interracialism promise writerly agency to male African-American authors at the cost of black female comrades, unaddressed in three-point plans for equality? Finally, how did black women connected with the party write their way through these triangles?

The last two chapters reconnoiter the early career and present reputation of Richard Wright to take a fresh look at African-American writing and Communism during the Great Depression. Chapter 5 mediates the debate between Wright and Zora Neale Hurston with reference to quarrels over the rural black folk within anthropology, sociology, and Communism. Wright's fascination with party ideas of a black southern nation, I maintain, temporarily powered a reinvestment in black vernacular culture close to that which Hurston derived from Boasian anthropology. The final section of the chapter tests this peacemaking against the representational violence of Wright's first book, the short-story collection *Uncle Tom's Children* (1938). It reinterprets climactic stories from this text as attempts to amalgamate the party's Black Belt Nation thesis with a revoicing of Hurston's folkloric fiction. Here, if not in a dismissive review of *Their Eyes Were Watching God* (1937), Wright's Communism did not keep him from rendering a Hurston also seen in the novels of later black women, "a literary forebear," notes Michael Awkward, "whose texts are celebrated even as they are revised, praised for their insights even when these insights are deemed inadequate" (8).

Chapter 6, the book's conclusion, relates the attachment between *Native Son* and Nelson Algren's *Somebody in Boots* (1935), the proletarian novel whose working title gave Wright's text its famous name. Though Wright and the white Algren were Chicago comrades and friends, their novels are antibuddy narratives. Each concludes with a black-white male pair failing to bond despite party prompting; each diagnoses infirmity in the New Negro–Old Left alliance initiated with the Harlem Renaissance. In the interracial interdependence of their sympathetic challenge to party interracialism, the novels nevertheless expose important gaps in the cautionary history of African-American writing and Communism, a history that Wright himself helped to frame and that the whole of this study hopes to unsettle.

My book-long reliance on "zebra vision"—seeing race in America as a program in black and white—matches the basic racial composition and racial imagination of interwar Communism. The patent blind spots produced by this binary lens are offset, I hope, by attention to the splits within the clumsy categories of whiteness and blackness and a persistent sense of these categories' mutable and mutual composition. My intermingling of tools drawn from African-American and "Eurocentric" theories needs less defense. Pierre Bourdieu and Henry Louis Gates, Jr., Hazel Carby and Eve Kosofsky Sedgwick cross paths in this book because of the previously crossed interracial history of modern radical thought. With Laura Doyle, I believe "it is not only that our theories are always already derived from white intellectual fathers, but also that 'their' theories have always already enfolded the social acts and intellectual insights of mothers, daughters, workers, servers, and Others" (preface n.p.). In the instance of the black leftists I consider here, such "social acts and intellectual insights" were not infrequently performed within the theory-producing bodies of the Old Left. Communist literary institutions, party headquarters, even the Kremlin closely witnessed black radical thought and at times consciously enfolded it within sanctioned Marxian policies and orientations. The theoretical combination perhaps most characteristic of this book's own analytical performance—ecumenical, unscientific Marxism plus various African-American historicist and vernacular modes—is thus not too unlike the combination deliberately, interracially produced when New Negroes came aboard the Old Left.

Though it centers on the dealings between Communism and African-American literary intellectuals, *New Negro, Old Left* is colored by several other controversies over attempts to grasp the present through the past. In the pages that follow, I directly address ongoing debates over the nature of the Harlem Renaissance, the gendered fault lines in interwar black culture, the balance of Soviet and local leverage in U.S. Communism, the recovery and periodization of African-American and proletarian literatures, and the mixed-race fiber of U.S. modernisms. I seek to do something about bisecting charges that African-American studies and a whole generation of humanists staring at the intersections of race, gender, sexuality, et cetera, rival the chamber of commerce in ignoring the social fact of class. Indirectly, I make a case for a literary history that neither flattens all walls between the literary and the historical nor inflates a wish-fulfilling politics of token cultural resistance. Finally, I hope to remind both reflexively anti-Marxist interpreters of black culture and race-weary proponents of economic fairness that many African-American modernists saw working-class interracialism as an arduous necessity, the final, elusive key to redeeming a society disfigured by racial slavery. At a juncture in which progressive intellectuals seek to connect the politics of identity with the politics of economic justice or to reconnect outright with unionism against spiking class inequality, the work of such New Negroes on the Old Left cannot be neglected with comfort; ironically, restoring their discounted contribution to this left's "failure" may ease the next left's successful arrival. Both the historical tragedy and achievement of U.S. radicalism are sounded in the dynamic black expression dedicated to the Old Left, a movement inspired and consumed by pro-Soviet choices and wider capitalist histories that it could not select. Even when surest of the faulty equivalence between socialism and the Soviet Union, this expression is frequently testimony to the African-American invention on which U.S. progressivism must draw: to borrow a rhetorical tic directly from the Old Left, it is no accident that the headiest days of U.S. anticapitalism were those of its tightest rapport with black art.

1 · Kitchen Mechanics and Parlor Nationalists: Andy Razaf, Black Bolshevism, and Harlem's Renaissance

The Negro is "seeing red."

> —Attorney General A. Mitchell Palmer, *Investigation Activities of the Department of Justice* (1919)

Of course, the thinking Negro has shifted a little toward the left with the world-trend, and there is an increasing group who affiliate with radical and liberal movements. But fundamentally for the present the Negro is radical on race matters, conservative on others, in other words, a "forced radical," a social protestant rather than a genuine radical. Yet under further pressure and injustice iconoclastic thought and motives will inevitably increase. Harlem's quixotic radicalisms call for their ounce of democracy to-day lest to-morrow they be beyond cure.

> —Alain Locke, *The New Negro* (1925)

The first extended musical allusion in Ralph Ellison's *Invisible Man* (1952), perhaps African-American literature's most insistently allusive and musical novel, involves a bluesy torch song with an axe to grind. Near the climax of the monologue that fills the novel's prologue, Ellison's unnamed, invisible narrator reveals a desire that would surely provoke his New York neighbors to violence if he lived anywhere but in an abandoned coal cellar. "I'd like to hear five recordings of Louis Armstrong playing and singing 'What Did I Do to Be so Black and Blue,' " he divulges, "all at the same time" (8). One recording won't do, because "there is a certain acoustical deadness in my hole, and when I have music I want to *feel* its vibration, not only with my ear but with my whole body" (8; emphasis in original). Yet Ellison's narrator is excited by more than the sensual pleasures of pumped-up volume. The alchemy to be heard as "Louis bends that military instrument into a beam of lyrical sound" offers this invisible man rare insights into time and history (8). Sampled along with a joint, Armstrong's version of "Black and Blue" can spark a surreal but illuminating descent into the racial past, complete with a rendezvous with slavery and a sermon on the elusive *"Blackness of Blackness"* (9; emphasis in original). Experienced under the influence of a legal dose "of vanilla ice cream and sloe gin," Armstrong's syncopated phrases can orchestrate the liquid, manifold awareness of time—"never quite on the beat"—that the narrator has come to recognize as the epistemological advantage of going unseen (8). "But what did *I* do to be so blue?" the invisible man asks in the prologue's concluding lines, annexing Armstrong's musical question as the key to his own history's meaning and casting the novel that unveils it as the libretto of "Black and Blue" (14; emphasis in original).

Apart from its status as an overture and narrative inducement, the version of "Black and Blue" heard by the invisible man earns its honored place among the novel's intertexts for its distillation of some of Ellison's abiding concerns: concerns with the masquerading of black tricksters who, like Satchmo, counter whites in visible and invisible blackface; with the attitudes toward history of those seemingly "outside the groove" of classical Marxism's teleological plottings (443); with jazz generally and the rehabilitation of Armstrong's post-bebop profile as a gifted Uncle Tom specifically. Given the novel's focal theme of black invisibility and its encyclopedic ransacking of black cultural archives, however, its failure to unveil the African American who first posed the overwhelming question of "Black and Blue" is at least ironic. Before Armstrong mock-innocently asked "(What Did I Do to Be So) Black and Blue?" the inquiry had been raised by Andy Razaf, who wrote the lyrics to the tune in 1929. Before the song appeared on any Armstrong disc, it had been the showstopper in a New York musical called *Hot Chocolates*, one of the many black revues of the decade that inspired Ziegfeld's *Follies* to grumble that "It's Getting Dark on Old Broadway." "Black and Blue" was the result of the kind of improvisational bravado that Ellison counted among the black gifts to American democracy. During rehearsals, Jewish mobster-impresario Dutch Schultz confronted the lyricist with a nonrefusable offer to add "a little 'colored girl' singing how tough it is to be 'colored' " (Singer 216). Razaf and his partner, Fats Waller, responded with what has often been called America's first popular song of racial protest.[1] In its original form, "Black and Blue" led with wickedly punning lyrics lamenting an interracial gentlemen's agreement from the point of view of a lonely, dark-skinned black woman. "Browns and yellers / All have fellers," went an introductory verse Armstrong would delete, "Gentlemen prefer them light. / Wish I could fade, / Can't make the grade, / Nothin' but dark days in sight." The choruses Armstrong favored issued their grievances from an ungendered angle available to all saddled with the myth of Ham:

> Just 'cause you're black, folks think you lack,
> They laugh at you and scorn you too,
> What did I do to be so black and blue?
> . . . .
>
> How sad I am, each day I feel worse,
> My mark of Ham seems to be a curse.
> How will it end?
> Ain't got a friend.
> My only sin is in my skin.
> What did I do to be so black and blue?

Why are readers of *Invisible Man* still unlikely to know that the novel unwittingly perpetuates Razaf's relative invisibility along with Armstrong's edit of "Black and Blue"?[2] Barry Singer, Razaf's biographer, attributes his subject's absence from a variety of historical repertoires to his anomalous career as a black song lyricist on Tin Pan Alley, a walking contradiction of the myth of the effortlessness of black musicianship and a hazard to the exploitation of black musicians that this myth threatened not at all (338). But Razaf's semiobscurity may also be due to his typicality. Some of the forgetting of Razaf, I believe, is an aspect of the forgetting of the black anticapitalists among whom he wrote and argued, New Yorkers who bid to direct a racial renaissance powered by the black working class years before Harlem's canonical vogue was declared in the mid-1920s. While Razaf's personal history seems bent on disproving that the self only signifies as a symptom, my concern in what follows is not to drag a singular popular artist up from the cellar of cultural history. Without regarding Razaf as a plaything of discursive or historical forces, I will consider him as a partial product and gauge of the place of black bolshevism within the cultural field of the Harlem Renaissance. It is with this field that my book begins, for it convened the first meeting of the New Negro and the Old Left as it freed a host of self-consciously modern currents in African-American intellectual life.

The Left in Harlem Renaissance History; the Left in the Renaissance Field

In contrast to Andy Razaf, anticapitalist radicalism is a topic that histories of the Harlem Renaissance have felt bound to raise. If, as George Hutchinson claims, virtually all criticism of the Harlem movement has pivoted on the evaluation of "its interracial dynamics" (15), much has also set the historical parameters of these dynamics with reference to the U.S. pro-Bolshevik left, the left that, capital "C" Communist or not, took comfort and inspiration from the Soviet Bolsheviks' revolutionary victory. Proudly identified with total revolution and the forced entrance of the future, readily envisioned as a perpetrator of radical historical breaks, the pro-Bolshevik left has regularly been sighted at scenes of the renaissance's birth and death. In many of the strongest general accounts of the Harlem movement, beginning with Harold Cruse's *The Crisis of the Negro Intellectual* (1967), the U.S. Communist Party or its allies are described as leading causes and beneficiaries of the rebirth's demise in the early 1930s. The "Harlem Background" chapter of Cruse's classic attack on the integrationist treason of modern black intellectuals argues that "the Harlem Renaissance had too much to contend with in the new Communist left-wing and the new Garvey nationalism" (53). By the chapter's last sentence, any Garveyite contribution to the movement's dissolution is ignored in favor of Communism's unique place as a fatal supplement to the renaissance's intellectual deficiency: "Unable to arrive at any philosophical conclusions of their own as a *black intelligentsia*, the leading literary lights of the 1920s substituted the Communist left-wing philosophy of the 1930s, and thus were intellectually sidetracked for the remainder of their productive years" (63; emphasis in original).

While distancing itself from 1960s-style black nationalism, David Levering Lewis's elegant *When Harlem Was in Vogue* (1981) recapitulates Cruse's analysis of Communism in a manner both less direct and more dramatic. The "last days" of the Harlem Renaissance, Lewis affirms, were spent in the company of Langston Hughes, Louise Thompson, and twenty other representatives of the younger Harlem intelligentsia, new enthusiasts for Communism who sailed from New York for the Soviet Union in 1932 (288). Although Lewis never explicitly claims that the renaissance could not survive its replanting in Russian soil, he presents a quasi-allegorical reading of the expedition in which the fracturing of the liberal coalition that braced the renaissance is first revealed in the seat of Communism. In the bickering and eventual disintegration of the Hughes-Thompson troupe once in the Soviet Union, he finds "an ideograph of Afro-American politics in the thirties," expressing both the breakup of "the old entente cordiale of Jewish notables, Negrotarian publishers, and civil rights grandees" and the turn of "more artists and intellectuals . . . with more or less enthusiasm, to communism" (291). Lewis's detection of this ideograph appears to be dramatically motivated; with it, he may frame his book's historical territory between two spectacular mirroring journeys, one to and one from Harlem. Much as his study concludes with New Negroes making an exit (stage left) from the city of the renaissance in 1932, it opens with the 1919 entrance into Harlem of the decorated, all-black 369th Infantry, "New Negroes in uniform" returning from the battlefields of World War I (288). But Lewis's bookends for the Harlem Renaissance are notable for more than their symmetry. In their vivid, compressed narrativization of the idea that the rebirth stalked off to Russia to die, they give life and style to the premise that Communism breached black cultural production with the Depression of the 1930s, dooming the first wave of black modernism and its imagined inspiration, audience, and author, the so-called New Negro.

Elsewhere, Lewis has classified the pro-Bolshevik left as less the renaissance's rival and executioner than part of a prehistory it must crush to be born. His introduction to *The Portable Harlem Renaissance Reader* (1994) presents a birth story in which the aesthetic renaissance proper is a consequence of antiradical "repression" as well as "metropolitan dynamism" (xxiv). Drawing from psychoanalytic vocabulary and positing an intensely political postwar black unconscious, Lewis claims that "the Red Summer of 1919, a period of socialist agitation and conservative backlash following the Russian Revolution, produced the trauma that led to the cultural sublimation of civil rights" (xxiv). This diversion of radical political arousal into tamer cultural labors ensured that the renaissance would surface as an elitist and multiply idealistic "cultural nationalism of the parlor" (xv), though one for which the securing of African-American civil rights remained the ultimate justification. Minus a few of the hints of emasculated domestic retreat, the heart of Lewis's position can be found in an anthology of renaissance texts with which his now competes, the late Nathan Huggins's collection *Voices from the Harlem Renaissance* (1976). Nearly twenty years before Lewis, Huggins's introduction proposed that Harlem's rebirth began when the New Negro who absorbed the anticolonial lessons of World War I took stock of the red scare and determined that he or she "could best thrive as a cultural being, not as a political force" (9). "In an atmosphere of political repression," Huggins maintains, black intellectuals oversaw "a channeling of energy from political and social criticism into poetry, fiction, music, and art" (9). In so many words, both Huggins and Lewis finger red-chasing Attorney General A. Mitchell Palmer and his young Bureau of Investigation pupil J. Edgar Hoover as accidental nurturers of black cultural awakening.

Even new historicist criticism aiming to break the Huggins-Lewis head-lock on memory of the renaissance retains their line on its birth. Henry Louis Gates, Jr.'s often-cited essay "The Trope of a New Negro and the Reconstruction of the Image of the Black" (1988) situates the Harlem movement in relation to the *longue durée* of "black intellectual recon-struction" between 1895 and 1925 (131). With a chiefly textual focus that separates him from history department residents Huggins and Lewis, Gates casts the renaissance as the fulfillment of this lengthy self-recon-struction project, during which the trope of a New Negro dallied with sev-eral black rebirths before discovering one truly "suitable to contain [it]" (132). Gates's challenge to the pair's construction of a unique, short-form renaissance is nonetheless coupled with respect for their thought on its derivation. He traces Alain Locke's ability to instigate a suitable black rebirth to his success in retouching the immediate postwar portrait of the New Negro, a forbidding depiction of a "militant, card-carrying, gun-tot-ing socialist who refused to turn the other cheek" (147). Echoing Huggins and Lewis's accent on New Negro metamorphosis, not creation ex nihilo, Gates claims that Locke's kinder, gentler New Negro had by 1925 "trans-formed the militancy associated with the trope and translated this into an apolitical movement of the arts. Locke's New Negro was a poet, and it would be in the sublimity of the fine arts, and *not* in the political sphere of action or protest poetry, that white America . . . would at last embrace the Negro" (147; emphasis in original).

Despite its attractive conceptual economy, the account of the renais-sance's postwar emergence through radical sublimation has meaningful weaknesses, not the least of which is the equivocal formula for a move-ment distinguished by both a culturalist repression of politics and a pur-suit of politics by cultural means. As Gloria Hull and Cheryl A. Wall argue, assigning any post–World War I birth date to the movement strands part of the work of Jessie Fauset and all of the work of several significant female poets, justifying Hull's dictum that "women writers are tyrannized by periodization" (30).[3] Most important, if only to my purpose, is the weakness that arises when the account of birth via radical sublimation is fused with the tale of death by communism: the pro-Bolshevik left is ren-dered a controlling presence at the renaissance's start and finish but nowhere in between. We might extrapolate that this left, sublimated to launch the renaissance, lay quiet in the rebirth's unconscious until desub-limated by the economic catastrophe of the 1930s, a return of the repressed with lethal results. Cruse and Lewis make it plain, however, that the Com-munism they associate with the close of the movement was a force external to it, an alien entity at the time of the renaissance's passing. If, like a guilty absentee parent, the pro-Bolshevik left thus abandoned the movement at its birth and reappeared only at its death, several questions are begged: Where was this left during the movement's maturity? Were it and the Harlem Renaissance not just distinct but antipathetic modern projects?

With their understandably selective interest in the movement's articulations with nonracial intellectual traditions, the treatments of the renaissance discussed above provide only sporadic clues with which to answer these questions. George Hutchinson protests in his imposing, archive-scouring intellectual history *The Harlem Renaissance in Black and White* (1995) that work on the movement has "been framed within limited parameters, with too exclusive a focus upon issues of race, inadequate notions of American modernism, insufficiently particularized narratives of the intellectual and institutional mediations between black and white agents of the renaissance, and curiously narrow conceptions of the larger 'environmental conditions' . . . in which those agents acted" (3). Hutchinson's own antidote to these perceived failings of narrowness and generality is to consult French sociologist Pierre Bourdieu's increasingly eye-catching theory of the "cultural field." For Bourdieu, the cultural field is the field of forces and struggles in which literature and its producers are cultivated. While a distinct social universe relatively autonomous from the political and economic fields, the cultural field remains a field of forces because it encompasses a dynamic "network of objective relations between [the] positions" occupied by cultural producers, a network tied to a particular distribution of cultural capital ("The Field" 30). It is a field of struggles because these producers, or "agents"—individual artists, schools and tendencies, publishers and other cultural institutions—enter the field of forces to compete for capital enough "to impose the dominant definition of the writer," literary culture's grand prize (42). Even though agents are thus compelled to submit themselves to the field of forces in order to be recognized as contestants in the literary game, they are not condemned merely to be played by these forces: in the struggles among agents for the capital specific to the literary field, objective relations in the field of forces may be preserved or altered. As a result, the configuration of the cultural field at a given historical instant depends on the relative position of both the capital and human catalysts within it; both objective social relations and the unprescribed maneuvers of agents make and remake the field.

Hutchinson's deployment of Bourdieu's un-unified field theory results in impressively full, subtle, and dynamic reconstructions of the domain in which agents of the renaissance competed and by which agents of the larger, intersecting U.S. cultural field became convinced that the rebirth was genuine. Many of the literary institutions of the renaissance receive Hutchinson's illuminating attention, not excepting *The Liberator*, home to some of the first publications of Claude McKay and Jean Toomer but previously drummed out of the rebirth for its Marxism and majority-white editorial board. Even so, Hutchinson's map of the movement's contending forces is insensitive to many signs of renaissance radicalism. The problem lies with two related stances: his selection of a governing problematic for the renaissance cultural field and his lack of interest in what Bourdieu retains from Marxism. While Hutchinson's account of the renaissance is ultimately more helpful than its predecessors in addressing the question of the movement's full relationship to the pro-Bolshevik left, it is not because of his committed search for an answer; rarely, in fact, does he devote the attention that Cruse, Huggins, and Lewis pay to this left's whereabouts during the renaissance's birth and death. His work is of greater use because it proposes a model through which the renaissance can be seen as an outwardly focused yet internally divided ensemble, and the ability to define the movement might be viewed as an honor fought for by a variety of cultural agents, not excluding Andy Razaf and others affiliated with Harlem anticapitalism.

With the stipulation that "appeals to national identity could challenge the dominant, racist consensus," Hutchinson claims that "the issue of American national identity" was not just thick in the air from the 1890s through the 1920s but the "dominant *problematic*"—or unavoidable stake of competition over literary capital—"structuring the literary field relevant to the Harlem Renaissance" (13; emphasis in original). It is possible to find this problematic quite problematic without objecting that Hutchinson's epoch of U.S. national self-consciousness is also the epoch of U.S. empire or that he is too quick to enfold a distinctly black cultural nationalism back into the consensus-obsessed American ideology. Concurrent with the nationalization of African America in the early twentieth century grew an internationalizing imagining of blackness, institutionalized in the United States by the Pan-Africanism of W. E. B. Du Bois, one founder of the nationalized NAACP, and by Marcus Garvey's immensely popular Universal Negro Improvement Association, or UNIA (accent on the "Universal"). Many of this imagining's eminent architects, including Garvey himself, were Caribbean newcomers to Harlem, the "Negro Metropolis" that absorbed about two-thirds of those who doubled the nation's immigrant black population between 1900 and 1910 (Hill vi). Schooled under Eng-

lish, French, Dutch, or Spanish colonialisms, thrown together in the
packed black city within a city, migratory black intellectuals clashed over
much but jointly regarded the oppression of blacks as a transnational ill
requiring transnational remedies. They were hard pressed to regard their
adopted city as the capital of *The Negro World* (the name of Garveyism's
multilingual journal) and the Harlem Renaissance as a chance to define
the international soul of modern blackness; by 1925, after all, about one in
four Harlemites over the age of fifteen was foreign born (Gutman 453).
Alain Locke's landmark *New Negro* (1925) anthology affirms that the
immigrants' perspective impressed renaissance builders born in the USA.
"The pulse of the Negro world has begun to beat in Harlem," boasts Locke
in the volume's preamble; "In terms of the race question as a world problem, the Negro mind has leapt, so to speak, upon the parapets of prejudice
and extended its cramped horizons" ("The New Negro" 14). At best, then,
Hutchinson's selection of American national identity as the master problematic of the renaissance cultural field discounts one operative sense of
what fighting over the movement meant fighting for. At its least productive, it decrees that some of the most influential black internationalists be
severed from the renaissance. Du Bois's Pan-Africanism might be found
compatible with a saving vision of "the Americanness of the American
Negro," but "Garvey's insistence on separation from American culture and
society" places him beyond the pale, outside Hutchinson's meticulous
topography of the movement (146).

Hutchinson's excision of black internationalists from the Harlem
Renaissance ironically demands not only the banishment of Garvey and
the cultural work produced in his name but the premature dismissal of
many of those who became his most vocal and effective Harlem enemies:
namely, Razaf and the rest of the earliest black bolsheviks. This loose collective shared Garvey's black diasporan prospect while rejecting what they
considered his racially exclusive nationalism, his ill-fated ventures in black
capitalism, and his quasi-imperial ambitions for a repatriated Africa.
Caribbean immigrants or their close associates, they were initially drawn
leftward by the Soviet Union's bids to the colonized world and convinced
by Lenin's idea that imperialism was the highest (and last) stage of capitalism, the true cause of world war but the bearer of the preconditions for
worldwide socialist revolution. When they considered the nationalization
of American and African-American phenomena, they presupposed the
simultaneous consummation of the capitalist world system and the emergence of an emboldened, equally global anticapitalist opposition. In the
estimation of Harlem's communists, the arrival of the black renaissance

was thus inextricable from the advent of a vastly expanded, more sharply disputed field of class relations, a social field that Hutchinson overlooks but Bourdieu, for one, glimpses beyond the horizon of the cultural.

Hutchinson rightly holds that Bourdieu's theory of the cultural field carefully distinguishes itself from social and economic determinisms, especially of a Marxist stripe. Bourdieu pronounces the cultural field a "peculiar universe" on which the "external determinants . . . which the Marxists invoke can only have an effect through resulting transformations in the structure of the field" ("Principles" 181–82). While mediated by prismatic "*refraction*," or the distinctive, transfiguring force of the cultural field, these external determinants nonetheless pierce this field, and there organize effects (182; emphasis in original). When Bourdieu elucidates his theory in spatial terms the social fields in which external determinants arise are thus shown to *contain* the cultural field. In the programmatic essay "The Field of Cultural Production" (1983), Bourdieu offers both the expected caveat about the cultural field's relative autonomy and a diagram that illustrates this field's relative dependence by displaying its embedding within both the wider field of social (read economic and political) power and the all-encompassing field of class relations (38–39). What Bourdieu's diagram conveys graphically is a posture toward the process of cultural change that, for all his stress on the clash of motivated human agents, is much obliged to theories of structural causality drawn from Althusser's antihumanist Marxism. The outcome of struggles within the cultural field, Bourdieu believes, depends on "the correspondence they may have with the external struggles between the classes (or between the fractions of the dominant class) and on the reinforcement which one [internal] group or another may derive from them" (57). This correspondence is based not on direct cultural reflection of external conflicts but on "homology and the consequent synchronisms" (57). In the interest of concreteness, Bourdieu offers the example of a common type of cultural struggle whose results fully depend on a homologous relationship with external struggles:

> When newcomers [to the cultural field] are not disposed to enter the cycle of simple reproduction . . . but bring with them dispositions and position-takings which clash with the prevailing norms of production and the expectations of the field, they cannot succeed without the help of external changes. These may be political breaks, such as revolutionary crises, which change the power relations within the field . . . , or deep-seated changes in the audience of consumers who, because of their affinity with the new producers, ensure the success of their products. (57–58)

Razaf and his black bolshevik comrades did not abstract the Harlem Renaissance cultural field from what Bourdieu calls the field of class relations. They assumed that the successful break with the norms of production in African-American culture known as the Harlem Renaissance was indebted to the revolutionary crisis of the capitalist world revealed and intensified by the Russian Revolution. They reckoned that the fate of their own "position-takings" within the renaissance—their stance on the movement as manifested in artistic and other texts—rested on their ability to address an urbanized, working-class black audience, an audience that, like them, was versed in the full range of modern, mass-cultural forms. To chart the renaissance cultural field without reference to the surrounding field of class relations is hence not only to overestimate the "post" in Bourdieu's post-Marxism; it is also to underestimate the number and efficacy of anticapitalists within renaissance territory. Like the choice of American national identity as a master problematic, such selective isolation or formalization of the movement ensures that the position of most of these radicals will go unrecorded. One doesn't have to share their enthusiasm for Leninism, or even regret their omission from the history of the renaissance for its own sake, to find this a significant loss. In the case of any cartography of the movement representing the competitive situation of its agents, the absence of black bolsheviks distorts the modeling of present features. As Bourdieu observes, "every position [occupied by an agent in the cultural field], even the dominant one, depends for its very existence, and for the determinations it imposes on its occupants, on the other positions constituting the field" ("The Field" 30). Full understanding of the differential positions assumed by more familiar makers of the renaissance therefore requires a determination of the place of the black bolsheviks among them.

Through the window provided by Andy Razaf, this chapter will establish the position and position-takings of the first black bolsheviks inside a Harlem Renaissance cultural field restored to its location within the field of class relations. It will show that while the black bolsheviks' position was only briefly—if ever—dominant, the intellectual practice it yielded was felt throughout the full dispute over the movement's definition. Necessarily, then, this chapter distinguishes itself in several ways from existing renaissance histories. In passing, it will offer new angles on the relationship among the renaissance, jazz and blues music, and mass culture; on the identities of renaissance intellectuals and Harlem masses; and on the transactions between these two, often overlapping camps. Centrally, however, it will challenge interpretations that either banish anticapitalist radicalism from the renaissance field or confine it to a negative presence at the field's creation and disintegration. I will be suggesting that bolshevism was an invited guest, not an interloper, at the birth of Harlem's rebirth; that black bolshevism's position-takings in the renaissance field included expressive culture with a configuring impact on high and low African-American art; and that reports of Communism's responsibility for the death of the movement are thus greatly exaggerated.

Duke Razaf Goes Harlem

Casting Andy Razaf as a window onto Harlem Renaissance–era black bolshevism is counterintuitive: he was of royal birth, and he could swing. Born in 1895 with the Malagasy name of Andreamen*en*tania Paul Razaf*in*keriefo (the italicized letters are silent), Razaf was a living, breathing New World scion of African royalty. Barry Singer's genealogical research confirms that Razaf's father, Henri Razafkeriefo, was not only a native Madagascan but a nephew of Madagascar's queen, Ranavalona III. His mother, Jennie Maria Waller, sprang from the African-American aristocracy attached to the post–Civil War Republican Party. She was the daughter of John Louis Waller (no relation to Razaf's songwriting partner, Fats), a lawyer and government official who survived slavery in Missouri, advanced through the party of Lincoln, and was rewarded with an appointment as U.S. consul to Madagascar in 1891. Had French colonial policy not interfered, Andy might have attained the elevated position in Madagascar his mother and grandfather foresaw for Jennie's children-to-be when she married into one of Africa's few intact monarchies. As it happened, however, 1895 saw Razaf's grandfather dragged aboard a steamship and imprisoned in Marseilles, a victim of French resistance to his campaign to strengthen official U.S. ties to the island and, failing that, to transform the French protectorate into "Wallerland," an African-American settler colony on the model of Liberia. John Waller was released by the French after U.S. protests mounted; news accounts in prominent papers at home forgave his race and freelance colonization proposal long enough to fashion him as a symbol of injured national sovereignty. Waller's son-in-law, the Madagascan father whom Razaf would never meet, was much less lucky, killed while leading troops against the French military. Razaf's mother was forced to return to the United States, where she settled in Washington, D.C., and delivered her first child not as the mother of a noble line that might rejoin Africa and its diaspora but as an isolated, fifteen-year old widow with a workaday future (Singer 6–23). "Greed took thy kingdom," Razaf would write of Queen Ranavalona and, by extension, of his mother and himself ("Ranavalona—Dead," l. 1).

The teenaged Razaf's response to his prenatal dispossession was apparently to conceive an ambition to become a self-supporting poet-lyricist. His aspiration seems an odd compensation for his stolen life as a Pan-African royal until one remembers that his boyhood coincided with the songwriting successes of the two most prominent, dignified race and verse men in the turn-of-century United States. As Singer recalls, Paul Laurence Dunbar, poet laureate of post-Reconstruction African America, took time in 1898 to write the libretto and lyrics to the musical *Clorindy, the Origin of the Cakewalk*; James Weldon Johnson, meanwhile, wrote dozens of songs for the New York stage with his brother, J. Rosamond, prior to serving as U.S. consul to Nicaragua and Venezuela and publishing *Fifty Years and Other Poems* (1917).[4] Thanks in particular to the Republican official Johnson, an artier surrogate of Grandfather Waller, Razaf saw evidence that songwriting might pay the way of a self-respecting black poet, provided that he or she could broker the claims of the rising culture industry and the foremost black American art with signifying wit.

From the time he was seventeen, running an elevator in a Tin Pan Alley office building and hawking his lyrics between floors, until his death in 1973 at seventy-seven, Razaf outdid his precursors by composing the words to more than eight hundred jazz- and blues-flavored popular songs. Nat "King" Cole, Duke Ellington, Ella Fitzgerald, Paul Robeson, Frank Sinatra, and Bessie Smith followed Fats Waller in recording from his song book, the highlights of which include "Ain't Misbehavin'," "Honeysuckle Rose," "Memories of You," "This Joint is Jumpin'," "Stompin' at the Savoy," and "In the Mood."[5] Despite this enormous volume of lyrical production, Razaf never stopped writing in support of the left wing of progressive black politics, perhaps because his mature career as a professional lyricist never stopped colliding with the voluble racism and fraud of Tin Pan Alley music publishers. In the late teens and during the twenties, Razaf frequently published protest verse in Marcus Garvey's *Negro World*, Cyril Briggs's *Crusader*, and A. Philip Randolph's *Messenger*, Harlem-based radical magazines that led the postwar celebration of a self-assertive, comfortably modern New Negro. For much of his adult life, he contributed playful but trenchant essays and poems to the *Amsterdam News* and other African-American papers, more than once lambasting McCarthyism, calling for a black songwriters' union, praising the employment of dark-skinned black actresses, and—like August Wilson after him—protesting the inadequate material footing for an independent black theater (Singer 29–347).

This remarkable profile makes Razaf's absence from most Harlem Renaissance commentary far more mystifying than his absence from Ellison's *Invisible Man.*[6] The soberest historians might be forgiven for holding him at arm's length, as early publicists inflated the accurate improbabilities of his birth with the jazz-age version of tabloid royals gossip. A breathless 1928 newspaper story, for instance, revealed that "because Duke Andre Paul Razafkerie [*sic*] . . . has chosen song plugging as his career, his mother, the Duchess Christian, has refused to have anything to do with him" (qtd. in Singer 196). All the same, it would be difficult to invent someone who could better serve as a confluence of disparate renaissance energies: Razaf, who worked as a Harlem telephone operator in 1914–15, mimicked a switchboard through which many of the movement's contraries were patched. Renaissance oppositions meet in the exiled African nobleman turned poetic and musical purveyor of Harlem: the typically divided modernist enthusiasm for ostensibly premodern, primitive zones (Africa) and for modern, metropolitan ones (Harlem); the simultaneous achievements in formal literature (especially poetry) and popular music (especially jazz); the often dissimilar uses and significances of this music in Harlem and on Broadway and Tin Pan Alley; and the usually inimical conceptions of the Harlem movement as a rebirth of black cultural autonomy and a renewal of white appreciation for black culture's entertainment value.

In the early 1920s it appeared that this talent for mediation had won Razaf a place on the renaissance literary roster. Robert T. Kerlin's *Negro Poets and Their Poems*, a pathbreaking 1923 anthology of the "renaissance of the Negro" now overshadowed by James Weldon Johnson's *Book of American Negro Poetry* (1922; rev. 1931), praised Razaf's verse for its "great variety of forms[,] . . . moods and traits" (51, 199). Kerlin, a white professor at Lincoln University, lumped Razaf with Langston Hughes as "verslibrist[s] of individual quality" (197) and printed three poems by the poet with a "strange name" (199). The last of them, "Rainy Days," was chosen to close the collection for its "very good philosophy of life—which is especially the Afro-American's" (263). By the second half of the decade, however, Razaf's disappearance from any place whatsoever in renaissance literary anthologies would barely be noticed, a prediction of his unremarked absence from most scholarly histories of the movement. A volume of selected poems, perhaps enough to challenge this vanishing, was contracted in the 1950s but never saw print; Hughes's introduction, complimenting Razaf as a democratic "philosopher-poet" with "a talent for the concise line," languished along with it (*Poems* 2).

Razaf's literary disappearance, best understood in conjunction with a

larger realignment of renaissance forces, can begin to suggest why this singular figure also furnishes a stage from which to view Harlem Renaissance
bolshevism. In the mid-1920s, the declining fortunes of Razaf's poetry
matched the worsening position of anticapitalism in the renaissance cultural field. And for good reason: though Razaf never seems to have carried
a party card, most of this poetry had its objective social origin in Harlem's
postwar subculture of antiimperialist agitation; some of it had been composed in Razaf's capacity as a staff member of the Harlem journal that pictured the straightest of roads from Soviet Moscow to New Negro New
York. Sometime in the fall of 1918, Razaf became the house poet at *The
Crusader*, a monthly launched in September by Cyril V. Briggs with the
slogans "Africa for the Africans" and "an equitable solution of the Race
Problem" ("Aims of *The Crusador* [*sic*]" 4). *The Crusader* mixed political
and cultural reportage with imaginative literature and was attentive both
to international news and most aspects of Harlem's quickening life. Regular editors and contributors included John "Grit" Bruce, Ben and
Theodore Burrell, Bertha De Basco, W. A. Domingo, T. Thomas Fortune,
Gertrude Hall, Hubert H. Harrison, Richard B. Moore, Arthur Schomburg, and at least one informant from the proto-FBI (Kornweibel 137). J.
Ralph Casimir, Claude McKay, and Lucian B. Watkins filled out the
poetry pages with Razaf. All indications are that Razaf was a funny,
admired coworker. He starred in one of the journal's "Men of Our Times"
features, which toasted him as a "poet, songwriter and leading Afro-American humorist, whose poems and humorous articles monthly add to the
joy of living for several hundred thousand people throughout the world"
("Men of Our Times" 20 [see fig. 1]). Razaf likely found *The Crusader's*
office at 2299 Seventh Avenue a good vantage point on his musical and
political Harlem. Just a few blocks down on Seventh was Connie's Inn, the
nightclub that would first mount his musical *Hot Chocolates*; one block
west, at the corner of Lenox Avenue and 135th Street, was the sidewalk that
he and other radical orators built into black New York's speakers' corner.
If only for *The Crusader's* part in the inception of the Harlem Renaissance,
its Seventh Avenue home should join these locales in the practical historical geography of the movement, the mental map of a modern race capital
that is one lasting afterimage of renaissance criticism.[7] In November 1918,
seven years before Alain Locke's *New Negro* anthology and Levering Lewis's
"Year 1 of the Harlem Renaissance" (*When Harlem* 117), the publication
was already promoting what it called "a renaissance of Negro power and
culture throughout the world" ("Aims of *The Crusader*" 1). *The Crusader's*
advanced sponsorship of this renaissance as well as Razaf's early poetry

calls for a close look at its editorial posture, something missing even from Hutchinson's detailed anatomy of the magazines hosting the movement's competing positions. Among other things, such a look suggests that the cultural field of the renaissance was partially constituted through the cultivation—not the repression—of a communist New Negro.

The Crusader: Bolshevism, Nationalism, and Renaissancism

The Crusader's precocious sighting of a black renaissance prompted Razaf in the direction of 2299 Seventh Avenue, but so did the journal's special blend of race and class consciousness. From several angles, the magazine appears to be a typical organ of World War I–era black radicalism. It, too, strived to plot changes in the landscape of the black urban North during a period of massive in-migration, a crowded space in which mass self-defense and self-organization still found unheard-of room for cultivation (E. Allen 49). Like its peers, it refused to credit the opposition by which the last generation of middle-class black intellectuals had divided and defined itself; *The Crusader* was not unique in deciding that Booker T. Washington's in-group entrepreneurialism and Du Bois's advocacy of full civil rights had equally slighted the economic predicament of the black masses (E. Allen 52). As *Crusader* compiler and historian Robert A. Hill observes, however, Briggs's publication distinguished itself from the socialist *Messenger* and the Garveyite *Negro World* by articulating two strains of black nationalism—the romantic-didactic and the modern militarist—"to the revolutionary ideology of Bolshevism" (xxxiii). This original ideological alloy provided the backbone of the position that Razaf and other New Negro bolsheviks would occupy in the renaissance cultural field.

Some manifestation in *The Crusader* of a romantic strain of educational nationalism could have been predicted from the sources of its start-up capital. The initial $200 donation was not "Moscow gold," which arrived in disappointingly small amounts a few years later (Kornweibel 148), but the gift of the West Indian merchant Anthony Crawford, who volunteered that Briggs might care to use it to disseminate "propaganda of 'Africa for the Africans' [and to] educate the caucasian in African History" (qtd. in Hill xvii). *The Crusader*'s early issues thus echoed the redemptive counter-research of George Wells Parker, whose revelation of the African origins of classical Greek civilization, *The Children of the Sun* (1918), foreshadows recent claims to a Black Athena. Hill notes that the "Race Catechism" in *The Crusader*'s first issue was a distillation of the homilies fortifying Parker's rediscovery of the African past (xix–xx). "Why are you proud of your race?" asked this catechism; "Because in the veins of no human being does there flow more generous blood than in our own; in the annals of the world the history of no race is more resplendent with honest, worthy glory than that of the Negro race" ("Race Catechism" 11). Razaf's inaugural contribution to *The Crusader*, the poem "Why I Am Proud," does the catechism one better: for those less acquainted with African nobility than was his family, it versifies race patriotism into memorizable quatrains:

> My color stands for Achievements,
>   The greatest the world has known;
> A race, which for its endurance
>   Will ever stand alone. (ll. 9–12)

The Crusader's instructional offerings in cultural nationalism nonetheless broke from Parker when it came to the subject of black self-defense. The art nouveau–toned drawing on the covers of the March and April 1920 issues is a clear illustration of the journal's desire to cement romantic-didactic and militant strains of black nationalism: the titles of the major articles within each issue are emblazoned on the circular shield of a spear-carrying African warrior; at either side of his headdress balance smaller crests bearing images of the pyramids and the sphinx, icons of a monumental black past that have persisted into present-day Afrocentrism (see fig. 2). Here, the alignment of liberating modern African-American thought (the journal's contents) and the best of African civilization before racial slavery (the Egyptian icons) is shown to pivot on the recovery of a martial African persona (the warrior with his shields). The cover thus announces *The Crusader* as a magazine of fighting words and, more importantly, as the herald of a black renaissance that would include military exploits in the ledgers of African achievement.

The major stimulus behind the journal's militarizing of Afrocentric nationalism and black renaissancism was the global war it came to regard as a European scramble for African territory. After President Wilson proclaimed in April 1917 that the United States would help make the world safe for democracy, Briggs quickly registered for the draft; within months, however, he and his *Crusader* were beyond disillusion. The East St. Louis race riot of July 1917 indicated that violent white anxiety over competition with migrating black labor would not be put on hold for the war's duration. The secretive August hanging of thirteen black soldiers, court-martialed for mutinying against abusive white officers and citizens in Houston, suggested that a U.S. Army uniform gave its black wearer no unusual protection against lynching. Razaf encapsulated *The Crusader's* disappointment with the war in the poem "A Parting Word," written in the bitter voice of a black combatant disturbed by the compromised safety of democracy in America:

> If after all my sacrifices and pain,
> Your segregation laws would still remain—
> Then better would it be for me to crave
> A little spot in Flanders as my grave.　(ll. 5–8)

What was left for the journal was thus to ensure that another unappreciated sacrifice of black soldiers for the nation's welfare would also somehow serve black interests. The November 1918 issue contained a short, unsigned piece, "A Different Meaning," channeling surplus patriotic gore into the wish that black troops would bring the war home. Approvingly quoting a white writer who had predicted "that the word 'nigger' will have a different meaning after the war," the article anticipated that " 'cracker' will have a different meaning after the war also[,] as the one-time timid, harmless and conservative 'darky' backed by his hardening, man-killing experiences on the battlefields of Europe, will be prepared to make that word stand either for a reformed heathen or a dead one" ("A Different Meaning" 17). While "A Different Meaning" is no full-bore fantasy of war as the health of the strong, it prays that the trenches will deliver a healthier, stronger race. If things went *The Crusader's* way, black participation in World War I would thus become a major irony of U.S. racial history, in which fearful, undercompensated African-American mercenaries would inadvertently be transformed into the firepower of a remasculinized black nationalism.

Another name for this desired visitation of history's irony, of course, would be the transition from a timid Old Negro to a brave New Negro, the latter the presiding subject of *The Crusader's* Harlem Renaissance and practically everyone else's. As Henry Gates's and Hazel Carby's tropological histories of the New Negro reveal ("The Trope"; *Reconstructing* 163–66), neither *The Crusader*, nor Alain Locke, nor the greater Harlem–New Negro Renaissance can take credit for inventing this rhetorical figure and social template. The incarnate modernism of New Negro discourse, siting obligatory novelty in the self, not in aesthetic form, actually seems to predate Anglo-American high modernism, the academically favored reaction to modernity that once inclined renaissance critics to debate their subject's belatedness. Gates notes that around 1895 "the image of a 'New Negro' " began to serve "various generations of black intellectuals as a sign of plenitude, of regeneration, of a truly reconstructed *presence*," a sign answering the coding of blackness "as . . . a truly negated *absence*" ("The Trope" 130; emphasis in original). While Gates does not say so, 1895 may mark the conception of the New Negro image because it also marks the acme of "retrogressionism" in postemancipation racial discourse, the belief that unsupervised free blacks, unable to modernize themselves, were slouching toward barbarism (Gutman 531–44). Despite its likely origins as a negation of retrogressionist thought, the notion of a New Negro steeped in presence logically required that of an Old Negro hollowed out by deficiency, whether or not this relic was seen exclusively as a white figment. "The two . . . figures," Gates remarks, "can . . . be said to have a certain cause-and-effect relation" (130). Because of the engrossment of end-of-century racism in evolutionary theory and black bodies, the passage from Old Negro cause to New Negro effect was typically denoted by physical refinement, a representational habit with resonance as far afield as 1952's *Invisible Man*, with its half-Joycean, half-New Negro play on "creating the *uncreated features of his face*" (354; emphasis in original).

The *Crusader*'s specific contribution to New Negro discourse maintained some emphasis on black physiques as canvases of racial modernization, fashioning World War I as bloody training in which black men hardened into threats to "cracker" terror. It kept the relationship of opposition and causation between the Old Negro and the New and conceived of the old variety as both imaginary and real, generic and individual; this token of the black past could be found in the stereotype of the cringing, insipid "darky" and in the person of particular aging black leaders. "The old Negro and his futile methods must go," the journal insisted, "After fifty years of him and his methods the Race still suffers from lynching, disenfranchisement, jim-crowism, segregation and a hundred other ills" ("The Old Negro Goes" 9). Still, there were elements in *The Crusader*'s remodeling that made over the New Negro trope. The usual insistence on newfound dignity and aggressiveness was taken to hazardous extremes. Having "imbib[ed] the spirit of liberty," cheered *The Crusader*, its hero was "willing to suffer martyrdom for the Cause [of racial freedom]" (9). "He'll straightway [*sic*] seek his rights with murder in his eye," added Razaf ("The New Negro" l. 7). Newest of all, however, was the fact that this fire-breathing New Negro sought kinship with a "New Crowd" of white anti-capitalists. In the opinion of the *Crusader*, the white left did not menace a fully formed New Negro from without but inhered within the mix of modern positions and movements that compelled this model's creation and ensured its dangerous novelty. Here—not in a surrender of black autonomy to a stable, crafty Communist Party—can be located the earliest significant program to affiliate the New Negro and the Old Left.

The Crusader never defined its variation on the New Negro trope against white radicals; whenever it considered the relationship of African Americans to organized labor and its political expression, it opened the possibility that the Old Negro/New Negro divide was shadowed by the opposition between an "Old Crowd" of white conservatives and their radical children. A 1919 editorial headed "Make Their Cause Your Own" showed the need for a combination of New Negroes and white labor radicals to be as obvious as the economic exploitation of the vast majority of blacks and almost as airtight as a syllogism:

> No race has less of the idle non-producing rich than the Negro race.
>
> No race would be more greatly benefited [*sic*] proletariat than the Negro race, which is essentially a race of workers and producers.
>
> With no race are the interests of Labor so clearly identified with racial interests as in the case of the Negro race.
>
> No race would be more greatly benefited by the triumph of Labor and the destruction of parasitic Capital Civilization with its Imperialism incubus that is squeezing the life-blood out of millions of our race in Africa and the islands of the sea, than the Negro race.
>
> Is the lesson clear?
>
> We need not fight alone if we breast the sea upon the irresistible tide of liberalism that is at present sweeping the world. (6)

Although *The Crusader* was impressed by indigenous outfits like the IWW, the white Marxist party to clinch the idea that New Negroes need not fight by themselves was born in the Soviet Union. Editor-in-chief Briggs, a native of Nevis island who arrived in New York in 1905, was one of the Caribbean immigrants who built the Harlem outpost of an internationalized conception of blackness. The race he hoped to rally stretched from Africa, through the "islands of the sea," and into the United States in no small part because of the dispersal effected by its worst enemy, "Capital Civilization with its Imperialism incubus." Briggs's understanding of a black diaspora created and bled by capitalist imperialism warmed to the Soviet Bolsheviks, the revolutionary socialists who prevailed in the Russian Revolution, for a lucid reason: as early as the founding congress of the Soviet-led Communist International in March 1919, they were topping Wilson's postwar principle of national self-determination with outright calls for revolution in the colonial world, backed by promises to aid it. The first agreements the Soviet Union reached with emergent non-European states testified that these promises were not antiimperialist window dressing. In 1921 Briggs's *Crusader* judged that Soviet treaties with Persia and Afghanistan were fit to reprint for the benefit of "thoughtful Negroes, who must of necessity be vitally interested in the liberation of Africa" ("Russia and Self-Determination" 11–12). "Soviet Russia is the only Power in the world which puts into execution the principle of 'self-determination' in its dealings with weaker peoples," the journal announced, "and Soviet Russia does this regardless of the color of the people with whom she is dealing" (11).

Revolutionary Bolshevism, the third and most distinctive strain within *The Crusader*'s ideological alloy, thus initially appealed to Briggs and company because it seemed nearly as likely as World War I to give teeth to a cosmopolitan black nationalism. In their eyes, revolution Soviet style offered militant New Negroes both support against the economic generator of the imperial system and a pattern of egalitarian social organization even George Wells Parker might find congruent with African attributes. The Communist commonwealth, explained one smitten, anonymous *Crusader* writer, "has the advantage for the Negro race of being along the lines of our own race genius as evidenced by the existence of Communist States in Central Africa and our leaning towards Communism whenever the race genius has had free play" ("The Salvation of the Negro" 8). Unlike many nineteenth-century white American workers, devoted to the language of civic republicanism, the *Crusader*s therefore talked labor politics in unembarrassed internationalist-socialist accents. It would be tough, they bet, to red-bait a population too familiar with race-baiting: "Don't mind being called 'Bolsheviki,' " they cracked, "by the same people who called you 'nigger' " ("The African Blood Brotherhood" 22). For the benefit of readers unconvinced that New Negroes could trust even revolutionary whites, they proposed the kind of acid test later adopted by the Black Panthers, another group of gun-owning, coalition-seeking black Marxists. That test, the *Crusader*s related, "is simply whether [the white] person is willing to see the Negro defend himself with arms against aggression, and willing even to see Negroes killing his own (white) people in defense of Negro rights" ("The Acid Test" 9).

This erection of martial standards for both New Negro membership and white radical sincerity meant that *The Crusader*, however worthy in combating racist violence, whet a taste for wholly masculinized ideologies of redeemed blackness. There is little doubt that the journal hoped to dismantle the historical whiteness of working-class identity in the industrial North. From at least the mid-nineteenth century on, workers from diverse European immigrant populations had periodically struck against the commutability of blacks and white laborers, knitting themselves together over black bodies in manly entertainments from race riots to blackface minstrelsy.[8] There is also little doubt that *The Crusader* had few objections to the virility inherent in this working-class identity or to the disappearing act it performed on white and black women, the latter of whom were breaking into northern factory jobs just as the journal developed a column called "Helpful Hints for Women and the Home." When pursuing allies for its New Negro, *The Crusader* offered white male workers the chance of fraternity with equally manly black male peers; the Great War and the great black migration to northern industrial cities, the journal calculated, placed black male workers in an unprecedented position to forge interracial working-class identities opposed to feminized forms of capital. The *Crusaders* here distinguished themselves from the Black Power advocates of the 1960s, who also "turned repeatedly to the historical legacy of race and gender in order to define and articulate a strident black masculinity" (Wiegman 85). Briggs and company did not pit black masculinity against a solid mass of submasculine white men; instead, they reserved their charges of effeminacy for a white and black, capitalist or procapitalist Old Crowd. As they saw it, black manhood suffered "not only from alien political oppression but from capitalistic exploitation by members of its own group as well" ("The Salvation of the Negro" 8). The clash between proletariat and bourgeoisie was thus conflated with an oedipal battle between interracial brothers and fathers, an only-in-America recasting of Freud's fraternal mob squaring off against the primal patriarch (*Totem and Taboo* 143). This peculiar Marxian-oedipal logic carved out some place for a biracial working class within the venerable black modernism of the New Negro, even as it undertook to bridge the black-white divide within the U.S. proletariat, piling shared familial, generational, sexual, and gender roles on top of a common place in the production process. What it did not resist was the temptation to hedge a hard-to-sell language of black-white affiliation with deference to exclusionary manhood. In this, *The Crusader* set the homosocial terms through which New Negro–Old Left fusion was most often pursued during modern black writing's long engagement with Communism.

The Crusader's Service

Did *The Crusader's* New Negro bolshevism have other lasting effects? In a kind of international interpellation via publication, the journal succeeded in realizing its black diasporan outlook through its subscription list. Most copies were sold in Harlem, but mail orders were sent to the American South, the West Indies, and Africa, thus attracting the worried notice of British intelligence (Kornweibel 133, 136). According to Briggs's most upbeat figures, however, *The Crusader* reached only 32,700 people at its peak, or about one-third of those who subscribed to the NAACP's *Crisis* in 1920 ("Rally to the Cause" 11). The Red Summer, named for the seven or more brutal race riots that flared throughout the United States from May through September 1919, made it less simple for the journal to convince even this concentrated pool of readers that "the negro's place is with labor" ("The Negro's Place" 7). The culpability of white unionists in triggering the riots was more difficult to judge than in the East St. Louis explosion of 1917, just days before which the city's Central Trade and Labor Union officially declared that "drastic action must be taken . . . to get rid of a certain portion of [black migrants]" (qtd. in Meier and Rudwick, "Attitudes" 46). Yet it was hard to avoid the postriot message that white factory workers, jealous of the price of labor and ushered into segregated locals by the American Federation of Labor (AFL), did not welcome the entrance of blacks into the northern proletariat that both wartime industrial expansion and *The Crusader* had urged. When programmatic violence reorganized every dimension of urban public space along racial lines, some of these workers had shown themselves capable of doing everything imaginable to terrorize black newcomers back into the labor reserve or the sunny South. The grim reaction of local white elites to the formation of the Progressive Union of black sharecroppers, the immediate cause of the September riot in Phillips County, Arkansas, was to be expected; the well-documented joining of white stockyard workers in the July–August Chicago riot, where twenty-three blacks were killed, was something else (Waskow 38–142). If not in industrialized, unionized, and radicalized Chicago, where was an American cousin of *The Crusader*'s New Crowd bolshevik to be found?

The journal responded to the frustration of its opening arguments for New Negro–Labor partnership not only by upping the rhetorical ante but by forming the African Blood Brotherhood (ABB) in the fall of 1919, a political and paramilitary force that pragmatically divided its slight membership into cells in New York, Chicago, perhaps other U.S. cities, and the West Indies. The Brotherhood's eclectic models included Garvey's UNIA, black benevolent orders, Leninist avant-gardism, and the Irish Republican Brotherhood, the secretive nationalist group behind the failed Easter Rising of 1916 (Hill xxvii–xxxiii). Its statement of aims, a barely chastened derivation of *Crusader* editorials, instructed members to "adopt the policy of race first, without, however, ignoring useful alliances with other groups" ("The African Blood Brotherhood" 22). The ABB's reply to the Red Summer was dual and somewhat contradictory: on the one hand, it formalized the lessons in self-defense that black veterans of World War I appeared to have offered black migrants; on the other, it counseled patience and black working-class self-organization while working to hasten the day of interracial labor atonement. The Brotherhood's advocacy of the disciplined defense of black neighborhoods indeed became less and less formulaic: after the Tulsa race riot of 1921, the *New York Times* joined *The Crusader* in attributing the high white death toll to ABB coordination (Hill xxxiii). With help from the national attention that Tulsa provided, Briggs took the ABB's offer of interracial fraternity directly to union leaders, using the group's stationery to seek donations and caution that labor's victories would be impermanent if black "unorganized workers pouring North [were not] reached with the message of Unionism!" (qtd. in Foner and Allen 39). There is no sign that checks flowed in response to these requests, and the warnings about the high costs of segregated unionism would go largely unheeded until the 1930s. Such defeats nevertheless eased the way for the *Crusader* group's major practical accomplishment: the installation of a hot line between Harlem anticapitalism and the Third International marshaled by Soviet Communists, a development with crucial effects on the history of both black radicalism and Harlem's renaissance.

The difficulties the *Crusaders* discovered in forming alliances with U.S. labor resulted in their looking ever more hopefully to the Bolsheviks and their U.S. representatives, the American Communist Party, for assistance in the good fight against "Capital Civilization" after 1919. As the twenties wore on, Briggs and company came to turn exclusively to Soviet-affiliated Communism for a commendable agreement between the left and the New Negro, thus establishing something of a rule among interwar black Marxists. A pact with the Third, or "Red," International, they reasoned, could supplement the sputtering alliance between black and white U.S. labor with a contract more favorable to the New Negro's antiracist and antiimperialist terms. Such reasoning went hand in hand with a firmly Moscow-focused understanding of communism's meaning and tendency. Briggs himself recalled in 1960 that he was galvanized to join the U.S. party by Soviet developments and the likelihood of their American translation: "I entered . . . [in part] because . . . of the solution of the national [or ethnic] question in the Soviet Union and because I was confident that the American Party would in time take its lead on that question from its Soviet Party" (qtd. in Hill xxvi). To this way of thinking, the inverse of that which sees Soviet direction as fatal to freewheeling indigenous radicalisms, sovietization stood to guarantee the special interests of U.S.-based black bolsheviks. If Robert Hill is correct, Briggs's ABB was hitched to the American Communist Party from the beginning (xxiii–xxvii). At the very least, it was members of the *Crusader* circle, particularly those who joined the Brotherhood, who became the party's first black recruits and some of the U.S. radicals most welcome in the young Soviet Union. Otto Huiswoud and Arthur Hendricks, black West Indian immigrants and ABB officers, were charter members of the U.S. party at the time of its formation in September 1919 (Hill xxvi). All told, more than half of the Brotherhood's national council became Communists in good standing (Kornweibel 145). Along with fellow ABB member and *Crusader* contributor Claude McKay, Huiswoud was an early guest of the Communist International, or "Comintern," in Moscow, and—as I will argue in chapter 2—a parent of the Third International's approach to the Negro Question between the wars.

There were fixed expenses related to the *Crusader* group's felt proximity and privileged access to the Soviet Union. For starters, it secured the harassment of federal intelligence agencies, which concluded that Briggs was a "radical of the worst sort" (qtd. in Kornweibel 146) and that "the ABB was the worst of the black radical groups" (145). J. Edgar Hoover, a *Crusader* reader who shared distressing editorials with the State Department, used the journal to stoke his weighty conviction that civil rights militancy was Communist-inspired (139–40, 174–82). The greatest expense of the *Crusader* group's Soviet orientation, however, involved its own failure to credit intelligence. Briggs and later black Communists, Ellison not excepted, were slow to give credence to reports of Soviet failings and crimes that disturbed black socialists like A. Philip Randolph, especially where Soviet ethnic policies were concerned.

Despite this steep long-term cost, there were immediate gains to be had from the Soviet connection. With an assist from the Third International and the Marxism it claimed to incarnate, *The Crusader* suggested that black urban proletarianization, not U.S. national identity, was the problematic around which the cultural field of the Harlem Renaissance should be contested. Briggs and company were certain that capitalism's unknowing contribution to this renaissance—the Great Migration that brought over one million blacks to the urban North by 1930—would equip Harlem with a modern proletariat, something far more valuable to black culture than the migrants' purported deliveries of rural soil to uprooted artists. From the editorial pages on unionization to the reviews of new films showing in Harlem theaters, the journal taught that it was metropolitan black workers, their numbers swelling with southern and Caribbean migrants, who would snatch the baton of the New Negro from World War I veterans. The *Crusaders'* stake in this problematic for the Harlem movement was transparent: to budge Harlem's working-class renaissance as far toward the Communist left as it would go. Briggs's journal argued for a "renaissance of Negro power and culture throughout the world" that would help unravel the global net of capitalism ("Aims of the *Crusader*" 1), thus committing itself to a black rebirth even more ambitious than that which would ease U.S. racism through proofs of black artistic excellence. It supposed that its aims were more bold than fantastic because of the 1917 victory of the Bolsheviks and the two years of European revolution and near-revolution that followed. What was then widely feared or applauded as the beginning of the end of capitalist history offered the journal's position on the renaissance viability and momentum. Considered in Bourdieu's terms, the epochal social transformations signaled by the Great Migration and the Russian Revolution seemed more than able to "change the power relations within the field" of African-American culture ("The Field" 58). For *Crusaders* who brought "with them dispositions and position-takings which clash[ed] with the prevailing norms of production and the expectations of the field," these transformations augured the external changes in near and far arenas of class battle necessary to pilot black cultural renovation (58).

From Razaf's perspective, *The Crusader's* renaissance must have seemed both grand and commonsensical. Its internationalist brand of black nationalism chimed with his intimate connections to Africa; its soaring socialist program was rooted in the facts of Harlem economic life as he knew them. During his stint at the magazine, his plans to reconcile vocation and avocation through songwriting were not yet realized; he could only moonlight as a writer and editor. Like Richard B. Moore and other poorly paid *Crusaders*, not to mention a greater percentage of the renaissance's talented tenth than is usually acknowledged,[9] Razaf earned his rent money working at some of the unskilled labor and service jobs that then occupied around seven out of ten Harlem men (Gutman 453). Between 1913 and 1920 alone he put in time as a telephone operator, a butler, a "coater" in a Chinese laundry, a custodian in a government building, and an elevator operator shuttling audiences to the roof of the New Amsterdam Theater, home of Ziegfeld's *Follies* (Singer 44–57). To adapt E. P. Thompson's adage, class was "something which in fact happen[ed] . . . in [the] human relationships" these jobs thrust on Razaf (9). In his elevator and similar workplaces, personableness was mandatory; Razaf was alienated from his moods—even his facial expressions—along with his labor.[10] Catering to the *Follies* stars and audiences who later sang his words, he shouldered both the historical burden of African-American servitude and the cost of having nothing to sell but a smile and unsolicited song lyrics. *The Crusader's* renaissance promised to remove some of the weight. For one thing, it recognized that most Harlemites were not dusty, still rural-minded folks but metropolitan wage workers; even those whom the Great Migration had lured from the American South, like Washington, D.C.–born Razaf, were more than likely to have been city-dwelling, nonagricultural employees before the move (Marks 32–41). For another, *The Crusader* celebrated this state of affairs, projecting urban proletarianization as the motor for its renaissance rather than as a sidelight or hazard to the main business of upgrading the vernacular culture of black folk. In the orbit of the journal, Razaf was revealed as Briggs's kind of Harlem Renaissance man: an intellectual as organic as he was public, solidly grounded in the political movement of black bolshevism, and consciously working out "the principles and problems raised by [his class]" (Gramsci 330).

Renaissance stars from onetime chauffeur Zora Neale Hurston to onetime busboy Langston Hughes occasionally suspected that Harlem's rebirth was as much in service to white New York as was Harlem's workforce. Their suspicion has been passed down to renaissance criticism, where it lurks behind numberless discussions of the deforming effects of white artistic patronage.[11] Razaf, though troubled by the estrangements inherent in running both *The Crusader* and an elevator, learned that service jobs could finance contributions to institutions servicing black liberation. He did his bit for *The Crusader's* renaissance in the knowledge that service work and advanced cultural work might accommodate one another; the fact that *The Messenger* could have been named after a common Harlem job description did not long faze him. Some of his wittiest and most audacious early writing would thus trump even *The Crusader's* proletarianism and suggest that Harlem service workers were authoring renaissance culture as they earned their wages.

"A Wondrous Symbol": Razaf Versus the Literary "Nadir"

The poetry Razaf composed for *The Crusader*—unstudied until now—pleads that cultural history is doubly mistaken when it proposes a clean breach between a superstructure-averse, anticapitalist prerenaissance and a Harlem Renaissance proper of cultural sublimation and aesthetic heroism. First, Razaf's verse indicates that the supposed prerenaissance was nearly as convinced of the political use-values of black literature as Alain Locke and other framers of the "civil rights by copyright" position (Lewis, "Parallels" 29). Second, it affirms that the literary position-takings of the *Crusaders* played a role in jump-starting renaissance writing by helping to detach it from an unusable portion of the black literary past.

Whatever the influence of chosen exemplars such as James Weldon Johnson, Razaf cut his poetic teeth during a moment when the nineteenth-century genteel school enjoyed a final flash of prestige. What U.S. poets and critics imagined as the spiritual pressure of World War I coincided with a boom in poetry sales and in the genteel notion that "poetry has a practical function that resides, paradoxically, in its idealizing influence" (Harrington 498). The union of the poetic and the ideal was in full effect, yet it was not understood as the purchase of autonomy at the price of material irrelevance. Poets were workers in an "essential [war] industry," argued a 1918 issue of the *Literary Digest*, for their products could enable consumers at once to transcend and modify difficult material circumstances; versemakers had showed "a very genuine effect in uplifting the hearts or stiffening the courage of thousands of readers" (qtd. in Harrington 498). Even those radical poets who opposed the war and courted censorship were not immune to the poetics of the "practical-ideal" (498). They gladly "joined poetic 'uplift' with economic and political uprising," notes Joseph Harrington (499). Insofar as Razaf designed his poems to pique black rebellion by hailing and ennobling black souls, he was right among this crew. His understanding of poetry was thus markedly different from that of Huggins and Lewis, later renaissance historians whose sense of literature as a realm apart owes as much to training in the social sciences as to any formalism. Razaf proceeded on the assumption that radical political intervention was both amenable to the poetic and reliant on the ideal with which the poetic communed.

This is not to say that every instance of Razaf's verse for *The Crusader* was a lyric on the spirit-warming qualities of black bolshevism. The diversity that anthologizer Robert Kerlin praised in the whole of Razaf's early poetry is not hard to find in the magazine. Some of his *Crusader* poems took what can only be called an editorial-occasional form, built not just to suit the particular themes of monthly issues but to plug holes in layout. "Labor Lines," a collage of satiric couplets and quatrains that appeared in the Soviet-oriented January–February 1922 issue, is evidence of Razaf's attachment to *The Crusader's* bolshevik strain.[12] It is also an example of the modular quality of his editorial-occasional poems, suitable for extension or contraction according to the copy editor's need:

> Hark to the song the money-hogs sing:
>   "Keep them idle, unemployed,
> Till their morale is destroyed
>   Then they'll work for anything."
>
> The worker dared to use his head
> And for the crime was called a "Red."
>
> One servant should be made to do
> (For one man's pay) the work of two. . . .
>
> "Are Bolshevickies [*sic*] really bad?"
> Asked little Charlie Capers.
> His father chuckled, "Yes, my son,
> According to the papers."   (1–8, 19–22)

Other poems by Razaf were topical verse essays in cultural criticism and/or theater chat. Such blends of the poetic and the journalistic were not uncommon during the interwar heyday of light verse, in which book reviews, even sports news, might be rhymed (Furia 8). The same *Crusader* issue that included "Labor Lines," for example, contained Razaf's lauda-tory (and corny) poetic review of Eubie Blake and Noble Sissle's *Shuffle Along*, the 1921 musical from which Langston Hughes and James Weldon Johnson would date Harlem's renaissance. However tame in themselves, both the medium and the content of the text challenge the assumption that a radical prerenaissance preceded or dismissed new energies in African-American art:

> Dusky maidens, snappy and cuteiful [*sic*],
> All in costumes, gorgeously beautiful;
> Dances, abundantly flavored with novelty,
> Heart-gripping, side-ripping, clean, wholesome comedy.
> Voices, melodious, characteristic
> In Negro-sweetness, soulful and mystic.
> Songs that will capture you, haunt and enrapture you,
> Scenes that will please your eyes,
> Each one a real surprise.
> MILLER and LYLE, SISSLE and BLAKE

What a wonderful quartette these clever boys make!
They didn't go wrong when they created—
"SHUFFLE ALONG." (" 'Shuffle Along' ")

The lion's share of Razaf's more considered poems for *The Crusader,*
however, did their utmost to link uplift and uprising. I would like to con-
sider one such poem in some detail, a ballad entitled "Don't Tread on
Me." First published in April 1919, this poem draws on the insignia of the
Fifteenth Infantry, the all-black New York regiment whose heroism in
France won them the Croix de Guerre and the nickname the Harlem
Hell-Fighters:

There is a wondrous symbol
Which has come from 'cross the sea
It's worn by every member
Of the Fifteenth Infantry:
A snake, curled up, prepared to strike—
And one can plainly see
That by its threat'ning attitude
It says, "DON'T TREAD ON ME!"

O! race! make this your battle-cry—
Engrave it on your heart
It's time for us to "do or die,"
To play a bolder part.
For by the blood you've spilled in France
You must—and will—be free
So, from now on, let us advance
With this, "DON'T TREAD ON ME!"

Even after repeated, convincing arguments for the contingency of aesthetic value and the politically interested repressions of the modern U.S.
poetic canon, it is initially difficult not to read this text as a case for the
old-time modernist religion of complexity, ambiguity, and nonmetro-
nomic rhythm. Matter-of-factly exhortatory, with a sing-song ballad measure that predicts Razaf's success as a song lyricist, "Don't Tread on Me"
seems to ask readers simply to internalize its identical title and refrain. The
poem's insistent iambs and happily masculine endings efficiently sloganize
The Crusader's scheme for postwar black militancy. The first stanza elucidates the meaning of a "wondrous symbol" of self-defense and self-determination that has returned to Harlem in the possession of heroic black

troops. The second stanza apostrophizes the race to which these troops rightly belong, pleading that African Americans inscribe the meaning just where the ideal and the practical join to motivate social action.

To put brakes on interpretation here, however, would be to ignore the intersection between Razaf's verse and that believed to have opened the floodgates of Harlem Renaissance literature. At the very least, "Don't Tread on Me" stands out for its insistence that the U.S. army–supplied image of "a snake, curled up, prepared to strike" is fit for engraving on all black hearts. As David Roediger has observed of a different text, "a greater appreciation of African American patterns of resistance might have argued for using Brer Rabbit" or another of the nonvenomous trickster creatures who get the last laugh in New World black oral literature (*Towards* 168). Yet Razaf's contention that the time had come for all of black America to imitate its most honored returning soldiers and "play a bolder part" in securing liberation required a symbol of active and even predatory resistance, not one associated with the caginess the hunted are compelled to use against their hunters. A less subtle, ultimately less symbolic mode of black struggle called for an immediately readable icon of the intent to secure emancipation by any means necessary, and the uniforms of the Fifteenth Infantry had come preequipped. In "Don't Tread on Me," the transition from Old Negro to New Negro is accordingly premised on a transfer of black identification from Brer Rabbit to Brer Snake.

Just as important, Razaf's poem suggests that the rearticulated significance of the "Don't Tread on Me" snake should be expressible and interpretable both inside and outside the race. The slogan to be used as a "battle cry" in the public campaign for freedom is no different from that to be written on the private "heart" of black combatants; this script of black resistance is neither hermetic nor double-voiced, and it is designed to minimize misreading among those without easy access to African-American hermeneutic codes. Houston Baker has argued that renaissance verse in conventional (meaning Western or white) form stealthily adopts a black modernist discursive strategy he calls the "mastery of form." The faithful English sonnets and ballads of poets such as Countee Cullen and Claude McKay, claims Baker, "are just as much mastered masks as the minstrel manipulations of Booker T. Washington and Charles Chesnutt" (85). Driven to display the outward signs of Anglo-American formal competence, these poems in whiteface nonetheless live to effect a "denigration of form—a necessary ('forced,' as it were) adoption of the standard that results in an effective *blackening*" (85; emphasis in original). Readers in the know can detect the dark tones beneath the ivory surfaces, just as they would have eyes to see the African-American trickster-hero's rebellious face beneath the pious mask. Perhaps Razaf's employment of the ballad is a sign of such poetic "denigration." His seizing of the "Don't Tread on Me" snake and legend from Revolutionary War patriots, Confederate secessionists, and a segregated World War I American Expeditionary Force is an inspired act of black appropriation. But the overriding project of Razaf's poem declines the mastery of form along with the motif of the grinning, lying mask woven throughout turn-of-century African-American poetry. "Don't Tread on Me" is a brief for black literary and political *un*masking, an impatient thematization of the belief that black belligerence must reveal itself in an interracial public sphere most impressed by displays of strength. The poem embodies not so much a fugitive mastery of white literary form as an unmistakable request to begin contesting white mastery in its chosen language of force. And why not? The primary environment of the poem's production and publication—*The Crusader*—forced neither the adoption of Western poetic forms nor a cryptic advocacy of civil rights.[13] The journal's readers, black internationalists by conviction or temporary editorial conjecture, even had reason to appreciate the ballad form as the poetic lingua franca of the English-speaking black diaspora.

What may be most noteworthy about "Don't Tread on Me," however, is what now seems least remarkable about it: its synthesis of standard English and the expression of black militancy without tears. Several months before the Red Summer prompted Claude McKay to write "If We Must Die," African-American literature's canonical statement on black regeneration through violent resistance, "Don't Tread on Me" had enacted the tectonic shift in black poetry's diction and thematic range that would soon be seen as McKay's achievement. Much like McKay's furious yet decorous sonnet ("If we must die, let it not be like hogs / Hunted and penned in an inglorious spot" [ll. 1–2]), Razaf's ballad smashes what Melvin Tolson called the "mold of the Dialect School and the Booker T. Washington Compromise" (288). The subject of "Don't Tread on Me," replacing black accommodation with either liberty or death, anticipates the farewell in "If We Must Die" to the Bookerite gospel of racial progress through forbearance. Razaf's diction banishes the "hyeah"s and "chillen"s representing black linguistic difference in Dunbar and the turn-of-century Dialect School, installing a standard English less soaked in the idiom of English romanticism than McKay's and probably more cognizant of its break with dialect's forced ties to Confederate nostalgia (a prose poem Razaf published on the same *Crusader* page as "Don't Tread on Me" insisted that he couldn't "see why colored folk keep singing 'Dixie' songs" ["Dixie

Songs"]). With the same enthusiasm as "If We Must Die," "Don't Tread on Me" thus takes on the job assigned to renaissance verse in Weldon Johnson's preface to *The Book of American Negro Poetry*: replacing an over-taxed approximation of rural black speech chained to plantation apologetics with "a form freer and larger than dialect" (41). Several early (and warring) audiences thought the similarities between the McKay and Razaf texts were evident. *The Crusader* reprinted both poems to point up the moral of its September 1919 riot issue, while a Department of Justice report on black radicalism introduced the pair as being of equivalent "significance in the record" of New Negro subversion (qtd. in "We 'Rile' " 6).

For present-day audiences, the similarities between the poems ought to make it harder to believe that the literary sea change traditionally associated with McKay flows from his typewriter alone. Beginning with Johnson's anthology, the McKay of "If We Must Die" has been viewed as "one of the principal forces in bringing about the Negro literary awakening" (168). Accounts of renaissance literature often identify the sonnet and its likenesses, collected in *Harlem Shadows* (1922), as definitive ruptures with the age of Dunbar and invitations to New Negro letters. Placing "If We Must Die" next to "Don't Tread on Me" suggests, however, that in shrinking the earliest campaign of renaissance literature to a duel between New Negro McKay (Harcourt, Brace, and Company) and Old Negro Dunbar (Dodd, Mead, and Company), we reproduce an artificially foreshortened relationship between the two poets and ratify their major white publishers' nearsighted views of the black poetic landscape. McKay and Razaf, each *Crusader* readers, contributors, and role models, built their poetic projects in conference with each other and with the position of the journal in the renaissance cultural field. The "mold of the Dialect School and the Booker T. Washington Compromise" that McKay is said to have shattered was exactly the mold the journal's New Negro defied. In a sonnet that advertised this New Negro as a necessary archetype, McKay stood on Razaf's shoulders to present the Harlem Renaissance with a literary calling card. "If We Must Die" did not set a single direction for renaissance poetry, let alone renaissance literature: Langston Hughes and Sterling Brown would save dialect poetry from the Dialect School, just as Zora Neale Hurston rescued dialect narrative. To the extent that the sonnet's cry for self-defense helped clear the ground for the plurality of renaissance literary forms that followed, however, it did so by adapting the frank and proper language of New Negro militancy employed by *The Crusader* and similarly carved into verse by Razaf. McKay may have provided African-American writing with the officially recognized break from a literary "dark ages" that the logic of cultural renaissance demanded, but not without the aid of black bolshevism and another of its preferred poets. Razaf himself backhandedly suggested this debt in the poem "A Harlem Rhymster," which explicitly invited comparisons with McKay while justly confessing a relative lack of metrical sophistication and lyrical "greatness" (l. 4).

Locke, Razaf, and the Sense of an Ending

It is tempting to conclude that Harlem Renaissance bolshevism ends with this chronic twentieth-century irony: an avant-garde aspires to depose capitalist relations and succeeds in overthrowing a cultural style it successfully pronounces reactionary. By the mid-1920s Razaf was writing fewer poems and spending more time with midtown music publishers than with black Marxists. *The Crusader* had ceased publication with the January–February 1922 number, and the ABB had effectively merged with the Communist Party by 1923, one year before Razaf met the prolific Fats Waller. The timing of Razaf's increased devotion to music neatly correlates with two developments that paved the way for Langston Hughes's disappointed quip that "ordinary Negroes hadn't heard of the Negro Renaissance. And if they had, it hadn't raised their wages any" (*The Big Sea* 228). The first was a political double whammy obvious to the U.S. left by 1925. The wartime wave of U.S. labor militancy had been sent to a historic defeat between 1919 and 1924 (M. Davis 49–51), just as the prospects for revolution in European capitals had collapsed. Several of the alterations in the fields of political power and class relations on which *The Crusader*'s renaissance banked had thus changed for the worse. The second development— made easier by the first—was the spectacularly successful transvaluation of Harlem's rebirth instigated by Alain Locke's 1925 *New Negro* anthology, a volume commonly read as the birth certificate and blueprint of the Harlem Renaissance. With aid from the NAACP, the National Urban League, and well-connected white liberal Negrotarians, *The New Negro* redefined the type invoked in its title as someone more likely to turn to Fauvists than Bolsheviks when consulting the muses of Europe. In the process, Locke's anthology assembled a model that has commanded the description, marketing, and consumption of Harlem's renaissance for over seventy years and remains the proving ground for revisions of the movement's history.[14]

The takeoff of Razaf's music career in the middle of the 1920s thus appears to be a sign of the concurrent rout of renaissance bolshevism, done in by forces inside and outside black New York. But such a conclusion is not suspicious enough of the desire to acknowledge the renaissance's complex history in the least complicated manner, not wary enough of the shortcut of constructing a contested, nonstatic movement that still unfolds in an orderly progression of discrete, uniform stages. By 1925 the position of black bolsheviks in and on the renaissance was suffering. They were short of one species of capital they actively sought, the kind collected by those able to define the meanings and stakes of black renovation. The distinctive stance on the renaissance of these bolsheviks had not simply vanished, however, exiled once and for all by a Lockean renaissance of artistic suasion. Their proposals for urban, working-class leadership would inflect renaissance culture produced following the ground-clearing gestures of McKay's poetry, itself reposited in *The New Negro*, and their position in the renaissance field, though weakened, would make itself felt into the 1930s. Deep-seated changes in the Harlem audience and population, if not red victories, continued to license their ventures.

So that these claims won't be dismissed out of hand, I would like to take an immediate look at Locke's contributions to *The New Negro* anthology and the issue of *Survey Graphic* magazine on which it was based, the very texts that might be presumed to have buried Harlem bolshevism on contact. In these 1925 essays deciphering the meaning of the New Negro, as in most later renaissance criticism, the Great Migration of the black masses away from a southern, agricultural destiny is treated as a necessary cause of Harlem's rebirth. All the same, Locke's explorations of the roots of the Harlem movement go on to highlight a transaction between a cluster of black metropolitan intellectuals and what he colorfully labels "the racy peasant undersoil of the race life" ("Negro Youth Speaks" 51). Locke suggests that it is the traveling masses' peculiar task to carry the folk basis of the race to Harlem in mint condition, as if it could be packed along with clothing and photos safe from the hard knocks of dislocation. "A railroad ticket and a suitcase," he asserts, work "like a Baghdad carpet," offering swift and smooth transport of selves and cultures "from the cotton-field and farm to the heart of the most complex urban civilization" ("Harlem" 630). Once in the city, it is the peculiar fate of the migrants to continue to embody the folk essence and its peasant matrix even after immersion in urban labor and culture. Although Locke casts the migrants' journey as "a jump of two generations in social economy and of a century and more of civilization," he suggests that their integral Harlem function is to "provide an exceptional seed-bed for the germinating contacts of the enlightened minority" (630). Locke here figures the migrants not merely as once-and-future peasants but as a kind of human soil that has carted itself northward, presenting a feminine agricultural resource to be fertilized and cultivated by Harlem's modern farmers, "the Negro poet, student, artist, thinker" (630).

Some of the best recent discussions of Locke have emphasized his intimacy with the modern antiessentialist currents of philosophical pragmatism and Boasian anthropology.[15] Locke's apparition of the "racy peasant undersoil" beneath Harlem reminds us, however, that his sense of a voluntary "cultural racialism" did not preclude an indebtedness to older streams of romantic literary nationalism ("Resume"). After a term as the first African-American Rhodes scholar, Locke did graduate work in Berlin, where he had every opportunity to absorb J. G. Herder's brew of untutored folk culture, formal literature in the vernacular, and the spirit of the nation. A distinctive feature of *The New Negro* is indeed its sponsorship of a Herderian national literature based in black New York, albeit one without a definite political telos. "Harlem has the same role to play for the New Negro as Dublin has had for the New Ireland or Prague for the New Czechoslovakia," Locke insists, explaining that the uptown "race capital" in which the folk mind meets the black literati presently seeks only U.S. citizenship, a merely cultural nation within the nation ("The New Negro" 7). This hedged deployment of Herderian rhetoric is not unrelated, I believe, to what congressional tax debaters call "class warfare."

Locke's silken title essay in *The New Negro* is harassed by visions of Garveyite nationalism and race-conscious Marxism in the *Crusader* grain, both of which are more than absent presences in the text. Near the argumentative and literal center of the piece, Locke grants that the new spirit alive in the black masses has made for a "shift in popular support from the officially recognized and orthodox spokesmen to those of an independent, popular, and often radical type who are unmistakable symptoms of a new order" ("The New Negro" 8). Closer to the conclusion, he acknowledges that black thinkers have "shifted a little toward the left with the world trend, and there is an increasing group who affiliate with radical and liberal movements" (11). While Locke goes on to dub the African American a selective or " 'forced radical,' a social protestant" overwhelmingly concerned with racial justice, he ends with the caution that "under further pressure and injustice iconoclastic thought and motives will inevitably increase. Harlem's quixotic radicalisms call for their ounce of democracy to-day lest to-morrow they be beyond cure" (11). His consideration of the New Negro's move to the left thus works at vigilant cross-purposes, aiming both to subdue and to preserve the reputation of Harlem radicals outside their home base. He assures his implied non-Harlemite reader of these radicals' atypical extremism while painting them as heralds of a dim future should interracial democracy—and his program for winning it through black "cultural recognition" (15)—be denied.

Seen in the context of these controlled warnings, Locke's weak-Herderian renaissance born from the black artist's cultivation of the folk looks like a tactical substitution of prototypes for the exchange between Harlem intellectuals and restless masses. Locke's hoped-for channel of spiritual commerce between city-dwelling black peasants and their artistic interpreters supplants but mirrors the *Crusaders'* desired interchange between black urban workers and black bolsheviks (not infrequently the same people). A similar maneuver of reflect and switch can be seen as Locke addresses a major venue of interracial dialogue promoted by the left-wing renaissance. To counterbalance the fact that "in the Northern cities manual laborers brush elbows in their everyday work" ("The New Negro" 9), he endorses "the re-establishment of contact between the more advanced and representative classes" of each race (10). Locke may have pictured race-rioting mechanics checked by antiracist highbrows when arguing "that the only safeguard for mass relations in the future must be provided in the carefully maintained contacts of the enlightened minorities of both race groups" (9). An invitation for integrated "advanced . . . classes" to offset the potentially leftward orientation of ground-up, working-class interracialism cannot be missed, however, given the nearby alarms that Harlem would go red if not dosed with democracy. Locke's contribution to a manifesto genre that, in Janet Lyon's words, typically ignores "the historical presence of competing radical groups" (101) thus feels compelled to address Harlem leftism by name and to counter specific terms and proposals drawn from its armory. It is only the great rhetorical and institutional success of Locke's competition with Harlem communists and other renaissance agents that has permitted us to ignore that his *New Negro* was produced as a stab at rearticulation. The anthology is neither the originating moment nor the final truth of the Harlem movement but a brilliant assortment organized by an editor who admits he has rebuilt to a less radical design. Within a decade, Locke himself would disown the elitism of his masterly reconstruction and offer the black anthological torch to Communist Nancy Cunard, whose *Negro* (1934) collection he privately esteemed as "the finest anthology in every sense of the word, ever compiled on the Negro" (qtd. in Chisholm 221).

Thus, despite Locke's self-proclaimed status as the "midwife" of the Harlem movement, the renaissance as redefined in his *New Negro* was not free from the competitive pressures exerted by Harlem anticapitalism, incubator of black rebirth since the war's end. Neither, moreover, was all worthy and popular post–*New Negro* renaissance art unmarked by the values of black bolshevism. The song lyrics Razaf composed after 1925, for example, bear the imprint of "Don't Tread on Me" and the subculture-cum-political tendency in which it took shape. Eric Sundquist, one of the few renaissance commentators to show an active interest in Razaf, has lately wondered in print if the words to 1929's "Black and Blue" might not be the Harlem movement's best poem ("Red, White" 114). This lyric's fusion of canny internal rhymes, revealing color puns, and ironic but unmistakable antiracism, so reminiscent of Razaf's verse in *The Crusader*, is typical of only a fraction of his mature songwriting.[16] In its unwillingness to segregate the properties of renaissance literature from the black music that helped capitalize the modern U.S. culture industry, however, "Black and Blue" is indicative of Razaf's basic lyrical aesthetic through the 1930s. A provider of Harlem-themed love tunes to the highest bidder, he was professionally aware of the low degree of generic blurring the song market would bear, but he preferred keeping no strict account of the differences between popular song and renaissance poetry, profit-minded mass culture and politically minded working-class culture.

Razaf gradually developed an intimate critique of mass-market music drawing on African-American sounds, a critique based on his own intercession between Harlem and the Tin Pan Alley song-publishing industry as its product began to dominate Broadway, Hollywood, and the radio. He came to complain of the repetition compulsion of the thirty-two-bar chorus, the unfair trade in African-American innovations, and the paradox that the relatively democratic interracialism of urban musical audiences was not reflected in the relations of paid musical production. During his renaissance days, however, Razaf's anger at such binds was outweighed by the conviction that black-authored popular music could stand with the best in the black rebirth. Renaissance criticism tends to protest that, outside of Hughes, Hurston, and Sterling Brown, Harlem's literary ascendancy missed the boat on jazz and the blues, thus missing the most sensitive modern registers of black aesthetic experiment. David Levering Lewis, for example, regrets that when Du Bois and colleagues anticipated a cultural revival based on the art of black folk, they "fully intended to exclude the blues of Bessie Smith and the jazz of 'King' Oliver," favoring the spirituals as more authentic vernacular material and superior evidence of black humanity (*The Portable* xvi). When the various blues-singing Smiths and Oliver's second trumpet, Louis Armstrong, began to "impinge inescapably on Renaissance high culture," Du Bois's troops supposedly "made a virtue of necessity; they applauded the concert-hall ragtime of 'Big Jim' Europe and the 'educated' jazz of Atlanta University graduate and big-band leader Fletcher Henderson" (xvii). Placing Razaf back within our renaissance sights makes this nose-pinching relationship with commercial jazz and the less educable blues seem a little less typical and much less fundamental to the Harlem movement. It is not that Razaf balanced Du Bois by forecasting a literary high renaissance less proud of "Go Down, Moses" and patterned on "St. Louis Blues." It is that for him, as for most *Crusaders*, blues and jazz records and sheet music might themselves be considered renaissance documents. No less than McKay's sonnets on black resistance, they were fair game for New Negro recruitment.

In contrast with Du Bois, born in 1868, Razaf was of the first African-American generation raised along and in sympathy with twentieth-century urban mass amusements, from films and broadcasting to records and vaudeville.[17] Nothing that he and his generation confronted in *The Crusader* was designed to convince them that their affection was unworthy. An evening out for a young, working-class Harlemite during the renaissance years might begin with a visit to the Lafayette Theater on Seventh Avenue, where on a good night Hollywood silent movies were actively, "ethnically" received with the help of Fats Waller's organ playing, between-reel stage plays, and blues artists to close (Singer 143; Vincent 42–43). The cultural wing of Briggs's journal in essence asked to join this variety program and sharpen its usually latent class identifications. *The Crusader* regularly reviewed films shown at the Lafayette and hyped the theater's black acting company at every chance, perhaps because it once extended Briggs a dancing part and was unafraid to produce plays dealing "with Socialism and the relation between capital and labour" (qtd. in Vincent 42–43).[18] The magazine was a delighted agent of the blues boom that followed the huge sales of Mamie Smith's "Crazy Blues" in 1920. Poems on black labor nestled close by notices praising blues entrepreneur W. C. Handy and classic blues singers such as Lucille Hegamin; full-page advertisements for blues recordings faced tributes to Soviet anticolonialism.[19] Unlike the black socialists at *The Messenger*, some of the first Marxists to hear improvising saxophones as capitalist distortion, the *Crusaders* also paid their respects to jazz. Richard Strauss's esteem for the form was the subject of bragging (Henry 32), and jazz was the main drawing card and social lubricant at the Liberty Dances the journal organized to provide itself with a financial cushion (Vincent 138).

With all this, Ted Vincent is not wrong to speculate that "there may not have been another Marxist journal on the planet with [comparable] support of pop culture" (159). *The Crusader's* vision of a renaissance for Harlem's working class seems to have encouraged a liking for many of black New York's actual cultural affections, not solely those centered in print, or traceable to the rural South, or obviously hostile to remuneration and mechanical reproduction. The journal was thus less anxious than most renaissance contenders and modern leftists over workers' cocktails of mass and radical, musical and literary enthusiasms. A bit like Ireland in relation to Britain, *The Crusader's* Harlem was a "race capital" indefinitely separated from the capital of the "colonizing" enemy, thus allowing "a paradoxical circulation of [blackness] back into the metropole, politically, culturally, and economically" (Wicke 605). In these close quarters, as in the Ireland of Joyce described by Jennifer Wicke, there was "a slippage in the alterity" of majority-aimed mass culture that a minority "modernity [could] make use of" (605). But there was also something in *The Crusader's* renascent Harlem unparallelled in Joyce's anticolonialism. Surveying Columbia Records ads that granted black performers the title of artist and featured photos not unlike the models of black deportment on *The Crusader's* covers, Razaf and comrades saw mass culture as a blossoming category of black production, not as the consumptive slough customarily imagined in the modernism/mass culture split. By this I do not mean that *The Crusader* envisioned black bolsheviks productively rereading mass cultural texts for signs of racial ideology and utopia; I mean that the journal viewed mass culture, especially its musical sector, as a relatively open domain for the production of black authorship and a militantly modern black urban working class.

The heart of this attitude, and its implications for Razaf's later lyric writing, are on display in his contribution to the Crusader Music Company, a short-lived music firm that was run from the *Crusader* offices. In 1919 Razaf composed a song entitled "The Fifteenth Infantry" and convinced Briggs to foot the publishing bill. Like an early rap promoter selling records from a car trunk, Razaf personally sold the sheet music to Harlem block by block, demonstrating his creation with the aid of a piano mounted on a rented truck (Singer 52–53). His song's subject was along the lines of "Don't Tread on Me": the proper lesson to be drawn from the return of Harlem's heroic World War I regiment:

> The Fifteenth Infantry is marching thro'
> Just listen to their band the best band in the land;
> 'Twould almost make you grab a gun, grab a gun, join them too.
>
> (qtd. in "Biggest Song Hit")

If anything, these lyrics squeeze a bolder insinuation from the repatriation of the Harlem Hell-Fighters than does "Don't Tread on Me." In broad strokes, Razaf paints the music of James Europe's regimental band as a soundtrack to New Negro conversion back in the USA, a more potent temptation to "grab a gun" than any sidewalk oratory at Lenox Avenue and 135th Street. The firearm-happy chorus is plain communication of the *Crusaders*' trust in the radical uses of jazz. Razaf's Hell-Fighters play it like the journal talked it, wedding the advanced sound of urban blackness with a black militancy first feted in Paris, reigning capital of the modern. In a fantastic fulfillment of the idea of the avant-garde, his Fifteenth Infantry has returned to Harlem scouting the future both militarily and musically. Razaf's chorus no less plainly reveals the blurred lines between his renaissance poetry and song lyrics and the fact that the latter's attachment to transient musical commodities could open room for the expression of New Negro militancy.

One of Razaf's major efforts in 1930 proves that these blurred lines did not firm up with the retreat of radical labor and the publication of Locke's *New Negro*. In that year, he was commissioned to compose the book and lyrics for a floor show at Ed Smalls' Paradise, a 1,500-seat Seventh Avenue nightclub just below the Cotton Club and Connie's Inn on the Harlem pecking order. Smalls' was a genuine "black and tan," a spot opened by its black owner—another former elevator man—to Harlemites as well as white tourists (Singer 174). James P. (Jimmy) Johnson, the dean of Harlem's bounding stride-piano style and the mentor of Fats Waller, was hired to provide the show's music. What emerged from Razaf and Johnson's collaboration was *A Kitchen Mechanic's Revue*, a plotless but tightly themed musical celebrating male and female service workers as Harlem's fountain of wealth, sanity, pleasure, and art. From one perspective, the *Revue*'s tribute to maids, porters, and cooks ("kitchen mechanics," in Harlem slang) seems to be a repetition of Razaf's *Crusader* history as farce. Take the resolutely offensive lyrics of a number called "Sambo's Syncopated Russian Dance":

> Both Lenin and Trotsky
> They do the Kazotsky
> To Sambo's syncopated Russian dance.
> This hamsky from Bamsky [Alabama]
> Is now the man what-amsky,
> All through his syncopated Russian dance.
> Once they were about to shoot him

Where the Volga flows,
Now the Soviets salute him,
Ev'rywhere he goes;
They say this tarsky,
Will soon be the Czarsky,
All through his syncopated Russian dance.

As Eric Sundquist proposes, it is not too hard to imagine this song playing in the background of a painful scene near the close of *Invisible Man*,
the same novel that leads with an allusion to Razaf's "Black and Blue"
(*Cultural Contexts* 116). In one set piece of the invisible narrator's serial disillusionment, Tod Clifton, a gifted African-American ex-communist, is
caught peddling dancing Sambo puppets on a New York street, abjectly
satirizing his manipulation by the Brotherhood, Ellison's facsimile of the
party. It is more difficult, however, to reconstruct the satiric object of these
lyrics as performed for the racially integrated clientele of Smalls's, the original and paying audience for the tale of Lenin's dance coach. At what,
exactly, does Razaf take aim with his absurd and ingenious "-sky" rhymes,
inventing a synthetic Afro-Soviet dialect from dizzy cross-cultural juxta-
positions? Perhaps he focuses on radical Harlem's beeline for the Soviets
and thus on an aspect of his *Crusader* self. As I will detail in chapter 2,
Claude McKay made a triumphant pilgrimage to Moscow in 1922–23,
launching a trend among Harlem Marxists. Lovett Fort-Whiteman, an
ABB member who journeyed to the Soviet Union in the mid-1920s and
returned there to die in Stalin's gulag a decade later (Klehr, Haynes, and
Anderson 218–27), continued wearing Russian costume when back in
Harlem (Naison 13–14). The 1929 stock market crash and official Comintern resolutions on the Negro Question in 1928 and 1930 only increased
the enthusiasm for things Soviet. The satiric target behind Sambo's Soviet
tour might thus be this escalating Russophilia and the related impression
that Communism required disconnection from black cultural wealth.[20]
What should we make, though, of the likelihood that the performance
through which Razaf's Sambo gains fame is as indebted to the Black Bottom as the Kazotsky? It's the syncopation of his Russian dance, and thus
his capacity for cultural syncretism, that is stressed. Razaf's Sambo invents
moves that fit somewhere between Lenin and Trotsky's habitual steps and
his own; he is a compulsory but wildly successful cultural arbitrator,
another fact suggesting that the song is self-ironizing. Like the protagonist
of his lyrics, Razaf was practiced in negotiating between Bolsheviks and
jazzbos, comfortable in both radical Harlem and a Tin Pan Alley

untouched by multicultural sensitivity training. The song's satire also homes in, however, on the Communist state "where the Volga flows." Razaf gives us a Bolshevik pantheon that succumbs to syncopated rhythms despite itself, in the process hinting at the hypocritical squareness of those Soviet officials who refused to welcome black music along with treasured African-American comrades. Novelist Maxim Gorky had denounced jazz as the "music of the gross" in 1928, while other protectors of Soviet proletarian culture tried to ban the saxophone and succeeded in frightening prospective importers of U.S. jazz records with six months in jail (Gorman 133). "Sambo's Syncopated Russian Dance" jokingly protests such censorship with a narrative germ close to the rock-and-roll films of the 1950s, in which authorities ban but then helplessly dance to the kids' music. More gravely, the song intimates that Soviets were now responsible for crimes against humanity, not just the saxophone. Only the dancing skill of Razaf's hero, after all, keeps him from being shot in the manner of an enemy of the state and puts him in the running for the anachronistic but rhyming post of "Czarsky."

What is to be done with such fuzzy, multidirectional satire? The remainder of *A Kitchen Mechanic's Revue* answers that the irresolution of "Sambo's . . . Dance" was one price Razaf paid to lend a left accent to genuinely popular Harlem theater. Theophilus Lewis, *The Messenger*'s iconoclastic theater reviewer, may have been isolated among renaissance-era critics in arguing that any African-American drama worth its salt would have to build from black stage performance as working-class Harlem knew and liked it. He thus instructed proponents of an indigenously black renaissance theater to study the comic revue, an entertainment George Hutchinson nicely describes as "modern, urban, erotic, both morally and culturally 'impure' . . . , [the] 'illegitimate' offspring of an illegitimate, patently racist (though subconsciously miscegenationist) . . . 'white' American drama," namely, blackface minstrelsy (311). Lewis seems to have sparked at least one black artist to put his proposals to the test. As an author of comic musical theater, Razaf was equally unawed by Lockean folk authenticity and the kind of proletcult solemnity in which Lenin never dances and never sins; he knew he wrote for a nightclub audience, not the rock-solid unionists who took in James P. Johnson's later musical *The Organizer* (1939), a collaboration with Langston Hughes commissioned by the International Ladies' Garment Workers (Denning 311). Yet Razaf still hoped to produce purposeful dramatic amusement, discreetly slipping doses of the *Crusaders*' working-class renaissance into voguish Harlem club life. The *Revue* accordingly took up an impure, if not illegitimate, task: breeding the casual, risqué, and urbane theatrical mode that ruled Harlem evenings with the service work that filled most Harlemites' days. The opening song, "Kitchen Mechanic's Parade," sets the tone by showering praise and vacation time on black New York's domestic rank and file:

> That kitchen mechanics' parade
> Puts all the rest in the shade,
> Porters, butlers, cooks, and maids;
> There'll be no work done today,
> Bosses have nothing to say,
> Step back, give them plenty of room,
> Heroes of the mop and broom . . .

A later verse allows the club's kitchen staff to flaunt its musical readiness:

> We're the chefs of the Paradise
> We're here at a fancy price,
> To cook you a musical stew for this review.
> Soon you'll learn when you take a look,
> What we cook isn't in the book,
> Our recipes are melodies—
> We serve them as we please.
> We know our bass and treble clefs,
> For we're the musical chefs,
> We're the musical chefs.

These lines to be sung by "musical chefs" qualify as advertisements for Smalls', whose wait staff was famous for dancing perfect Charlestons as they served drinks. Yet the silencing of the bosses insists that the lines also promote something grander. The *Revue*'s opening number entertains dreams normally undreamt by the white clubbers who "like Van Vechten, / Start inspectin' " in Razaf's song "Go Harlem" (qtd. in Singer 239). What might happen, Razaf asks, if Harlem service workers were permitted less circumspection about their artistry, if their melodies could be served when and as they pleased? What if the black working class represented by Smalls's kitchen crew could unveil itself as the prime mover of the vanguard sounds of the twentieth century ("What we cook isn't in the book") and be rewarded for its effort ("There'll be no work done today")? The most interesting implication of this fantasy is not that a gifted musician emerges each time a Harlem cook takes off an apron; the many fusions and confusions of cooking and composing also suggest that assiduous labor goes into Harlem service and Harlem rhythm, that those who know recipes can also "know . . . bass and treble clefs," and that these knowledges don't always war with each other. Through its conceit of an ultimate servant's night off, "Kitchen Mechanic's Parade" crosses a carnivalesque inversion of class rank with an erasure of all the distinctions between Harlem's menial and cultural labor. Razaf's own employment history shows beneath the song. His lyric both remedies the social concealment of the black service work he once performed and protests the fetishism of seemingly laborless black musical commodities that might obscure his lyric writing. In a critique of political economy you can dance to, he spotlights the Harlemites behind services luxurious and common and reveals the black work—preferably purchased "at a fancy price"—hidden within salable Harlem melodies.

The *Revue's* biggest hit, "A Porter's Love Song to a Chambermaid,"[21] does a similar job of exposure:

Tho' my position is of low degree
And all the others may look down on me,
I'll go smiling thru,
That's if I have you;
I am the happiest of troubadours,
Thinking of you, while I'm massaging floors,
At my leisure time, I made up this rhyme:

I will be the oil mop,
If you'll be the oil,
Then we both could mingle
Ev'ry time we toil.
I will be the washboard,
If you will be the tub,
Think of all the Mondays
We can rub-a-dub.
I will be your shoebrush
If you'll be my shoe,
Then I'd keep you bright, dear,
Feeling good as new.
If you'll be my razor,
I will be your blade,
That's a porter's love song,
To a chambermaid.

Through their bluesy double entendres, one of Razaf's specialties, these lyrics re-sound the Marxian overtone of "Kitchen Mechanic's Parade":

underpaid black labor, not the ingenuous talent of the Sambo figure, is the breeding ground of the African-American art that "Jes Grew" from Harlem to the land where the Volga flows. Much like the opener's musical chefs, Razaf's porter needs little prodding to rival Cole Porter and composes a clever rhyme at the drop of a mop. The bawdy results, though couched as the product of a pure proletarian writer, could well have been taken as an insult to the puritan element in the U.S. cultural left, which analogized "jazz hounds and sex degenerates" (qtd. in Gorman 116). The main motive for the porter's off-color composition is not opposition to conventional proletarian culture circa 1930, however. His rhyme is an extended play on the multiaccentuality of the word "work" in modern African-American speech, where it can signify "dancing, labour, sexual activity or any nuanced combination of all three" (Gilroy, "There Ain't" 203). The porter's introductory lines emphasize work as mere drudgery, but his love song then diverges from Prufrock's and becomes a catalog of the domestic chores and erotic acts a maid and porter could share. We might think that this transition from preface to catalog, from work alone to work as sex, coincides with a move from necessary, sexually repressive labor to erotically fulfilling, voluntary artistic production. The introduction indeed presents a lonely porter reckoning with his paying "position . . . of low degree," whereas the verses that follow represent his autonomous, pleasurable creation. But Razaf's worker-writer can't quite bring himself to segregate eros and labor, unalienated song composition and alienated service work. In 1924's *The Gift of Black Folk*, W. E. B. Du Bois argued that African Americans had given all U.S. workers a precious donation in "the idea of toil as a necessary evil ministering to the pleasures of life" (79). Razaf's porter might agree with Du Bois but add that another gift worth giving was the idea that the pleasures of life could minister to—and mingle with—toil. He figures eroticism in terms of his wage labor, concentrates his desire on a fellow employee, fantasizes a relationship unfolding on the job as well as on Mondays off, and describes himself as "the happiest of troubadours" while attending to his cleaning. Like the young Razaf, this lyrical porter has learned to dissolve the worst tensions inherent in mixed hours of desire, intellectual effort, and service obligation. The sliver of utopia within the slightly dirty joke of "A Porter's Love Song to a Chambermaid" is thus not the promise that sexuality and art might escape cleanly from the discipline of the wage but the prospect that the common labor in making love, "massaging floors," and devising rhymes could be freely acknowledged and enjoyed.[22]

It would be too cute to propose that *A Kitchen Mechanic's Revue* consciously works to synthesize Marx's secret of surplus value with popular forms of African-American labor resistance. Razaf's Moscow-on-the-Harlem pageant nevertheless suggests that his contact with the renaissance of Harlem bolshevism allowed his songwriting to draw on two distinct "counter-cultures of modernity":[23] Marxism, with its materialist accent on labor's primacy and exploitation under capitalism; and the vernacular arts of the black diaspora, whose utopian politics Paul Gilroy distills as a "desire . . . to conjure up and enact the new modes of friendship, happiness, and solidarity that are consequent on the overcoming of [modernity's] racial oppression" (*The Black Atlantic* 38). The *Revue* draws from black music's "posing [of] the world as it is against the world as the racially subordinated would like it to be" (36), evoking the deliverance of Harlem's "heroes of the mop and broom" through parades and songs of liberation from dormant bosses. It draws from Marxism as it discloses the personal yet still hidden and naturalized labor of service work. It braids the two borrowings together in its suggestion that black emancipation might emerge through a generous enrichment of productive labor, a proposition as distinct from most black radical thought, forged in the memory of slavery, as from the severe work ethic of Booker T.-ism.[24] "Sambo's . . . Dance" affirms that the Razaf of 1930 was less infatuated with the Soviet Union than were his *Crusader* comrades, many now party officials; he would not follow his common-law wife, leftist singer Minto Cato, on the international tours for which she was eventually blacklisted (Singer 375). All the same, the whole of the *Revue* bespeaks his continued infatuation with the *Crusader* group's understanding of Harlem's rebirth. Razaf filled the floor of Smalls' with a performance of renaissance culture ardently devoted to the manual and artistic labor of Harlem's working class. Through his rhyming porters and singing chefs, staged versions of his *Crusader* self, he attested that renaissance culture was this class's performance.

Renaissance Time (Again)

Crucial Harlem Renaissance texts from *Fine Clothes to the Jew* (1927) to *Home to Harlem* (1928) might be added to the case I have pursued through *A Kitchen Mechanic's Revue*. Neither Hughes's cooks and elevator boys nor McKay's uninhibited, pro-union longshoreman Jake seems to believe that the renaissance of Harlem's proletariat had failed entirely by 1925. The sweep of Razaf's renaissance radicalism alone, however, should serve to suggest that black bolshevism is best seen as a fluctuating but consistently fertile position within the full history of the renaissance cultural field.

The primary aim of this conclusion does not need belaboring at a moment when the history of the renaissance is back in vogue and back in flux. Under the combined pressure of black feminism, various new historicisms, and what I have elsewhere called the "new integrationism" in modernist studies ("Black and White"), the self-defeating and melodramatic problem of the movement's "failure" has finally been tabled. Clearly, I intend my work to join the reopened questions of the renaissance's parameters and balance of power. I hope it is just as clear that the retrieval of Razaf and the *Crusader*s at the core of this work is not intended to provoke unreflective nostalgia. Not every aspect of the renaissance promoted by Razaf and the black bolsheviks inspires loving resurrection. The specifically political edge of this renaissance was dulled not only by historical forces beyond its jurisdiction but by a willed hypermasculinism and a general unwillingness to question a special relationship with the Soviets. Why, then, should we believe that recovering Razaf is valuable to endeavors other than more accurately mapping the Harlem movement?

For at least four reasons, I submit. First, retrieving Razaf argues that we have just begun to explore the continuities between putatively disjoined and hostile periods of black cultural life: the renaissance of the 1920s and the black proletarianism of the 1930s sustained by the Great Depression, the Federal Writers' Project, and an aggressively antiracist Communist Party. Might the crash and the resulting reorientation of political and economic capital in fact have forced a weakened renaissance position—black bolshevism—into dominance and equipped it to install a compelling problematic for black literary culture? Second, retrieving Razaf argues that the engagement between the New Negro and the Old Left was commenced much earlier than usually thought, and by parties usually deemed passive in its grip. The pages of *The Crusader* testify that this engagement was first proposed during the dawning of a self-conscious Harlem–New Negro modernism and at the instigation of black intellectuals who never suspected that Communism and black renaissances were bad neighbors. Third, retrieving Razaf argues that we go awry in assuming that the meeting of the New Negro and the Old Left is purely an installment in the history of modern interracial organization or black-Jewish relations. As the sparring renaissance position-takings of Locke and the black bolsheviks suggest, this meeting was from its inception also played out within African-American cultural ranks. Fourth, and finally, retrieving Razaf argues that we have little reason to fear that intellectual freedom was necessarily compromised when African Americans eyed Communism as a fraternal relation. From the *Crusaders'* renaissance, we learn that the canonical modern unveiling of such freedom—the Harlem Renaissance—tapped and accommodated Communism with liberty. For all these reasons—the details and consequences of which will require subsequent chapters to explore—Razaf should not remain an invisible man.

2 · Home to Moscow: Claude McKay's *The Negroes in America* and the Race of Marxist Theory

Young comrades,

        keep eyes on Moscow,

                train ears

to Russian consonants, vowels.

Why,

    were I a black

        whom old age hoars,

still,

    eager and uncomplaining,

I'd sit

    and learn Russian

        if only because

it

  was spoken

    by Lenin.

        —Vladimir Mayakovsky, "To Our Young Generation" (1927)

Claude McKay's "If We Must Die," the poem most often judged to be the inaugural address of the Harlem Renaissance, was first printed above an article on Bolshevism and religion in the July 1919 *Liberator*. In the eyes of its author, however, the sonnet was unveiled before a group Andy Razaf might have styled as the renaissance's chefs: the black employees of the Pennsylvania Railroad dining car where McKay waited tables. "It was the only poem I ever read to the members of my crew," McKay claimed, and "they were all agitated" (*A Long Way* 31). The excited response of McKay's coworkers was to be echoed by the dozens of African-American journals that reprinted the poem repeatedly into the 1920s. *The Crusader* hailed "If We Must Die" with speed: its September 1919 issue featured the sonnet a few pages ahead of a reprise of Razaf's martial ballad "Don't Tread on Me."

The pressing historical stimulus for *The Crusader*'s embrace was the Red Summer, whose color McKay ecumenically traced to "the outbreak of little wars between labor and capital and, like a plague breaking out in sore places, between colored folk and white" (*A Long Way* 31). The immediate goal of the republication was to spark further black boldness in all these battles. To the *Crusader*s, McKay's sonnet was the ideal text for a militant sampler. With steely propriety, the poem put forth the creed of a New Negro whose modernity rested on self-defense as much as on Marxism and the metropolis:

> If we must die, let it not be like hogs
> Hunted and penned in an inglorious spot,
> While round us bark the mad and hungry dogs,
> Making their mock at our accursèd lot.
> If we must die, O let us nobly die,
> So that our precious blood may not be shed
> In vain; then even the monsters we defy
> Shall be constrained to honor us though dead!
> O, kinsmen! we must meet the common foe!
> Though far outnumbered let us show us brave,
> And for their thousand blows deal one death-blow!
> What though before us lies the open grave?
> Like men we'll face the murderous, cowardly pack,
> Pressed to the wall, dying, but fighting back!

Though "If We Must Die" famously does not designate the racial identities of "kinsmen" and their enemies—nowhere is the "foe" of the speaker revealed to be an "ofay"—it must have struck the *Crusader*s as a poem written to their specifications. Appearing in the wake of the armed African Americans who had made race rioting unprecedentedly dangerous to whites, the sonnet was hard to dissociate from the journal's plea that the weapons of interracial warfare stay double-edged swords. The "I" of the modern lyric, opposed to the collective, if not free from the social determination of individuality itself, here became a "we" promoting the visceral comradeship the *Crusader*s likewise tied to a willingness to die for imagined "kinsmen." The correlation of suicidal retribution with martyrdom on behalf of a blood brotherhood; the rhetorical performance of an evolution from potential animal fear ("If we must die, let it not be like hogs"), to certain masculine fortitude ("Like men we'll face the murderous, cowardly pack"), all seemed to render *Crusader* policy into iambic pentameter. From the moment "If We Must Die" was reprinted in the journal, McKay was stamped as a *Crusader* poet of choice, a fluent historian of the magazine's postwar code of radical remasculinization.

McKay was not Briggs and company's sole poet of choice, however. As we saw in the previous chapter, "If We Must Die" was less a revelation than a confirmation to *Crusader*s acquainted with poems such as "Don't Tread on Me." Razaf's early verse affirms that McKay was not the only postwar Harlemite merging calls for black insurgency with standard English and regular forms drawn from the Anglo-American inventory. Considered alongside Razaf's lines, McKay's resistance to both dialect and free verse is less easily read as either an isolated renaissance-launching triumph or an aberrant antimodernist refusal of formal innovation and black vernacular infusion. Still, pairing Razaf and McKay cannot level all the distinctions between the "Don't Tread on Me"s and the "If We Must Die"s. The *Crusader*s welcomed McKay not just because his poetry seemed to rhyme with Razaf's and summarize their New Negro's creed; it also seemed to elaborate *Crusader* poetics with an eye to European literary history and thus to entertain the tastes of readerships otherwise unmoved by black bolshevism. Unlike Razaf, McKay was determined to show the rise of the self-defending New Negro as a productive problem for the lyric sonnet of Petrarch, Shakespeare, and Keats. Many of the best-known poems collected in *Harlem Shadows* (1922) explore the social history and continued value of this song form without failing its requisites. "America" broaches the question of whether a black rebel can stand within pentameter walls without "a shred / Of terror, malice, not a word of jeer" (ll. 9–10). "In Bondage" is a pastoral sonnet worrying over the mode's unpaid debt to the sweat of agricultural slaves. Surprisingly emphatic in McKay's U.S. verse is self-examination of the "flaw" found by generations of McKay critics: the questionable fit between the New Negro's self-determination and the baggage and scaffolding of the sonnet form.

Consider "The White City," originally printed in the October 1921 *Liberator*. In lieu of the application in "If We Must Die" of negative emotion to the positive end of joining kinsmen in struggle, this sonnet argues for hate as good medicine for a single black soul:

> I will not toy with it nor bend an inch.
> Deep in the secret chambers of my heart
> I muse my life-long hate, and without flinch
> I bear it nobly as I live my part.
> My being would be a skeleton, a shell,
> If this dark Passion that fills my every mood,

And makes my heaven in the white world's hell,
Did not forever feed me vital blood.
I see the mighty city through a mist—
The strident trains that speed the goaded mass,
The poles and spires and towers vapor-kissed,
The fortressed port through which the great ships pass,
The tides, the wharves, the dens I contemplate,
Are sweet like wanton loves because I hate.

This poem obviously savors conceptual inversion. Like the young Louis Farrakhan's calypso tune "A White Man's Heaven Is a Black Man's Hell," McKay's text declares "the white world's hell" a heaven (l. 7); hate not only feeds the speaker's "vital blood" (l. 8) but makes the monuments of the white city's power look "sweet like wanton loves" behind a scrimlike, Eliotic urban mist (l. 14). The structural motivation behind the sequence of reversals is not only the binary logic of contradictive black and white worlds but also the production of a loyal sonnet—the West's archetypal variety of love lyric—about titanic hate. This latter motivation is clarified at the close of the first quatrain, designed to ambush those anticipating another rehearsal of love's powers. The identity of the emotion "Deep in the secret chambers of [the speaker's] heart" is not revealed to be "life-long hate" until the middle of line three; even then, line four goes on to cast this hate as something the speaker will bear as thousands of other sonnet voices have borne unrequited desire: "nobly," while playing an assigned "part" in a theatricalized test. In the second quatrain, the program of imagining hate as an enabling emotion for the sonnet speaker is given specific historical resonance by the news that this hate is a punningly "dark Passion" (l. 6) directed at the "white world's hell" (l. 7). The third quatrain, joined grammatically with the concluding couplet into a virtual Petrarchan sestet, drops the hate-for-love substitution during a series of aestheticized metropolitan perceptions: "strident trains" (l. 10) rumble beneath "vapor-kissed" skyscrapers (l. 11). The final lines, however, return the negative image of the sonnet's ruling emotion to the fore of the poem's ironic repertoire. The nonwhite speaker enjoys a type of futurist gaze unveiling the loveliness of the white city's steel, crowds, and byways, but only with the X-ray glasses of race hate, corrective lenses that supply glimpses of reckless pleasure: "The tides, the wharves, the dens I contemplate, / Are sweet like wanton loves because I hate" (ll. 13–14).

The attitude of "The White City" toward the sonnet form is less severe than its stance toward those who own the "poles and spires and towers," manifestations of urban beauty and aspiration that in themselves recall the "ships, towers, domes" of Wordsworth's 1802 sonnet "Composed Upon Westminster Bridge" (l. 6). McKay's inversion of sonnet conventions necessarily evokes and depends on these conventions for its success. More pointedly, his poem's speaker is an inheritor of the sonnet persona that had developed along with the fourteen-line formula. True to type, the voice of "The White City" appears to have discovered a way to live deeply with intense emotion through the process sonnet historian Paul Oppenheimer calls "dialectical self-confrontation" (183). Even as the poem's first two quatrains instill and thwart the expectation that love is locked in "the secret chambers of [the speaker's] heart" (l. 2), they gesture to a barely concluded controversy over hate's powers of (self-)creation. The poem's initial line— "I will not toy with it nor bend an inch"—marks the public resolution of a private argument, a just-decided inner debate discernible in this same line's formal declaration of determination and in the melodramatic self-reassurance of the second quatrain:

My being would be a skeleton, a shell,
If this dark Passion that fills my every mood,
And makes my heaven in the white world's hell,
Did not forever feed me vital blood.   (ll. 5–8)

The staging of the conclusion of this internal argument warrants Adorno's contention that in the modern lyric "the historical relationship of the subject to objectivity, of the individual to society, must [find] its precipitate in the medium of a subjective spirit thrown back upon itself" (42). McKay's "I" reveals that he has learned to thrive on the subjective experience of socially instilled antagonism not by appealing to this emotion's object or to his implicit audience but by resolving a difference within his "secret . . . heart" (l. 2). Significantly, such resolution relies on the lyric sonnet's provision of more than a "shell" in which "dark Passion" may be poured (ll. 5, 6). The speaker's praise of the explosive emotion with which he now refuses to "toy" (l. 1), along with his willingness to bear "life-long hate" in noble if actorly style (l. 3), suggests that he has found in the sonnet persona one model for the New Negro who accepts anger's formative power.

"The White City" thus shows the lyric sonnet's merit for the New Negro—and vice versa. With the latter demonstration, the poem makes itself accessible to readers schooled to respect lyric confessionalism above the insertion of black enmity into interracial discourse. Those who first introduced McKay to nonradical white U.S. publics indeed praised his equal possession of old-line lyricism and indelible blackness. As *Liberator* editor Max Eastman put it in his introduction to *Harlem Shadows*, McKay bucked his "age of roar and advertising" (xviii) to protect the quality of "all the poets that we call lyric because we love them so much": "the pure, clear arrow-like transference of . . . emotion into our breast, without any but the inevitable words" (xvii). His sonnets were thus for the singing and had "a special interest for all the races of man because they [were first] sung by a pure blooded Negro" (ix). This profile of McKay as the custodian of both full-throated lyric voice and full-blooded Negritude was among the earliest images of Harlem's renaissance projected outside uptown Manhattan. Whatever its racialist pitfalls, it was an image partially suggested by McKay himself, not by blundering into a constrictive white form but by forcing the encounter of the lyric sonnet and the *Crusader*-built New Negro. In stage-managing the "dark Passion" of a militant made black and bid to sing, McKay made hay from the form/content problem later ascribed to his reflexive failings and became a messenger of Harlem's radical rebirth to audiences who never believed that Communism would prove fatal to racism.

A less poetic aspect of McKay's work as a renaissance missionary will be addressed in the remainder of this chapter, work he performed on several fronts despite his public dismissal of "the highly propagandized Negro renaissance period" (*A Long Way* 154). In September 1922 McKay sailed for the Soviet Union, where his *Harlem Shadows* poem "Exhortation: Summer, 1919" had already discovered the sun of Africa's "new / dawn" (ll. 9–10). He came to sample the air of the world's first Marxist state and to convey to the original Bolsheviks the advice of their Harlem relations. The culmination of McKay's latter aim was a short book entitled *Negry v Amerike* (*The Negroes in America*, 1923). This still-obscure treatise allows a useful shift of attention from the career cost of McKay's expatriations to the imaginative dialogues and translations they mandated. In particular, *The Negroes* offers a rich site on which to consider one of the thorniest questions of McKay's—and renaissance Harlem's—encounter with the Third International: Was the Soviet-sponsored Marxian theory of the Negro Question underpinning the exchanges between New Negro and Old Left a clueless, domineering Russian import, innocent of or hostile to independent black thought?

Black Theory and/or Communism

Even before shelves filled with critiques of Marxism's "labor metaphysic," the first wave of historical scholarship on African Americans and the Old

Left answered this question with a resounding yes. Midcentury liberal historians of black-Red relations began with the conclusion that U.S. Communism was chiefly notable for its deference to the Soviet Union. As a result, African and other Americans were seen to affiliate with the party at the cost of all thoughts unattuned to Communist fealty. In a chapter instructively titled "Red and Black: Unblending Colors," for example, Wilson Record's *The Negro and the Communist Party* (1951) claimed that a black intellectual attracted to the Communists could anticipate "the compromise of his independence, the circumscription of his imagination, and the channeling of his idea-output into a rigid mould" (309). Those with leadership positions, such as Langston Hughes, onetime president of the League of Struggle for Negro Rights, could expect no better. "The Communist 'leader'—Negro or white—can lead only if he is willing slavishly to follow," declared Record (108). African-American Communists were thus little different from the naive or cynical white servants of Stalin who fleshed out the party.

Record's characteristic cold war assumption that U.S. Communism was umbilically connected to Moscow has ironically been reenergized by some of the initial historical fallout of the collapse of the Soviet Union. Newly opened Soviet archives have provided historians Harvey Klehr, John Earl Haynes, Fridrikh Igorevich Firsov, and Kyrill M. Anderson with evidence they believe shores up the premises of anti-Communist Communist history. In *The Secret World of American Communism* (1995), the inaugural volume of Yale's Annals of Communism series, Klehr, Haynes, and Firsov annotate ninety-two previously unavailable primary sources shedding light on Soviet funding of the American Communist Party (the CPUSA) and on covert activity by U.S. Communists linked to Soviet intelligence. In a follow-up volume, *The Soviet World of American Communism* (1998), Klehr, Haynes, and Anderson present ninety-five new documents concerning the close relationship between the CPUSA and the Comintern. *The Secret World* is justified in holding that its discoveries make it all but impossible to believe "that the Soviet Union did not fund the American party, that the CPUSA did not maintain a covert apparatus, and that key leaders and cadres were innocent of connection with Soviet espionage operations" (18). All points of interpretive nuance aside,[1] however, the evidence does not buttress the polemical judgment "that the widespread popular belief that many American Communists collaborated with Soviet intelligence and placed loyalty to the Soviet Union ahead of loyalty to the United States was well founded" (16). As Klehr, Haynes, and Firsov note at their book's close, "the overwhelming majority [of U.S. Communists]

had nothing to do with espionage" (323). Between introduction and conclusion, then, a well-founded "many" has become an underwhelming if
well-placed minority of Soviet spies.

The evidence contained in *The Soviet World of American Communism* is
similarly important, similarly compelling, and similarly harnessed to some
doubtful inferences. "At every period of the CPUSA's history," this evidence
establishes, "the American Communists looked to their Soviet counterparts for advice on how to conduct their own party business" (4). It is difficult to gainsay cables from the Comintern vetting candidates for U.S.
party leadership, telegraphs exhibiting the supervisory powers of Comintern representatives in the United States, and memos indicating that
U.S. Communists, black and white, did little to prevent the Gulag death
of accused antirevolutionary Lovett Fort-Whiteman. Matters are less
clear-cut, however, when Klehr, Haynes, and Anderson suggest that their
documents show the CPUSA to be "the American arm of Soviet Communism," plain and simple (6). The trio's metaphor of bodily attachment
opposes the New Left–leaning, grassroots-digging "new history" of the
party that in the 1980s began separating out the U.S. ingredient in U.S.
Communism. This new history may well be myopic when verging on the
claim that U.S. Communism was a homebound American democratic
politics like any other. The U.S. party, like all national parties affiliated
with the Comintern, was an internationalist organization obliged to apply
Moscow-centric resolutions and to render assistance to the Soviet Union.
Yet *The Soviet World* convincingly questions the import—not the valid-
ity—of the better part of such revisionism: the idea that domestic concerns as well as Soviet ones impressed U.S. Communists where they lived
and politicked.[2]

The discovery of domestic impacts on the U.S. party is in fact the hall-
mark of the best-regarded recent histories of African Americans and Communism. Mark Naison's *Communists in Harlem During the Depression*
(1983) and Robin D. G. Kelley's *Hammer and Hoe: Alabama Communists
During the Great Depression* (1990) share the new historians' intent to
rewrite Communist history from the bottom up, emphasizing the practices of the party's rank and file. While dealing with black spaces as distinct
as Deep South Alabama and New York's world symbol of black urbanism,
both books maintain that the infamous party line was subject to the transforming construal of African-American communities. Naison is accordingly concerned not only with the party's Soviet-sutured political history
but with the ways in which "the social and cultural atmosphere of Harlem
gave a distinctive cast to Party activity, creating problems and opportuni-

ties which Party 'theory' did not always anticipate" (xvii). He accentuates events dramatizing the autonomy of Harlem organizing, including a 1932 dance to benefit the Scottsboro boys, for which black party leaders were willing to engage gifted nonrevolutionaries such as Fats Waller and the Smalls' Paradise revue (Razaf must have been in the audience) (72). Naison judges that local Harlem leverage was most pronounced in the embracing, patriotic Popular Front period of 1935–39, the new historians' favorite party epoch. During this culmination of Harlem Communism, he claims, Harlem party activity at times foreshadowed 1960s protest movements, with a core of professional organizers mobilizing members and supporters united only by their respect for party-line basics.

The black Alabama Communists investigated by Kelley, meanwhile, were less impressed by the welcome wagon of the Popular Front but no more overwhelmed by commands from Moscow. Kelley paints a party branch "built from scratch by working people without a Euro-American left-wing tradition, . . . enveloped by the cultures and ideas of its constituency," not excluding the signs and prophecies of southern black Christianity (xi). A self-described youth in comparison to warring generations of ex–Old Left and ex–New Left historians, Kelley seeks to win the Alabama party for the new historians' cause while moderating the sharp struggle with anti-Communism. To his mind, none of the local inflections of Communism he discovers is incompatible with the position that party cadres jumped to accept Soviet guidance. Alabamians did what they could to enact the official line, "but because neither Joe Stalin, [nor American Party leaders] spoke directly to them or to their daily problems, Alabama Communists developed strategies and tactics in response to local circumstances that, in most cases, had nothing to do with international crises. Besides, if Alabamians had waited patiently for orders from Moscow, they might still be waiting today" (xiv). Distances of culture and communication made it impossible, then, to be at once a pawn of Stalin and a black Red in Birmingham or Tallapoosa County.

Both my approach to early Harlem Communism and my overall focus on black agency within the Old Left are sympathetic and indebted to the work of Naison and Kelley. All the same, I believe that the revisionist model of black Communists reworking and compensating for party directives has been slow to consider whether the ability of these Communists to recast party activity extended to the point of theoretical production. Did the social and cultural atmosphere of black communities breed not only "problems and opportunities which Party 'theory' did not always anticipate" (Naison xvii) but alterations of this theory that might rebound on international Communist policy? Did the meeting of black American life and the theory imperfectly transmitted from the Comintern to the U.S. party transfigure both? *The Negroes in America* is evidence that black revision of such theory was possible and forceful, at least when the distances between Moscow and Harlem were minimized by high-stakes revolutionary tourism. To say this does not mean I will be arguing that the official Marxism of the Third International was utterly decentered by New Negroes writing back to the Communist "metropolis." I will ultimately suggest, however, that Soviet-approved answers to the Negro Question did not take long to reverberate with the black voice McKay brought to Moscow in the early 1920s, the voice of Harlem Renaissance bolshevism. For this reason, above all, black Communists between the wars rarely worried that Soviet intervention threatened African-American autonomy: indigenous black interests were sometimes better represented in Comintern directives than in U.S. Communism at its most national. For these Communists, then, the opposition later at the heart of historical debate over the U.S. party—local issues and values versus Soviet administration—represented no great antagonism.

"The Magic Pilgrimage": A Working Vacation

What McKay called his "Magic Pilgrimage" (*A Long Way* 151) to the capital of communism was partly financed through the least fitting of sources: a fund-raising scheme in which his sonnets became a deluxe, limited-edition commodity. When McKay was scraping up the money necessary for the long voyage, James Weldon Johnson proposed that he offer *Harlem Shadows*, complete with a signed photograph and an inflated price tag, to the names on an exclusive NAACP donors' list. McKay took Johnson up on the idea, and any misgivings he may have had about becoming the dependent of a genteel circle faded as the checks began to augment his meager savings. Armed with a letter of radical introduction from Crystal Eastman, the prominent socialist feminist and sister of Max, McKay left New York in September 1922, working as a stoker on a Liverpool-bound ship to save money (*A Long Way* 153–54). Had Eastman and the NAACP angels understood that he would criticize both bourgeois racial reformers and actually existing U.S. Communism when he arrived, they might have been less helpful in getting him there. Once established in Moscow he declared himself a proud member of both the Communist Party and the African Blood Brotherhood and filled his public comments with sharp counsel to the first group drawn from the latter.

Despite McKay's later self-portrait as an accidental tourist, he was well prepared for his posting as radical Harlem's ambassador to Moscow, the city code-named "Mecca" in Communist dispatches (Klehr, Haynes, and Anderson 191 n. 29). Sure that the Russian Revolution was "the greatest event in the history of humanity" (qtd. in United States, 26 Jan. 1924), he had been promising himself a trip to the Soviet Union since 1920, when John Reed had invited him to visit with the Comintern (Tillery 63). He had honed his skills as a moderator between black and white revolutionaries when working for *The Liberator* in 1921–22, arranging discussions between interested white Communists and those he judged "advanced Negro radicals" like Cyril Briggs and Richard B. Moore (*A Long Way* 109). Even casual visitors to his Harlem apartment had come away with fistfuls of Communist and ABB literature and the impression "that the poet hosted communist meetings several days a week" (Kornweibel 148). McKay could not have been ready, however, for the ecstatic welcome he received in the Soviet Union: accounts of his reception resemble reports on a Western rock star's first perestroika-era tour. Before the spell was over, he had been carried along Moscow's Tverskaya Street on the shoulders of cheering crowds, granted the use of a driver, housed in some of the finest accommodations in the city, and toasted by units of the Red Army and Navy, whom he invited to join the "we" of "If We Must Die." While McKay only peeked at a sickly V. I. Lenin, Leon Trotsky granted him public correspondence and a private meeting; Grigori Zinoviev, the president of the Third International, stood by his side at a May Day reviewing stand; and the Moscow soviet made him an honorary member. He was dined by the commissar of education and arts, introduced to the constructivist theater director Vsevolod Meyerhold, and presented with an autographed collection of poems by Vladimir Mayakovsky. *Pravda, Izvestia,* and other Soviet publications competed for his articles, for which he received the best pay of his life. As if according to a *Crusader* master plan, the breakout literary voice of the New Negro became a celebrity in the nation of the New Crowd Bolsheviks (McKay, *A Long Way* 153–225; Cooper 171–92). McKay's complete success in the Soviet Union led him to the joking suspicion that the very whiteness of his hosts might now be challenged in the United States. "The anthropologists of 100 per cent pure white Americanism," he informed the NAACP's *Crisis,* "may soon invoke Science to prove that the Russians are not at all God's white people" ("Soviet Russia" 105).

From a handful of Russians, McKay received rock-star treatment because he was also thought capable of providing African-American–style entertainment. His autobiography recounts the insistence of Mayakovsky's wife that they "dance a jazz" in a Gypsy cabaret and the disappointment when he "did not measure up to the standard of Aframerican choreography" (*A Long Way* 187): his syncopated Russian dance impressed few Bolsheviks. Yet McKay traced most of his hosts' excitement to the fact that he was among the first blacks to enter the country after Red October and was therefore readable as an emblem of a whole race's sympathy for Bolshevism. He was treated "like a black ikon in the flesh," he thought, one fortunate enough to arrive when Lenin's market-friendly New Economic Policy was increasing the standard of hospitality along with the standard of living (168). McKay did not object to incarnating the symbol of his race within a new faith if his race was finally honored in the style it deserved. In a line destined to be echoed by later visiting African-American radicals, he swore that "never in my life did I feel prouder of being an African, a black, and make no mistake about it" (168).

Iconic status was also politically useful. Because McKay had not arrived in the Soviet Union as a registered U.S. Communist delegate, he was forced to find his own way into the Fourth Congress of the Comintern, a periodic policy-setting gathering of international Communist leaders that was one of the obligatory stations of his pilgrimage. Recognizing that the antiimperialist Soviets wanted blacks at the congress and could count only on the official U.S. delegate Otto Huiswoud, he "mobilized [his] African features" to gain entry into the inaugural session (*A Long Way* 173). For this mustering of physiognomy, he was rewarded with a seat on the main platform, a position from which his representation of the black proletariat could communicate itself to everyone in the hall. McKay refused when suddenly asked to speak on the Negro Question just reaching the floor, citing inadequate preparation. Before the end of the congress, however, he had composed and delivered a pointed address and broken dramatically with the role of seen-and-not-heard token (Cooper 177–78).

McKay began his formal "Report on the Negro Question" with the admission that he "would rather face a lynching stake in civilised America than try to make a speech before the most intellectual and critical audience in the world" (16), an odd compliment that deliberately or not invited comparisons between the Comintern and the Klan. Apologetic preliminaries were followed with strong criticism of what McKay saw as U.S. Communism's near-surrender to racism. The bitter truth about racial conflict in the United States, he insisted, was that it was "so ugly and terrible that very few people [there] are willing to face it" (16). Despite the coalition-building zeal of Harlem Marxists, it was the "reformist bourgeoisie" (read his friend Weldon Johnson's NAACP) who continued to lead the war against discrimination. The U.S. left had thus far "fought very shy of it because there is a great element of prejudice among [its ranks]" (16). McKay emphasized that the Negro problem was hardly an external or secondary issue for the U.S. party; it was "the greatest difficulty that the Communists of America have got to overcome" (16).

Solving Communism's own Negro problem was paramount for reasons of sheer political survival. "The American capitalists are setting out to mobilise the entire black race of America for the purpose of fighting organized labour," argued McKay (16). Just what he meant by "mobilise" was not specified but can be inferred from the frequent Harlem bolshevik contention that pitting black scabs against racially exclusive unions had become the preeminent class-war tactic of U.S. industrialists. Yet McKay's vision of what later radicals called a "racial capitalism," eager to inflate differences of color and culture into intractable intraclass oppositions (Robinson 9), spilled over U.S. borders. "The International bourgeoisie," he informed his Comintern listeners, "would use the Negro race as their trump card in their fight against world revolution" ("Report" 16). Imperial powers England and France had already created army divisions from among their African subjects during the world war and could easily exploit racial fears by throwing black troops against working-class uprisings in Europe. McKay's professed nervousness in facing the directorate of world Communism thus did not stop him from proposing an unorthodox trump card thesis that thrust the Negro Question from the far outskirts to the dead center of Communist strategy. To snatch a phrase from E. San Juan, Jr., he answered the Soviets' warm welcome with compliments and then dared them to view racial antagonism as the "Archimedean point of the class struggle" (77).

McKay's audacity seems to have been appreciated by the Comintern. "Red Red" Rose Pastor Stokes, an American mover and shaker of the congress's "Negro Commission," would report that he had captivated the delegates (31), and the text of McKay's speech was printed in the Comintern's organ of international public relations (McKay, "Report"). In any case, the magic of McKay's Magic Pilgrimage was undiminished after his address, and he was commissioned by the Soviet State Publishing House to expand his thoughts on the Negro Question to book length. The result was the Russian-language *Negry v Amerike* (1923), whose single copy in the United States was to sit forgotten on the Slavic language shelves of the New York Public Library until Wayne Cooper, McKay's fine biographer, dusted it off in 1973. In 1979 the book was translated back into a semblance of McKay's original, now-missing English text by Robert J. Winter and published under the title of *The Negroes in America*. Judging from the subdued reaction of U.S. critical theory, radical history, and African-American studies, this addition to Marxism after Marx might have remained inaccessible.[3] What the text has to say on the issue of the "race" of Comintern theory—the possibility of black alteration of official Marxism between the wars—is thus still news. In the section that follows, I will examine several innovative aspects of McKay's treatise, from its theory of African-American history to its thoughts on the preeminence of black Americans in U.S. class struggle and white-proletarian psychology. Consideration of McKay's outlook on black culture and white feminism, both conceived as medicine for what ails socialism in the United States, will lead into a final discussion of the implications of *The Negroes'* Marxist revisionism.

The Negroes' Argument

The Negroes in America was intended mainly as an African-American primer for Soviet beginners, although its pages thick with Cyrillic did not stop McKay from confessing to the additional "aim of explaining to black and white workers their close affinity, and of indicating to dark-skinned people their true place in the class struggle and their role in the international workers' movement" (*The Negroes* 3). The study's approximately one hundred pages are divided into a brief introduction, two appendixes, and eight chapters, which together predict both the expansive horizon and uneven adroitness of cultural studies at its most ambitious. Juggling economics, psychology, cultural critique, and political polemic, McKay is loath to exclude any facet of his topic save black Christianity, which he, like too many later secular radicals, mistakenly dismisses as an anachronism. His concerns thus range amply, from basic African-American history, to black art in the tracks of modernist primitivism, to the ties linking the Negro Question, the so-called Woman Question, and American sexual exceptionalism. McKay himself admits that his book is less than thorough even so, the output of a restless author "irritated by the fact that I have to stay in my room and write when I want to go everywhere, observe, and learn about the new life and constructive work of the Soviet Union" (6). Although he had access to only a few relevant sources—William Z. Foster's *The Great Steel Strike*, black socialist Hubert Harrison's *The Negro and the Nation*, Carl Sandburg's *The Chicago Race Riots*—he reduced his labor by seizing several long quotations from those at hand. Syndicalist leader Foster, IWW legend "Big Bill" Haywood, and Harlem bolshevik W. A. Domingo could have been listed as collaborators.

McKay nevertheless recognized that his hastily prepared, at times sloppy book was unprecedented and eventful. His was the inaugural "book or monograph" on African America written by a black author "from a class point of view," he claims, and he may have been right (3). McKay calculates that he got there first for a simple material reason: "other Negroes to whom it would occur to write about their race from a class point of view would [have met] with the same difficulties" as he did back in Harlem, above all, not being "able to tear [themselves] away from daily work in order to devote [themselves] to writing" (3). Perhaps only in the Soviet Union, he suggests, could the black worker–social scientist find the prerequisite of a proper book or monograph: a freedom from daily wage labor that need not bank on "the support of the reformist bourgeoisie" (3). McKay's engagement with the idea of proletarian letters thus cannot be reduced to his well-known dismissal of "doggerels from lumberjacks and stevedores and true revelations from chambermaids" (*A Long Way* 139). His first take on the benefits of living Communism highlighted Soviet patronage for his own—delightedly proletarian—nonfiction.

In the first chapter of *The Negroes*, "A General View," McKay's look at his "race from a class point of view" results in perhaps the first historical sketch of African America executed with the tools of historical materialism. His portrait of the black masses in the matrix of political economy anticipates W. E. B. Du Bois's much more sweeping and erudite *Black Reconstruction* (1935) in breaking with the idealist tradition in black history.[4] In one critical respect, however, McKay's introduction of Marxist categories into black historiography marks no advance over the great (black) men approach of the first African-American scholarly historians. The surveys of neglected black civilization builders produced by George Washington Williams (1849–91) and Carter G. Woodson (1875–1950) may have favored sermonizing narrative over materialist analysis but never doubted the ability of black people to act on their own fate.[5] By contrast, *The Negroes*' "General View" assumes that African Americans arrived late at historical agency, becoming self-directing historical players only during their twentieth-century flight "to the city and to a proletarian milieu" (12). With the exception of a season of striving following the Civil War, slavery and the first fifty years of Emancipation cast McKay's blacks as passive components in a deep-structural conflict adopted from Progressive history, a clash among the landowning South, the industrial North, and the farming West. McKay's staging of what Du Bois pointedly called Black Reconstruction, for example, features African-American freedmen and -women in the bit parts of "wards" of the North's "very expensive occupa-

tion army" and "victims of extreme bourgeois radicalism" (14). No quarter
is given Du Bois's arguments, premiered as early as 1909, that Reconstruction-era black legislators worked to provide the South with its first tastes
of democratic education and semidemocratic government.[6] *The Negroes'*
portrait of unprepared freed blacks at the mercy of Radical Republicans
may indeed seem too amenable to the frankly racist "Dunning School" of
Reconstruction history,[7] not to mention D. W. Griffith's epic valentine to
the Klan, *The Birth of a Nation* (1915). In fairness, however, McKay finds
"the Republican party and the northern bourgeoisie" guilty of a crime that
Columbia's William A. Dunning and his mostly white southern students
did not prosecute: betraying the Freedmen's Bureau and "depriving
[African Americans] of their lawful inheritance, the land—that land
which they had cultivated and . . . lived on for two centuries" (14). Dunning School products had spent the first few decades of the century
denouncing "Negro rule" even as they painted Negro rulers as the puppets
of northern wizards; McKay, it seems, sought to resolve the resulting paradox in the direction of consistent black powerlessness, pinning the blame
on northern Radicals who were finally not extreme enough. *The Negroes'*
reflections on the failure of even Radical Reconstruction to expunge the
productive relations of the slave South would not be pursued in earnest by
U.S. historians until the 1970s and 1980s.[8] McKay's prescience is bound
up, however, with the belief that African Americans lacked class consciousness—and thus true self-consciousness—before entering the North
and the factory door. To his mind, U.S. blacks do not lack a history but
dwell in its clutches until the proletarianizing Great Migration, a journey
toward the genuine self-activity reserved for industrial workers.

When McKay considers the revolutionary tinderbox the post–Civil
War South might have been, he is less ensnared by his era's witness of the
triumph of industrial production and by his safe bet on the historical
errand of industrial labor. *The Negroes in America* coolly poses Reconstruction as an abandoned program of economic transformation initially
closer to the October Revolution than the American Revolution. McKay
explores the briefly inverted world of the defeated Confederacy without
Du Bois's hyper-Marxian framework of a "dictatorship of labor in the
South" (*Black Reconstruction* 580). Twelve years before the avant-garde
Black Reconstruction, however, *The Negroes* likewise declares that "the
destruction of the southern Confederacy, which followed the Civil War,
was the single attempt at a genuine revolution in America," an ill-fated
effort to uproot the forced labor system haunting the entire nation's working class (13). What authorizes McKay's early assertion of Reconstruction's

magnitude is a vision broader than any abolitionism. "With the birth of American democracy in 1776," he argues, "the Negro Question became the main question," the key and motive to U.S. history before and after the Civil War (41). Like Du Bois, McKay stakes a pioneering claim to the centrality of African-American history in U.S. history; whatever Marxism's own historical and cultural constraints, it seems to have been a regular presence at the initiation of a black history presuming to explain U.S. development.

The bedrock of McKay's particular case for such a history is contained in chapters 3 and 4 of *The Negroes*, the book's contentious treatments of "Labor Leaders and Negroes" and "The Workers' Party and Negroes," respectively. While African-American workers may not have achieved the preconditions of class consciousness until the twentieth century, McKay suggests that they have been the outstanding pressure on U.S. class struggle since sometime in the seventeenth century. The two-party habit in U.S. politics can be traced to "the question of personal slaves" and the resulting combat between two ruling classes distinct in geography, property, and mode of production, "the commercial interests of the North and the slaveholding interests of the South" (42). The success of the abstract rights of man over the "rights of free labor in the United States" likewise can be located in slavery, which "disparaged and sabotaged" the aspirations of all U.S. workers (42). With the growing presence of black migrants in northern wage work, McKay contends, the pivotal position of African Americans in U.S. class history had become visible to the least trained eye. Labor leaders and the Workers Party, as the aboveground American Communist Party was then named, therefore faced a final fork in the road. The workers' movement "must choose one of the following two paths," McKay insists, "the organization of black workers separately or together with whites—or the defeat of both by the forces of the bourgeoisie" (44). This blessing of the contingency of a separate black labor movement stops short of C. L. R. James's better-known "Revolutionary Answer to the Negro Problem in the U.S.A." (1948), which identifies independent black struggle as the weathervane of U.S. socialism. McKay nonetheless reveals a Jamesian willingness to challenge socialist misgivings over black autonomy on socialist grounds, and this when James was still a schoolmaster in Trinidad.

McKay caps his do-or-die rhetoric on the necessity of black labor organization by bringing Harlem bolshevism home to Moscow more plainly than anywhere else in his study. Reprinted in "The Workers' Party and Negroes" chapter are large chunks of W. A. Domingo's article "The Main-

tenance of the Spirit of Radicalism Among White Radicals," an exceptional advice column for white comrades originally published in
Domingo's short-lived Harlem Marxist newspaper *The Emancipator*.
McKay seconds Domingo's motion that the commitment of white leftists
to black freedom is "the measure" of their radicalism itself, not just what
The Crusader labeled "The Acid Test of White Friendship" (qtd. on 40).
The reason, Domingo explains, is that "Negroes are sufficiently powerful
to maintain or destroy American radicalism. Their strategic position in the
industrial area gives them a power beyond their numbers. The Negro
workers' power, correctly understood and intelligently and disinterestedly
applied, could be used to obtain freedom for both black and white workers. And it is just this power which sooner or later will force white radicals
to speak out" (qtd. on 40). Given that in 1922 the Workers Party had
proven too cautious to advocate interracial "social equality" along with
other types of social equity, these claims were amazingly brash, the product of acute study of the Great Migration's class impact that had occupied
few outside the African Blood Brotherhood. Gone was the bean-counting
argument that African Americans now constituted an unignorable percentage of the industrial labor force. In its place was the assertion that the
freshly strategic position of African Americans made them the saviors or
executioners of U.S. socialism. What Domingo intended via the shorthand of "strategic position" was what McKay had probably meant when
he spoke of blacks being mobilized by capital in his speech before the
Comintern: that northern industry, with the self-destructive complicity of
discriminating white unions, had moved to employ arriving black workers
as a permanent wedge against organized labor. Yet this effort to transform
black workers into protectors of capital gave them a place within the proletariat as ambivalent as it was strategic: like palace guards, they could
secure this class's victory as well as its defeat practically on their own.[9]
Black industrial laborers, then, had as persuasive a claim to vanguardism
as did the Workers Party itself. Without Domingo's aid, McKay's "General
View" had answered the question of socialism's special absence from the
United States with reference to labor's lack of "a fraternal hand [for] the
black working force" (23). With Domingo's help, McKay proceeded to
charge that U.S. political development would remain exceptionally
arrested until leftists acknowledged that blacks wore the most "radical
chains" in the proletariat, the class, reasoned Marx, that could only break
its bonds by breaking humanity's. Among the most venturesome threads
in McKay's book—the idea that African Americans in themselves possessed the strength to clinch U.S. socialism—was thus also the most

beholden to Domingo and, through him, to the intellectual network of Harlem bolshevism.

Barbed and precocious as they are, McKay's thoughts on the prominence of African Americans in U.S. class struggle do not reflect much specific investment in Marxist theoretical controversy. Can it really be argued, then, that McKay's groundbreaking approach to African-American history is matched by creative work in Marxist theory? Undoubtedly, *The Negroes'* point of departure is a concrete, topical political dilemma: the depressed learning curve of the U.S. labor and Communist movements on the subject of African Americans. And yet the underdevelopment of Marxist thinking on race in the early 1920s required that McKay pragmatically renovate the Marxist theory he had studied most conscientiously during a London stay in 1919–21 (Cooper 110–11). Not every Marxist intellectual habit is subject to McKay's review, of course. As noted earlier, the author of *The Negroes in America* has few doubts about the millennial calling of industrial workers, black or white; his introduction suggests that "the Negro question is at bottom a question of the working class," exactly as the Marxism of the Workers Party would have it (10). But McKay also pleads that the odds for mass arrival at the bottom of the Negro Question are not improved when workers' parties reflexively sweep race into the dustbin of bourgeois wastes. For him, contra Stuart Hall, race is one modality in which class is *not* lived,[10] a refuge of scoundrels who would screen the U.S. working class from its own numbers and power; no less, though, is race a blindfold training practical social vision, a perceptual aid that the racially oppressed should surrender with care. With a then-rare Marxist emphasis on the grinding lived experience of racism, McKay argues that "the Negro in America is not permitted for one minute to forget his color, his skin, or his race" (4). As such, "it is very useful [for him] to be imbued with race consciousness," even if "it is still more useful for him to look at the problem which disturbs him from a class point of view" (4). Class struggle might be the determining battlefield of the Negro Question, just as, in something of a dialectical reversal, "Negroes are the Belgium of the American workers' movement, the battleground on which will be fought with unusual cruelty those battles which one can already distinguish on the American horizon" (44). The critical decision of African Americans to tackle racism on class terrain could not be guaranteed, however. In McKay's Marxism, a racially unified working class was neither predestined by the conditions of capitalist production nor compelled by the denial of racism's material effects on working-class understanding and activity.

McKay's deliberations on the race-class axis show a willingness to amend classical and Comintern precepts and distinguish him from nearly every Marxist of his day outside of Harlem. What distinguishes these deliberations from more recent academic boilerplate is McKay's assumption that the white working class had already accepted them as gospel. Many white workers, he believed, lived by the pragmatics of "race consciousness," and not simply because these pragmatics had trickled down as a solvent to proletarian unity. "When white firemen on the railroads of Georgia had a strike in 1919 with the demand to dismiss all black firemen," McKay notes, "they put out an appeal to the public in which they said, 'White people of this state refuse to recognize social equality' " (37–38). Whatever the hidden delicacies of their bargain, these strikers had engaged in a public campaign of self-racialization: their work stoppage in the name of white power could not be explained as a simple efflux of their bosses' short-term interest in profits and long-term interest in social peace. At their most aggressively and autonomously "workerist," it appeared, the firemen had been their most racist. Behind this disheartening scene, thought McKay, was something stranger than a white labor aristocracy investing in a split labor market. In a fascinating late chapter titled "Sex and Economics," he unveils his solution to the mystery of working-class racism: the white proletariat, led by its southern contingent, had internalized "an unusual neurotic fascination with the naked body and sexual organs of Negroes" (81). A thoroughgoing Americanized Marxism would logically need to develop not just a respect for the utility of race consciousness but a social psychology capable of grasping the effects of racial capitalism on working-class desires.

McKay's notes toward this social psychology lead with the claim that nearly all nonpetty crime in the United States, "be it class inequality, lynch law, or the exploitation of labor—is concealed by the fetish of [black-white] sex as behind a smoke screen" (76). The specter of interracial intimacy qualifies as America's distinctive contribution to the stock of ideologies obstructing a clear view of class insult: there is nowhere else, he reports, where "sex plays such a role in the economic struggle" (77). McKay's vision of a blinding sexual fetish complementing the fetishism of commodities on U.S. soil rests on the much-abused Marxist notion of ideology as false consciousness. At the same time, however, it demands a Marxist historical account unusually attentive to the specificities of racism in one country. McKay roots his sexual genealogy in the agricultural labor of the early southern colonies and the prohibition of all sexual attraction between physically proximate black slaves and white indentured and hired hands. By the nineteenth century, McKay pronounces, "hostile feelings between the races were fanned and magnified to a large extent by the sexual taboo" (79). Slaveowners had created a sizable interracial population and a paternalistic association with domestic slaves susceptible to a "false romantic tinge," as well as to the naive envy of whites outside the plantation household (79). "White workers," then, "could only look upon what the slave-owning class ate as forbidden fruit which they were not allowed even to touch" (79). Slave laborers, for their part, "constantly heard the contemptuous judgment of their masters about white workers, whom they called 'poor white trash' " (79). McKay's antebellum southern ruling class rivals Gramscian historian Eugene Genovese's in its high standard of hegemonic craftsmanship: by the Civil War, it "owned the bodies of white workers and black slaves . . . [and] the psychology of both races" (79). Progressive white southern workers had no choice but to migrate to the North or West; those left behind were easy recruits for the Confederate military and later for the deconstruction of Reconstruction through lynch law. A carefully cultivated "survival of the period when Negroes were slaves," the sexual fear and desire for African Americans had "acquired the force of an instinct" in the twentieth-century southern white working class (77). And the shallow identity of racial superiority this instinct provided had migrated northward: because of traveling headline news of black sexual "crimes," erotic Negrophobia had infected "the huge mass of the literate proletariat of the North" (82).

McKay's rickety history of racialized sexual fetish and taboo cannot be accused of excessive finesse or evidentiary detail. The claim about the white South's migrating radical workers, among others, lacks empirical support; the account of neurotic pollution through northern newsprint is abrupt and unconvincing; and the desire to ground white sexual psychology in the manufacture of race and class hegemony fades the further it gets from the slave South. Yet this imperfect chapter in the direction of a nonreductive, historically rooted Marxist understanding of white working-class racism still contains useful challenges for the exploding field of whiteness studies, a field opened to labor history by the work of David Roediger. In *The Wages of Whiteness* (1991) and *Towards the Abolition of Whiteness* (1994), Roediger explores the distillation of white consciousness amid wrenching economic change. Building on George Rawick's analysis of Anglo-American racism in the colonial era, he argues that the racial investments of the modern U.S. working class "took shape alongside the imposition of time discipline, the bastardization of crafts, the attacks on holidays, and the attempts to control sexuality and drinking characteristic of capitalist development in the second quarter of the nineteenth century" (*Towards* 64). European-descended workers caught in the painful transition to industrial wage labor began to project ambivalent longings for their own past onto purportedly lazy and inhibition-free blacks but were moved to deny the constitutive power of their dreamwork. As Rawick explains in a formulation Roediger often cites, the worker-racist built a "pornography of his former life. . . . In order to ensure that he [would] not slip back into the old ways or act out half-suppressed fantasies, he [had to] see a tremendous difference between his reformed self and those whom he formerly resembled" (qtd. on 64). Workers nostalgic for life prior to the estrangements of workplace sobriety thus defined U.S. whiteness and blackness simultaneously but acknowledged their attachment to the first creation only. They had made the racial Other but could not admit that their enemy was their "us."

McKay's much earlier hunt for the origins of a self-actualizing working-class racism similarly homes in on the coupling of compulsory work and prohibited sexuality. In distinction to Roediger, however, he traces the ancestry of the white laborer to the antebellum South and to the pornography of a life denied. White southern workers, McKay speculates, craved and resented the easy sexuality they attributed to black slaves, but not because they associated this sexuality with their own raucous past. Instead, they fantasized a fenced-off plantation of earthly delights, an interracial sexual garden from which they were barred. From one angle, this was a wrongheaded but resistant fantasy that refused to displace the sexual predations of the masters solely onto the bodies and desires of slaves.[11] Yet the very same fantasy was also the slaveocracy's secret recipe for labor peace, thanks to its willingness to weigh white working-class privation against sexually "favored" slave workers. Fatally, the white proletariat of the South mistook black resentment for black erotic—and economic—advantage.

Or so suggests McKay. Even as his history of U.S. "Sex and Economics" veers unsteadily from white to black southerners, from airy psychologism to old Marxist functionalism, it raises questions present-day whiteness studies might well explore. For instance, have archaeologies of whiteness been too eager to relegate the pre-nineteenth-century South to the "prehistory" of the white worker (Roediger, *The Wages* 24)? How was whiteness South and North shaped by the often brutal plantation practice of interracial sex? How might we grant this whiteness the status of a proletarian enterprise, relatively independent of ruling-class intrigue, without slighting its function as a salve for class wounds? How did African Americans witness and intervene in the manufacture and application of whiteness?

Was their protest of its violence preceded by an inadvertent assist in the making of "white trash"? Finally, has whiteness studies been overly wary of instructive Old Left echoes and insufficiently attentive to the long tradition of black radical thought on the white problem? McKay's chapter on "Sex and Economics" is in all likelihood the earliest history of the self-consciously white worker.[12] Along with the reflections of Du Bois, James Baldwin, and Toni Morrison, it carves out a spot in the "unsurpassed tradition of Black thought about white people and whiteness," a tradition that Roediger himself weighs against the perception "that 'whiteness studies' is a recent creation in which white scholars have pioneered" (*Black* xi).[13]

A still-lively question about whiteness directly addressed in *The Negroes* is where to find an antidote short of "a genuine revolution in America" (13). Given McKay's credentials as a poet, it is not shocking that one possible answer involves the modern upsurge of black culture. Cornel West has suggested that "Marcus Garvey's black nationalism made proto-Gramscians out of most Afro-American Marxists," in the sense that "the Garvey movement of the early twenties—the first mass movement among Afro-Americans"—taught the black left never to ignore "the cultural dimensions" of black liberation (20). Though McKay declared the Garveyites unstable dreamers, *The Negroes* confirms that he left Harlem with a pre-Gramscian conviction that culture was virtually as urgent a location for the black working class as its "strategic position in the industrial area" (qtd. on 40). Three chapters of McKay's book, over one-third of the total, are devoted to culture broadly, though not anthropologically, conceived. They are among his most international, for the paradox binding the modern African-American artist is not American alone: "Homage is rendered to dead Negro artists, while the living must struggle for the recognition of a just place for Negroes in the industrial society of the modern world" (64).

The dead artists getting the good notices, McKay explains, were brought to white attention by the circuits of empire; their carvings and bronzes, tributes to African kings and queens and rivals of "the greatest works of Greek art," had become gorgeous documents of imperial barbarism a second time with the European "fight over . . . African bones" (57). McKay identifies two main modes of the European imperial appropriation of African imperial artwork. The first, perfected by the English, can be called the ethnographic-piratic: in remarkably contemporary-sounding passages indicting the display of African art in Western museums, McKay protests the secreting of Benin bronzes within the ethnological section of the British Museum, "where the opportunity of seeing the most beautiful samples of the acquisitions of British piracy, exploitation, and deceit is presented to the gaze of the amazed spectator" (56). The second mode of appropriation, perfected by the French, can be called the aesthetic-counterfeit and grants the independent formal interest of African works to a fault. European modernist art was born, suggests McKay, with those who "followed the tricolor into the African jungles and returned to Paris with samples of Negro art" (57), samples whose social origin was immediately obscured through derivative avant-gardisms and that "genuine bourgeois thing, [the] art exhibit" (59). Through a fantasia of masks and idols speaking not as Parisian fetishes but with the voice of their departed creators, he envisions African art resocialized and repatriated, liberated from museum and market (if not from his own dipping into Montmartre Africanism): "In open places in the jungles near our huts, surrounded by wild beasts . . .[,] we worked in wood and clay without thinking about competition or reward or praise; some things we finished, others we carelessly set aside, having forgotten about them as now we are forgotten" (58–59).

McKay pairs his early satire of modernist primitivism with the efforts of the best living African-American artists to defeat obscurity and grandiose whiteness, whether in the sculpture studio or on the football field. In the chapter "Negroes in Sports," McKay prefigures C. L. R. James's cricket writing by approaching the boxing ring as an arena in which white supremacy is tested, viewing the fights as neither an antithesis to the fine arts nor a simple diversion from the real business of racialized wage differentials. While he regards heavyweights in less radiant light than James does his cricketers, ball-playing actors in "a dramatic spectacle" rivaling the opera (*Beyond a Boundary* 196), McKay treats responses to black champion Jack Johnson as texts to be combed for cracks in race relations. Any thought that "fist fights arranged for a commercial purpose" can settle racial disparities in full is absurd, however (55). Sport is a cultural institution in which African-American workers "exert all their efforts to gain the victory" (54) and another "large business . . . managed by corporations" that most often succeeds in setting the terms of black entrance and success (53). The dialectic between culture as a site of struggle with whiteness and culture as a white-owned industry is also to be found in McKay's section on "Negroes in Art and Music." There, black performers such as Charles Gilpin, the first Emperor Jones, are seen bursting "through the color barrier," in the process chipping at "the complete poverty and nullity of the American stage" (60). In "Negroes in Literature," McKay maintains that "the only [black] literature which merits any attention is that which has the character of national propaganda" (73) and shows this literature at war with white "novelists who depict Negro types" in the style of "biologists, anthropologists, purists, and criminologists, but not as artists" (72). His literary New Negro renaissance, the outgrowth "of a new spirit among the Negro masses" (73), is defined, like Razaf's and Weldon Johnson's, against "old dialect" (75). As a whole, the cultural chapters of *The Negroes in America* unveil McKay as a precursor—and Marxian pre-critic—of black cultural studies. They mingle high and low forms, culture, power, and national propaganda without yielding aesthetic valuation, the criterion of self-representation through artistic production, or a caustic awareness of the material limits on creative reception. They insist that the approach to culture as a site of struggle over the meaning of race will be impeded or exploited by those capitalizing the fights, the plays, and the novels.

After black cultural intervention, the second handy antidote to whiteness that McKay explores is white feminism, which to his mind faces a unique opportunity and responsibility to defuse the sexual taboo at whiteness's core. This taboo, he notes in "Sex and Economics," reached its ruinous peak in the South of the post-Reconstruction nadir and in the criminalization of contacts between black men and white women. The ex-Confederate patriarchy fought "all attempts to educate the liberated slaves and aid them in improving their position" with two bogies: "the fear of black rule and the defense of white women from rape by blacks" (81). Both flowed into the practice of lynching, which McKay dubs "that exclusively American national sport" (82) and theorizes, like Ida B. Wells before him, as a means to reestablish dominance over the entire freed black community.[14] Not to be denied, however, were the gender inflections that left the lynch campaign vulnerable to an uncommon crossracial understanding: black men and white women were fettered together in the manifest sexual content of the latent attack on Emancipation. Black manhood was therefore not the only prisoner of the myth of the rapacious black male; "the white man who parades his chivalrous views of a woman," McKay argues, "says to a white woman, 'You are under my protection and I can not trust you not to have relations with a colored man.' Thus, the white man directly confesses the white woman to be weak, and immoral in sexual conduct in her relations with a Negro man" (76–77). Feminism's success, McKay concludes, is contingent on the destruction of lynching and its ideological props. All (white) women were honor bound to "give [their] response to this open campaign against [their] virtue"; socialist feminists were obligated to stamp out all traces of suffragist racism and "to overturn the malicious assertion that their relations with colored comrades must necessarily be immoral" (77).

McKay's now-common injunctions on the logical necessity of feminist antiracism fall into bitter traps that are equally familiar. Though he briefly mentions the lynching of black women, his spotlight on violated black men and outraged white feminine virtue collates womanhood with whiteness and nourishes the public concealment of "the corporeal violence attending black female bodies" (Wiegman 84). Notwithstanding, McKay's proclamation that "the Negro question is inseparably connected with the question of woman's liberation" (77) represents a conjunctive insight much rarer in U.S. Marxism circa 1923 than in contemporary U.S. humanities departments. A combination of declared bohemianism, private bisexuality, and intellectual friendship with leftist feminists such as Crystal Eastman and Sylvia Pankhurst left the author of *The Negroes in America* unsatisfied by early Communist tributes to the reproductive services of the "Mothers of the Proletariat" (qtd. in Baxandall 146). Without surrendering the conviction that class is the elementary contradiction in capitalist society, this author thus invokes a Marxism in which sex and economics are contemplated in unison and the Negro Question and the Woman Question are inextricable first subjects, not incongruous exceptions to the rules of class struggle.

The Negroes' Legacy

McKay's Soviet book deserves better than the neglect or dismissal it has received since its English translation. During the Moscow leg of his globe-trotting as a sexual, political, and literary ultra, McKay made an appearance as an offhandedly creative figure in twentieth-century Marxist thought. The depth of the Marxist revisionism cultivated in renaissance Harlem is disclosed by his sure questioning of classical verdicts on the naturalness of class consciousness, the dependable arrival of proletarian victory, and the immateriality of culture, gender, and desire. With its chief emphasis on the pressure of race within U.S. capitalist development, *The Negroes* takes a place at the opening of Black Marxism, the theoretical articulation of European working-class radicalism and black resistance in the African diaspora that Cedric Robinson traces through Du Bois, C. L. R. James, and Richard Wright. McKay's pre-echo of more recent, more exclusively academic work in African-American history, whiteness studies, cultural studies, and a post-Soviet Marxism without guarantees is valuable for its challenges as well as its flattering symmetries. Yet the Marxism of *The Negroes in America* is to my mind most significant for its moments of unassimilability within contemporary dialogues and genealogies and for its honored place within currently unclaimed Soviet lineages. The paramount fact of the text's reception is the obscurity that flowed from its radical centrality, the publication in Russian commissioned by the Bolshevik state house that prevented its circulation within the flow of U.S. and black diasporan ideas. McKay's example in the question that frames this chapter—that of potential black clout on Comintern Marxism—was thus ironically hidden first by the Soviets' embrace.

The new availability of *The Negroes* in English makes McKay's own stance on this question less incredible. In a 1934 letter to Max Eastman, McKay insisted that the U.S. Communist Party had "carried on its propaganda among Negroes from the very acute angle of my position" since the Soviet visit (19 December 1934). This assertion of heroic influence pouring through the Soviets to the U.S. party came in the midst of an annoyed exchange but should not, I believe, be dismissed as simple bragging. Barring future work in decommissioned Russian archives, it is difficult to determine precisely how *The Negroes in America* affected the Bolshevik audience able to receive it. Evidence from presently accessible U.S. and Soviet sources does exist, however, to suggest that this audience esteemed McKay and the stances that impelled his book.

On the U.S. side, Max Eastman and the Bureau of Investigation (the FBI beginning in 1935) came to the same conclusion about McKay's Magic Pilgrimage: in the words of Eastman, who had observed the Fourth Comintern Congress at close range, McKay's work in the Soviet Union had rendered him "*the leading revolutionary figure in the Negro world*" (letter to Claude McKay; emphasis in original). McKay's FBI file, first procured by historian Tyrone Tillery, reveals that the bureau was confident that McKay had become nothing less than the "President of the Negro Section of the Executive Committee of the Third International" (United States, 19 Jan. 1923). It was less certain, however, that this post meant McKay would remain safely ensconced in the Soviet Union. Bureau chief William J. Burns personally warned agents in U.S. ports of entry that "it is possible that [McKay] may carry instructions and documents from the Communist International to the Communists in this country, together with a considerable sum of money" (United States, 10 March 1923). Another Burns directive passed on a report that McKay, receiving orders as "a Bolshevik agent," was "leaving for the United States with instructions to organize a colored Soviet" (United States, 24 March 1923). These warnings probably reveal less about McKay's actual duties for the Third International than about the bureau's persistent dread of the black left. Still, all the anxious vigilance over McKay's supposed leadership of the Comintern Negro Section and a black U.S. soviet is multiply instructive. It reveals one ignored reason why McKay may have hesitated to return to New York and enjoy the fruits of his renaissance fame; it suggests—along with *The Negroes in America*—that his Communism was far more riskily heartfelt and practical than his critics and autobiography admit. With its worry over the interchange of black nationalism and Communist internationalism, moreover, this vigilance captured some of what the Bolshevik leadership gathered from McKay's example.

The 1922 Fourth Congress of the Comintern that McKay addressed did more than propose the Negro Bureau that the proto-F.B.I. imagined as his fiefdom; it also installed international Communism's first Negro Commission and first binding stands on the Negro Question. McKay, invited to attend the commission's meetings along with ABB member Otto Huiswoud, appears to have affected its interests, rhetoric, and conclusions. The commission's final "Theses on the Negro Question" conjured up the Harlem Marxists' rendition of the New Negro, forged in the Great Migration and the Red Summer and proven in the defense of black Tulsa: "The post-war industrialization of the Negro in the North and the spirit of revolt engendered by post-war persecutions and brutalities (a spirit of revolt which flames into action when a Tulsa or other inhuman outrage cries aloud for protest) places the American Negro, especially of the North, in the vanguard of the African struggle against oppression" (29). The motivating gist of the "Theses" could have been taken as dictation from McKay's congress address: "The Negro problem has become a vital question of the world revolution; and the Third International . . . regards the cooperation of our Black fellowmen as essential to the Proletarian Revolution and the destruction of capitalist power" (30). The concluding points for implementation echo *The Negroes'* demand that Communism break the hold of whiteness on organized labor, if need be, through independent black unions: "The Communist International will use every instrument within its control to compel the trade unions to admit Negro workers to membership or, where the nominal right to join exists, to agitate for a special campaign to draw them into the unions. Failing in this, it will organize the Negroes into unions of their own and especially apply the United Front tactic to compel admission to the unions of the white man" (30). There was method, then, behind the decision of the Comintern's *International Press Correspondence* to run McKay's congress speech next to a report by Huiswoud offering a first glance at the "Theses."[15] The pair oriented Communism's earliest concerted outreach to black workers with the compass of a Harlem-made internationalist Marxism.[16]

In exchanges with the Comintern's inmost circle following his appearance at the Fourth Congress, McKay continued to press his attack on the Negro Question. In the introduction to *The Negroes in America*, McKay reproduces a February 1923 letter from Trotsky, previously printed in *Izvestia*, that responded to positions McKay had expressed in a personal meeting. Trotsky approved McKay's stand on the systemic damage done by racism to working-class awareness, agreeing that "the awakening of human dignity and revolutionary protest in the black slaves of American capital is one of the most important areas of [the] struggle against the capitalist corruption of proletarian consciousness" (qtd. on 8). The rise of African-American revolutionaries, the Red Army head affirmed, could doom racism's "enslavement of white as well as black workers" (8). Finally, Trotsky delivered an opinion on the extreme gravity of black organization that kept stride with his correspondent's: "*The training of black propagandists is the most imperative and extremely important revolutionary task of the present time*" (8; emphasis in original). Action followed Trotsky's emphasis. After 1922, blacks from the United States, the West Indies, and Africa were admitted for instruction in Communist theory and tactics at a Soviet institution named in the grip of prolet-chic, the University of the Toilers of the East (Robinson 306). A May 1923 personal letter from Zinoviev, the chairman of the Communist International, suggests that the business end of McKay's pilgrimage had convinced Bolsheviks beyond Trotsky that he was their conduit to black toilers everywhere: "Once more, *by you*, we call the Negro-workers to organise their own circles, to enter in the Trade-Unions, in every way to strive immediately to create their own mass-organization and to link up with other divisions of the fighting proletariat" (emphasis added). The Bureau of Investigation was wrong again when it alleged that the Soviets had "published the official instructions to Mackey [*sic*] for the organisation of the black race in the United States" (United States, 9 April 1923). But it would be equally incorrect to believe that McKay took his role as Comintern conduit lightly: he wrote Harlem Communist Grace Campbell from the Soviet Union "stressing Moscow's interest in American blacks and hope that they would 'show some spirit' in getting organized," and *The Crusader*'s national news service somehow wound up printing a bulletin emphasizing "Trotsky's plea for interracial revolutionary class consciousness" (Kornweibel 152, 154).

In 1928, the miraculous year he published the best-seller *Home to Harlem*, McKay could have detected the most dramatic evidence of his presence within the Comintern's intellectual system. By then, Stalin and the remaining Bolsheviks had fully registered the advice that bold moves would be necessary to draw many black workers to Communism (Robinson 306). At the 1928 Sixth Congress of the Comintern, *Crusader* editor Cyril Briggs's 1917 proposal that African Americans should formalize their status as a "nation within a nation" again reared its head,[17] this time as official Comintern theory extending the imagined benefits of Soviet nationalities policy to the African-American South. What was called the "Black Belt Republic" or "Black Belt Nation" thesis was in some ways the fulfillment of the analysis that McKay had promoted in Moscow in 1922–23; appropriately, its acknowledged coauthor was African-American Communist Harry Haywood, a former ABB recruit, fan of "If We Must Die," and student at the University of the Toilers of the East.[18] McKay's autobiography boasts that his remarks on southern U.S. conditions at the Fourth Congress "were more important than [he] imagined" and hints that he "precipitated" the Comintern's Black Belt approach (*A Long Way* 180).[19] It is more likely, however, that McKay anticipated the Nation thesis everywhere but along its southern axis. Leaving aside the issue of the feasibility of black self-determination in Dixie, the thesis granted the distinctiveness of both black culture and black oppression (Foley, *Radical* 173–79) and tightened the nexus of Marxism and modern black nationalism established by the *Crusader*s. As Cornel West allows, it was "antireductionistic and antieconomistic in character and nationalistic in content" (19). In it were flickers of many of the ideas animating *The Negroes in America*, from the centrality of African Americans—and the specificity of Negrophobia—in U.S. class conflict, to the political importance of African-American culture, to the possible alliance between black national propaganda and a Communist war on whiteness. As I will discuss in chapter five, the syntheses and generative contradictions of the Nation thesis encouraged Richard Wright, among others, to connect with the Depression-era Communist Party, the scene of the most familiar contacts between the New Negro and the Old Left.

What does it mean, at last, to lend credence to McKay's claim that Communism learned to approach the Negro problem from his "very acute angle"? McKay is surely not the solitary unacknowledged legislator of the "Theses on the Negro Question" and the Black Belt Nation line. These are best seen, I believe, as amalgams of New Negro and Soviet interests underwritten by the latter's dominance of the Comintern and by both parties' obligations to Lenin's and Stalin's teachings on the National Question.[20] Giving credit to McKay's claim of influence is instead to recognize that the crossing of Comintern and Harlem Marxisms altered the trajectory of both. Theodore Draper, the best of the "old historians" of American

Communism, identifies the Nation thesis as "the boldest effort ever made by the Russian party and the Comintern to demonstrate that they understood the dynamics of American society better than the Americans did" (*American* 354). Yet the Soviet understanding of African America that paved the way for the thesis was blessed and formed by grandly welcomed black pilgrims such as McKay, Huiswoud, and Haywood, equally certain that they grasped dynamics most Americans ignored. *The Negroes in America* is not just overlooked evidence of McKay's writerly reception of Marxist theory; it is documentation that a radical Harlem Renaissance position found a second home in Moscow, where it stretched the intellectual borders of the Black Atlantic and rephrased Marxism's Negro Question in the earshot of a receptive Kremlin.[21] Between the Fourth Congress of 1922 and the end of the 1930s, interracialism on the U.S. literary left would thus be boosted by Comintern theses that were themselves meaningfully interracial in composition, theses that borrowed most of their authority from the Soviets and a good deal of ingenuity from black bolshevism. In the next chapter, I will zoom in on one affected instance of interracialism involving McKay himself and the senior promoter of U.S. proletarian literature.

3 · The Proletarian as New Negro; the New Negro as Proletarian: Mike Gold Meets Claude McKay

Let the man of color distrust those false friends who mingle with him to get his money, who seek an alliance with him on the alleged common ground of "oppression," and who expose their whole hand when they urge him to that kind of Bolshevism found only in Moscow and on the East Side of New York.

—Henry Ford's *Dearborn Independent* (1923)

After a benefit for the Communist Party's *Daily Worker* at the Savoy Ballroom in Harlem in 1937, Mike Gold used his column in the newspaper to bestow two of the highest compliments he knew on the African-American social worker he had asked to jitterbug: "She could dance like a dream, and she was a Communist!" ("Doing the Big Apple" 7). As the second compliment indicates, Gold had been moved to praise by more than his partner's lessons in intoxicating rhythm. Unlike other white tourists who trekked to the Savoy to see what had become of the Lindy Hop, he had arrived raring to answer Sinclair Lewis's charge that Communists were as lifeless as their dreary proletarian literature.[1] In the bubbly atmosphere mixing Popular Front antifascism and a swing band that may have featured a young Dizzy Gillespie,[2] Gold had decided that the dance-floor skill of the social worker and other African-American comrades was not really evidence of the kinetic capacities of black folk. Rather, it was proof that rank and file party members stopped being alienated from their humanity the minute they left the workplace. His column praising the moves of the social worker went on to crow that the "floor [was] crowded with our comrades. Communists do the Lindy Hop, too, Mr. Hill Billy Sinclair Lewis. Communists laugh, breathe, drink highballs, kid each other, and even read your books. If you prick them, they bleed. If you spit on them, they feel insulted" (7). Black Communists performing black dances to black music at a ballroom built to capitalize on the black renaissance were emblems of the life of the party.

To be sure, some present-day readers might charge this symbolic appropriation of black dancers with ignoring the distinctiveness of an African-American cultural practice, subsuming race under class, and judging the Other in terms of the self. In Gold's peculiar revision of Shylock's plea—If you prick us Communists, do we not bleed?—African-American expression is cut from its specifically racial moorings and meanings. Yet this draft on what Michael Rogin calls "the surplus symbolic value of blacks" (14) makes African Americans represent nothing less than the fully human. Beneath the cutting of racial ties, Gold's symbolism thus rests on the same unconditional denial of black subhumanity that Ralph Ellison praised in his self-selected nineteenth-century ancestors. From the American renaissance to Mark Twain, claimed Ellison in 1953, the best of Anglo-American writing conceived of the African American as "a symbol of Man—the reversal of what he represents in most contemporary thought" ("Twentieth-Century Fiction" 49). Gold bids to enter Ellison's antiracist canon by recasting a stereotypic sign of black "animal spirits"—enthusiastic dancing—as a sign of the vibrant humanity of the interracial political party to which he belongs. Through this recasting, he implicitly acknowledges that his own humanity is threatened by racism and forgoes any humanism that would elevate European men over and against African "slaves and monsters" (Sartre 26).

My introduction of Gold into the dignified company of Ellison's godfathers is not meant to suggest that his Communism equipped him to detect all error in the racialisms of 1937. For example, even as his *Daily Worker* column discards some received ideas about black dance, it discriminates between authentic jazz and Tin Pan Alley mock-ups by describing a real thing bred in black "bones" ("Doing the Big Apple" 7). I instead want the flattering association to suggest that Gold's take on black expression is neither casual nor simply embarrassing to his Communism and the literary politics it engendered. While Gold may not be an ideal type of anything, his case qualifies as a strategic point from which to review the links between the self-conscious literatures of the New Negro and the Old Left. With his influential autobiographical novel *Jews Without Money* (1930), his ironic attachment to the modernist genre of the manifesto, and his ordained, belligerent arbitration of working-class literary excellence, Gold became a synecdoche for U.S. proletarian literature during his own lifetime. As this literature grew with the blessing of the Communist Party in the 1920s and 1930s, so did his reputation as a radical literary kingmaker. His disposition toward African-American culture has thus been considered a master key by those few critics who have examined the exchanges between proletarian literature and the Harlem Renaissance, the rebirth that brewed just a subway ride away from Gold's Greenwich Village as he first directed young writers "Towards Proletarian Art."

The habit of picturing Gold as proletarian literature incarnate marks Harold Cruse's *The Crisis of the Negro Intellectual* (1967), to this day among the most powerful studies of blacks and whites, ethnicity and class, on the twentieth-century U.S. cultural left. Gold lurks at the outset of Cruse's epic of white radical manipulation and black radical capitulation, first as the tormentor of Claude McKay, then as the standard-bearer of the Jewish Communists who supposedly hoped to remake New Negro literature in their own image. As Cruse notes, McKay spent the first half of 1922 scrambling the conventions of progressive interracialism, which then held that whites could staff black reform institutions such as the NAACP but rarely the contrary.[3] From January to June, he and Gold shared the position of executive editor at *The Liberator*, the resurrection of Max Eastman's *Masses* that synthesized its precursor's lyrical leftism with the more exacting, "scientific" Marxism following on the Russian Revolution. These coeditors sometimes disagreed over the direction of the publication, and McKay resigned from active duty a few months before his Soviet pilgrimage. To Cruse, McKay's departure from the executive editor post reveals "that Gold was either envious or fearful of McKay" (49). "Without a doubt," Cruse asserts, "Michael Gold was not sympathetic to McKay's literary work or anything coming out of the Harlem Renaissance" (49).

This lack of sympathy is not just a foible to Cruse. In *The Crisis of the Negro Intellectual*, Gold stands for the prudery, imperial design, and Jewish command of the Communist Party's congealing line on literature beginning in the early 1920s. Gold's attack on what he considered Carl Van Vechten's legacy to African-American writing—"Gin, jazz and sex . . . the gutter-life side of Harlem" ("Notes" 3)—is thus glossed as an "example of Communist puritanical puerility," not an ignorable local intervention but a "critical bomb" directed at the heart of the Harlem Renaissance (Cruse 50). For Cruse, who defines the United States as "a nation dominated by the social power of groups, classes, in-groups and cliques—both ethnic and religious" (7), Gold's effort to discipline New Negroes with a proletarian rod stemmed from the desire of Jewish Communist intellectuals to master their opposite numbers. The attempt to draw African-American writers into the proletarian camp was finally that of "another minority . . . [to] dictate cultural standards" to black intellectuals just as "they were on the ascendant" (52). "It should have been the [Langston] Hugheses, the [James Weldon] Johnsons and the McKays, who created the critical terms to be laid down on [the New Negro]," Cruse protests, "*not* the Michael Golds" (51; emphasis in original). Playing on "the weak-kneed, nonpolitical, noncommittal naiveté of many of the Negro intellectuals" (53), these "Michael Golds" supposedly speeded the default of the Harlem Renaissance, persuading black writers to abandon indigenous artistic criteria for another ethnic-religious group's criteria impersonating those of the entire working class. Gold/proletarian literature/the Jewish Communist expert on black culture was thus not merely guilty of opposing a movement that might have liberated African-American writers from extrinsic standards; this three-headed creature was also partially culpable for the movement's early death. According to Cruse, the damage inflicted during the 1920s paved the way for the more overt co-optation of African-American literature during the 1930s, when authors such as Ellison and Richard Wright were drawn to Communism by the Great Depression and the party's apparent place of honor for the Negro Question.

Any reopening of the related question of proletarianism's relationship to African-American expression needs to reckon with this portrait of the proletarian artist as an enemy of aesthetic decolonization. Clearly, Cruse's findings against Gold are somewhat compromised by an outsized fear of and respect for what he dubs "Jewish Nationalism" (167) and somewhat overdetermined by the demands of an ex–party member's turn to independent black nationalism. His monotone portrait of sheer difference and hostility between Gold and McKay hints at an anxiety of interracial influence, an unwanted dread that the crossed histories of the two writers might betray the interlacing of proletarian and Harlem Renaissance writing. Nevertheless, neither the substance nor the influence of Cruse's charges can easily be shrugged off. A work of passion and abundant scholarship, *The Crisis of the Negro Intellectual* continues to resonate, at its best placing painful historical weight behind now-ritual commands against class reductionism and speaking for the Other. Cruse-like attacks on Gold are elaborated even in two of the sharpest reconstructions of an un-Cruse-like interracial modernism, Walter Kalaidjian's *American Culture Between the Wars* (1993) and Michael North's *The Dialect of Modernism* (1994), the latter of which has Gold "forc[ing] Claude McKay to resign from the *Liberator* in 1919 [*sic*] because he insisted on greater coverage of racial issues" (193).[4] I will show here, by contrast, that the Cruse line relies on a highly selective account of Gold's interaction with McKay and the larger Harlem Renaissance while at *The Liberator* and neglects most of Gold's subsequent efforts to understand this interaction's significance for himself and for proletarian literature. More than the reputation of one well-known but hardly read white lefty, every Americanist's favorite Stalinist culture czar, is at stake in setting the record straight. To recover the complexity of Gold's interchanges with McKay and the Harlem movement is to challenge the edict that proletarian and New Negro writing are discrete, antagonistic schools. It is to acknowledge that the African-American presence within proletarian literature goes beyond a short list of Depression authors and into the very formation of the genre in the United States.

The *Liberator* and Interracial Editorship

Cruse is justified in claiming that Gold and McKay clashed during the half year in which they served as co–executive editors of *The Liberator*. On one occasion, the two were saved from a fist fight only by the pacifying effects of a bottle of red wine (McKay, *A Long Way* 140–41). Yet their disagreements did not seem to derive from Gold's race prejudice or envy of McKay's status as the first poet laureate of Harlem's renaissance. McKay reported to Eastman soon after leaving *The Liberator* that one source of tension had been "the race matter," by which he meant not some inborn hostility awakened by interracial collaboration but Gold's lack of "a comprehensive grasp of the Negro's place in the class-struggle" (letter, 3 April 1923). McKay charged his ex-partner with making "the race story in the June [1922] *Liberator* the basis of his attack on me" (ibid.). Gold's criticism had probably centered on the legitimacy of an article detailing a state-approved lynching in San Antonio. Its apparent author, a white Texan named Lucy Maverick, greeted publication with a letter to the editors protesting the use of her name and insisting that the piece was the work of a committee.[5] The ensuing controversy may have allowed Gold to score against McKay's proposal that because blacks composed 10 percent of the U.S. population and occupied a disproportionately critical position within U.S. class conflict, it was appropriate to devote to them 10 percent of a U.S. Marxist magazine. In a weird echo of present-day liberal caution over racial quotas, Gold and other white staffers were apparently worried that the 10 percent solution would lose them educable but presently white-proud readers. George Hutchinson notes that Eastman was convinced that "a presentation of 'materials on the race question' proportional to the population of Negroes . . . would cost the magazine . . . its existence, thus destroying the very organ that could most effectively address racial issues relative to the class struggle" (266). With this belief, white *Liberator*s showed themselves willing to indulge what they saw as the lingering bigotry of their white readership, trusting the old Socialist Party dogma that because racism was an exotic outgrowth of class oppression, direct attack could await the triumph of the class to end classes. As chapter 2 has shown, McKay would dedicate *The Negroes in America* to the proposition that such trust was one reason there was no socialism in the United States; in fact, until Eastman talked him out of it, he intended to provide the Soviets with a chapter on his *Liberator* disappointments. Less than a year after his resignation as executive editor, however, McKay declared himself insulted by Eastman's implication that he had fled the *Liberator* job because of "the race matter." It "was merely incidental to my quitting the executive work," he insisted (qtd. in Hutchinson 501 n. 68). For what it's worth, *The Liberator* itself announced that McKay was leaving his post for vintage reasons of romantic liberation: "to be free to write poetry and to see more of the world than is permitted to an office worker on a magazine" ("Liberator News" 27). Incontestable is McKay's consent to an unclean break: he packed for Russia as a *Liberator* contributing editor and lent his name to the journal's revival, *The New Masses*, when it was launched in 1926.

By the time McKay's *A Long Way from Home* appeared in 1937, all hints of "the race matter" had been excised from his official memory of editing with Gold. In this more public text, written during the transition to McKay's final, anti-Communist stance, two points of discord are stressed: first, what is characterized as Gold's alienating emotional intensity (he had suffered a nervous breakdown in February 1921 [Rideout 124]); and, second, Gold's heightening conviction that publishing a proletarian magazine meant "printing doggerels from lumberjacks and stevedores and true revelations from chambermaids" (*A Long Way* 139). McKay recalls sharing Gold's hard-lived insight into proletarian literature, a genre *The Liberator* first endorsed a year before the two started collaborating. No more than Gold was he a salon socialist, having also begun writing as "an ordinary worker, without benefit of a classic education" (139). When his first U.S. publications appeared in 1917, McKay was the most literal sort of proletarian writer, a poet who earned a bare living waiting tables at a women's club and on the Pennsylvania Railroad. Though the autobiography never admits it outright, he seems to have enjoyed the possibility that his joint editorship with Gold was a sign of the dawning of the "proletarian *period* of literature, with labor coming into its heritage as the dominating social factor," perhaps even a foretaste of an interracial dictatorship of the proletariat (139; emphasis in original). The text eagerly points out that McKay parted with Gold, however, whenever their empathy for the "peasant and proletarian aspirant to literary writing" threatened to devolve into special pleading (139). "I knew that it was much easier to talk about real proletarians writing masterpieces," he reports, "than to find such masterpieces" (139). As I suggested earlier, McKay may not have judged *The Negroes in America* a masterpiece, but he traced its portion of merit to its black proletarian authorship. He left Gold and New York behind, then, without abandoning the self-referential idea that the best working-class writing was of major value. The Olympian position ultimately reached in his autobiography—that "class labels were incidental" (139)—would be formulated later.

A look through the issues of *The Liberator* that McKay and Gold jointly supervised suggests that frictions over the gravity of race and proletarian authorship did not keep them from agreeing that racism was a threat to the entire proletariat. Hutchinson cogently argues that the journal cooperated in the making of the Harlem Renaissance. Even before McKay's arrival, *The Liberator* had displayed exceptional support for black self-defense and self-expression, honoring the militancy of returning black soldiers and publishing creative work by Mary Burrill, Fenton Johnson, and James Weldon Johnson (Hutchinson 262–64). The six Gold-McKay monthly issues did nothing to besmirch this record, featuring an increased number of items (if not quite 10 percent of the total) by and/or concerning blacks in the United States and the Caribbean. The January 1922 issue alone, for example, includes an essay answering the question "What Is Social Equality?" by Walter White of the NAACP; another comparing racial and wage slavery by frequent *Liberator* contributor Henry G. Alsberg; a book review by Hubert Harrison, the black socialist whose work McKay consulted in Moscow; and Daytie Randle's Whitmanesque poem "Lament," which opens with the line "I am a Negro woman," a vow of identity Mari Evans revamped in 1970's "I Am a Black Woman."[6] The March issue qualifies as an antilynching number. A two-page spread juxtaposes Onorio Ruotolo's sensitive sketch of a seated, grieving black woman and two poems: E. Merrill Root's "A Southern Holiday," a graphic arraignment of lynch law reminiscent of McKay's earlier poem "The Lynching," and Ralph Chaplin's sonnet "Wesley Everest," an angry antielegy for a murdered IWW activist that borrows the African-American figure of the lynch victim as crucified Christ. Taken as a whole, the grouping invites both mourning and organizing and associates sanctioned violence against African Americans with that against white radicals without completely collapsing one into the other.[7]

The Liberator's sharpened interest in race matters under the Gold-McKay partnership was not confined to its editorial policy. McKay's acquaintance Grace Campbell, one of the first blacks in the U.S. Communist Party, was prevailed on to recruit another black "first," referee Chris Huiswoud, as the star attraction for a March fund-raiser with "two black and white basketball games" ("2 Basket Ball Games"). A second interracial benefit held at Bryant Hall in May was a hit until crashed by a squad of police who found the crowd guilty of breaking the color line (Wood). McKay danced the shortened night away with Crystal Eastman, the pairing of the dark brown McKay and the very blonde Eastman causing a minor scandal in New York newspapers (McKay, letter to Nancy Cunard). However incompletely these events prefigured the color-blind society to be born in the death of capitalism, McKay's autobiography fondly remembers the "large freedom and tolerance about *The Liberator* which made such a mixing possible" (*A Long Way* 149). Though he wrote at a moment when Communist get-togethers in Harlem were common, he expresses regret that no radical cultural institutions after the journal had so thoroughly blended "all shades of radicals . . . pink and black and red" (148). Considered more cynically, the journal's gatherings probably succeeded in providing black intellectuals, red or otherwise, with some of the social capital they would invest throughout the 1920s to improve the material conditions in which black culture was produced and distributed. As Wayne Cooper suggests, the social orbit of *The Liberator* was among the first interracial scenes to introduce Harlem Renaissance cadres to impressionable white entrepreneurs (139).

McKay himself, of course, stood to profit from *The Liberator*'s enthusiasm for black intellectuals and their work. During the six months he ran the show with Gold, he unsurprisingly became one of the journal's leading contributors, publishing ten poems, five essays, and one short story.[8] Both before and after his term as co–executive editor, however, McKay was one of *The Liberator*'s signature poets. From 1919's "If We Must Die" to "Petrograd: May Day, 1923," many of McKay's most memorable poems were initially printed in *The Liberator*.[9] The journal was the first home of over one-third of the seventy-four poems gathered in *Harlem Shadows*; of the five poems by McKay included in Alain Locke's *New Negro*, three were first published by Eastman, Gold, and company. It initially seems strange that the same contribution to renaissance poetry embraced (and partly excited) by the *Crusaders* was rehearsed in a "white" magazine, even one Briggs's set declared to be "America's foremost white radical monthly" ("Claude McKay" 21). Yet *The Liberator* was among the handful of U.S. journals of any complexion then eager to consider Shakespearean sonnets beseeching "the avenging angel to consume / The white man's world of wonders utterly" ("Enslaved," ll. 10–11). When it came to something like "The White House," hymning the rage that tears the "vitals" of McKay's speaker while passing a building of no small political symbolism (l. 8), *The Liberator* was among the even fewer journals happy with immoderation. For instance, Locke admired the poem but altered its *Liberator* title to "White Houses" in the pages of *The Survey Graphic* and *The New Negro*, a change we can read as a miniature of his anthology's renaissance revision. While McKay's verse may have irked Eastman and Gold in its implication that interracial working-class unity was something to be built, not assumed, its performance of black anger within measured pentameter was readily accessible to them as fine modern verse. McKay's American poetry was informed both by Razaf and by jailed IWW poet Ralph Chaplin's sonnets blasting class tyranny. *The Liberator* published both McKay and Chaplin because each substantiated its vision of a progressive yet popular modernism, holding Pound's obscurantist troops at bay while rearticulating traditional forms with challenging political content.[10]

At least for the editors of *The Liberator* at the start of the 1920s—Gold included—the emerging categories of proletarian and Harlem Renaissance writing accordingly did not represent opposed aesthetics bound to opposing ethnic-religious interests. Gold's inaugural manifesto for proletarian culture in the February 1921 *Liberator* indeed hints that every artist should take a cue from folk-conscious New Negroes and bow before the earthy, not-so-common people. In the manner of a bolshevik Alain Locke, "Towards Proletarian Art" substitutes the socialist god-term of "the masses" for the Harlem Renaissance trope of "the black folk": "The masses are still primitive and clean, and artists must turn to them for strength again. The primitive sweetness, the primitive calm, the primitive ability to create simply and without fever or ambition, the primitive satisfaction and self-sufficiency—they must be found again" (66). As in Locke's invitations to "young Negro writers [to] dig deep into the racy peasant undersoil of the race life" ("Negro Youth Speaks" 51), Gold advises young proletarians to learn from those "never far from the earth" ("Towards" 66). McKay, in his corner, may have thought of Gold's earthy proletarian program when recommending "the new school of critics, chiefly Jews" to writers of New Negro spirit in 1923 (*The Negroes* 75). More certain is McKay's distance from the idea that Jewish critical standards were inimical to renaissance literary development. Rejecting "the decadent school of old critics who stubbornly cling to the old [black] dialect," *The Negroes in America* explicitly praises Jewish critics "who have a great heritage of racial community expression in literature" and thus have something to offer black writers in search of an uncompromised indigenousness (75).

Gold's contact with McKay at *The Liberator* in the first half of 1922 seems only to have strengthened his perception that proletarian literature and the Harlem Renaissance were allied. A May 1922 subscription offer that Gold must have written or approved, for example, testifies that he had no qualms over *Harlem Shadows'* proletarian standing. Dangled as a premium for new subscribers, McKay's collection is plugged as the work of "the foremost revolutionary poet of America. . . . [Its] passionate exhortations, even when most characteristically racial, are a stirring call to the oppressed everywhere." After McKay's departure, subscription bonuses in Gold's more emphatically proletarian magazine replaced *Harlem Shadows* not with a collection of worker's correspondence but with a translation of René Maran's *Batouala* (1922), the Prix Goncourt–winning novel that convinced some New Negroes that their literature was international (*The Liberator* August 1922). Nor did Gold's regime think it an offense against the working class to preview three ingredients of Jean Toomer's renaissance milestone *Cane* (1923). When McKay was en route to Moscow in September and October, *The Liberator* was running the poem "Georgia Dusk" and the stories "Becky" and "Carma." If Gold was as unsympathetic "to McKay's literary work or anything else coming out of the Harlem Renaissance" as Cruse argues, he had an uncharacteristically subtle way of showing it at *The Liberator*. Before, during, and immediately after McKay's stint as his collaborator, Gold acted as if proletarian and renaissance writing were analogous, sometimes blended injections of health into literature's tired bourgeois body. Despite the dubious fear of disaffecting white readers, he as well as McKay and Eastman helped to make *The Liberator* a conspicuous early presence on the border of the renaissance cultural field. After *The Crusader*, the journal was probably the leading host of the renaissance position that bound New Negro awakening to the dawning "proletarian period."

Itzok Granich's Civil War

While the toll of McKay's departure from *The Liberator* may have been steep, Gold did not attempt to erase the memory of their work together. Gold's first book, the pre–Popular Front patriotic hagiography *Life of John Brown* (1923), is an oblique commemoration of their joint editorship. As James D. Bloom notes, Gold's ostensible biography qualifies "at once [as] a covert autobiography and a plan for his own revolutionary career" (46).

"Who knows but that some time in America the John Browns of today will not be worshipped in like manner?" asks Gold, leaving no doubt about his own qualifications as one of "the outlaws of today, the unknown soldiers of freedom" who deserved the abolitionist's mantle (*Life* 60). If Gold was to be acknowledged as an inheritor of the spirit of Brown, it was only logical that McKay was to be recognized as a descendant of the five "dignified and manly" African Americans, carefully specified within Gold's list of Brown's companions, who joined the raid on Harper's Ferry (48–49). Regarded in the light of the historical imagination that Gold ascribes to a future socialist USA, his turbulent partnership with McKay becomes a shadow of the more perfect love among Brown's interracial band of brothers, "young crusaders, thoughtful, sensitive and brave," who also combined to provide ammunition for insurrection (46).

Had Gold never met McKay, he might still have treated his biography of Brown as a displaced confessional. Bloom points out that Brown was a constant presence on the "honor rolls . . . of writers and freedom fighters with whom Gold sought to affiliate himself and his agenda" (45). Bloom also observes that Gold always considered the abolitionist crusade against slavery as a type of and stimulus for the crusade against capitalism. In a 1953 autobiographical sketch, Gold claimed outright that "living echoes of the Civil War . . . prepared me for socialist ideas" ("The Writer in America" 183). Gold's very adult name was adopted from one of these living echoes, a Union Army veteran who came to mind as the antiradical Palmer Raids of 1919–1920 prompted Gold to choose a replacement for the birth name of Itzok Isaac Granich. Neatly enough, the Marxist *Liberator* for which the renamed radical went to work had borrowed its own name from William Lloyd Garrison's flagship abolitionist newspaper. Despite all the historical parallels, Gold's eagerness to define slavery as a horror "our class has suffered" distinguished him from many labor leaders of his namesake's generation, whose rhetoric opposing "white slavery" in the North bolstered proslavery ideology (Gold, "A Secret Meeting" 96).[11]

Gold's attachment to Brown derived from a variety of factors but none more important than the Jewishness his pseudonym did not strain to hide. Like thousands of Jews in the wake of the anti-Semitic Leo Frank lynching of 1915, Gold seized on traditional black Christian comparisons between African Americans and the Old Testament children of Israel; he became confident that the modern fates as well as the historical enslavements of the two peoples were linked, the concern of "our [single] class." While at the far left of left-of-center Jewish opinion, Gold was swept by the general conviction that black liberation was critical to the American errand of the chosen people. As historian Hasia Diner notes, this conviction was not free from all Jewish self-interest: it reflected a genuine belief in a common history of exclusion but also the hunch that battling racism might root Jews in the American grain. "When decrying racism, Jews could orate about how American they had become, how fundamentally they had internalized the principles of the Constitution, the Declaration of Independence, how well-versed they were with the 'true' meaning of American history" (Diner 237–38). Insofar as John Brown was a national martyr, a precursor of the socialist militant, and a scourge of the slavery to which Jews and blacks had been subjected, he invited Gold to Americanize both his Jewishness and his Communism, traits joined and made grounds for denaturalization during the Palmer Raids. In demonstrating he was a native son of Brown, Gold pleaded that a representative of seemingly alien religion and seditious politics understood American liberty more intimately than did citizens of old stock and safe opinion.

Whatever its uses in Gold's own rehabilitation, the notion of the shared fate of Jews and African Americans that led him to Brown also urged him to resist Americanization via black hating. While some second-wave immigrants were paying the ticket price of citizenship with professions of whiteness, Gold was exposing the bond between "Yiddish literature and music" and "Negro spirituals" ("The Gun Is Loaded" 226). Like a good materialist, he avoided loose speculation about the famously large souls of the two peoples, arguing that comparable cultures were formed by the same "ghetto poverty" (226). In a related spirit, he christened one of the Jewish heroes of *Jews Without Money* "Nigger," a volatile attempt to affiliate black and Jewish resistance by defusing the worst of racist language. Poorest of the poor but "bravest of the brave, the chieftain of [the] brave savage tribe" of street-tough young Jews to which the narrator belongs (43), Nigger is one of the text's few protorevolutionary models, a confirmation that organized defiance can be bred in the deprivation of the ghetto. It might even be claimed that Nigger proves racial differences to be flimsy, socially built, and thus made to be broken. A more attractive relative of the racially indeterminate hero of Melville's *The Confidence-Man* (1857),[12] Nigger "with his black hair and murky face" (42) muddles the purportedly clear boundary between black and white that stands in the way of Jewish–African-American identification. To reinforce this hotwired theme of racial category crisis, Gold wheels out a character who is Nigger's mirror image, a proudly pious, Hebrew-speaking black Jew from Abyssinia. Like the yarmulke-wearing Harlemites who captivated the *Jewish Daily Forward* in the 1920s (Diner 68–69), the Abyssinian leaves the narrator's father and friends wondering just who are "mere pretenders to the proud title of Jew" (Gold, *Jews* 175).

The idea that African Americans and Jews are united by impoverished representations as well as ghetto poverty makes an appearance in Gold's best-known post-*Liberator* statement on African-American writing: "Notes of the Month" on "Negro Literature" contained in a 1930 issue of *The New Masses*. Gold's first business here is denouncing Carl Van Vechten, the quasi-official liaison between Harlem and downtown intellectuals, as "a white literary bum, who has created a brood of Negro literary bums" (3). Van Vechten's sin is the mortal one of corrupting the young. In Gold's judgment, "this night-club rounder and white literary sophisticate" had succeeded in infecting "young Negro literatuers [*sic*]" with his appetites for "gin, jazz and sex" (3). Impressed by the great success of the novel *Nigger Heaven* (1926), Van Vechten's own controversial attempt to ironize the most hated racist epithet, many of these novices were "wasting their splendid talents on the gutter-life side of Harlem" (3). The result was an African-American fiction obsessed with night life and low life, a fiction that "slander[s] . . . the majority of Negroes who must work so painfully in the mills, factories and farms of America" by coddling the fantasy that black life is a cabaret (3). While Gold may have enjoyed stomping at the Savoy, he was certain that the place was not a proper metonymy for African America. Pretending otherwise for the sake of sales, he implies, helps uphold the gamut of ethnic and racial stereotypes, including those defaming Jews without money like himself: "The Harlem cabaret no more represents the Negro mass than a pawnshop represents the Jew, or an opium den the struggling Chinese nation" (3). Gold concludes that it is in the masses of "the revolutionary movement," rather than in the speakeasy, that "the Negro will at last find his true voice . . .[,] a voice of storm, beauty and pain, no saxophone clowning, but Beethoven's majesty and Wagner's might, sombre as night with the vast Negro suffering, but with red stars burning bright for revolt" (3).

As mentioned earlier, Cruse reads these "Notes" on Negro literature as a conclusive trashing of the Harlem Renaissance and an "example of Communist puritanical puerility." Taking up where Cruse leaves off, Hutchinson declares the piece "a fascinating study in cultural contradiction and attempted co-optation" and quotes it nearly in full (272). Gold's critique of the renaissance, Hutchinson asserts, "is integral with a vision of African American culture being in no essentials different from proletarian culture anywhere, a vision in which even jazz (as opposed to Wagner!) is perceived as little more than a product of the white capitalist culture industry, a minstrel-show travesty of black expressivity" (272). Cruse and Hutchinson have some excellent reasons for their fascinated distaste for the "Notes": the assumption that Van Vechten had fathered a "brood" of young black writers shows a Gold devoted to the white writer's generative burden. And yet a later comment indicates that Gold had a single figure firmly in mind as he reproached African-American artists for dulling their "splendid talents" to duplicate Van Vechten's success. I refer to Gold's old comrade McKay, who two years before the "Notes" had become the first best-selling black novelist of the renaissance with *Home to Harlem*, a text recommended by its publisher to "those who enjoyed *Nigger Heaven*" (qtd. in J. Wright 19). In the same 1953 sketch in which Gold unveils the influence of "living echoes of the Civil War," he describes McKay's novels as "badly affected by the time and the influence of white writers like Carl Van Vechten" ("The Writer in America" 188). Wielding a triplet of sin-drenched nouns almost identical to those used in 1930, Gold summarizes the lessons McKay had learned from Harlem's best-promoted white tour guide: "Negro authors could now reach a big audience among whites, but only if they forgot their people's wrongs and concentrated on *gin, sex,* and *the cabaret*" (188; emphasis added). The criticism of McKay is confined to the prose, however. The writer with whom Gold reminds us he "served as co-editor of the *Liberator*" is also praised as "a fine lyrical poet" whose "poems of the Negro liberation struggle are classics" (188). It is relatively easy game to point to further nuances and contradictions, textual and intertextual, that the Cruse line shaves even from the "Notes," Gold at his tone-deaf, racially paternalistic worst.

Consider Cruse's jab at Gold's "Communist puritanical puerility." It is noteworthy that Gold's attack on the cabaret metonymy and the "gin, jazz, and sex" infatuation recapitulates W. E. B. Du Bois's troubled reviews of *Nigger Heaven* and *Home to Harlem*. In the book pages of *The Crisis* in 1926, the not-yet-Communist Du Bois had also supplied a capsule sociology to disprove that "the black cabaret is Harlem" (rev. of *Nigger Heaven* 1216). "The overwhelming majority of black folk there never go to cabarets," he reminds Van Vechten. "The average colored man in Harlem is an everyday laborer, attending church, lodge and movie and as conservative and conventional as ordinary working folk everywhere" (1216). Du Bois hits *Home to Harlem* with worse, accusing it of sprinkling novelistic glitz on a decadent white projection of black life. McKay, he claims, "has used every art and emphasis to paint drunkenness, fighting, lascivious sexual promiscuity and utter absence of restraint in as bold and as bright colors as he can" (rev. of *Quicksand* 114). The presence of Du Bois in Gold's

"Notes"—conscious or not—argues that there was nothing peculiarly Communist or especially puerile in the thesis that Van Vechten encouraged New Negroes to uphold the old racism. While Cruse's crack about puritanism identifies a squeamishness about certain representations of sexuality that Gold shared with the more gentlemanly Du Bois, it does not reckon with the pair's main anticabaret premise, namely, that post-Freudian ideologies of the superiority of black license merely embroidered on past racial stereotypes. As Sterling Brown developed the idea, the jazz age stock character of the urbanized black primitive may have abandoned the "cabin" for "the cabaret" but guaranteed that "Negroes were still described as 'creatures of joy' " (*The Negro* 148). Gold, like Du Bois, had a special political anxiety that such stereotypes disguised the proletarian qualifications of the great majority of blacks. White workers needed no further encouragement to consign their black counterparts to the "*lumpenproletariat*," the reckless mass of "pickpockets, tricksters, gamblers, . . . brothel keepers, porters, *literati*, . . . [and] beggars" purportedly found at the base of reactionary movements (and near the top of *Home to Harlem*'s cast list) (Marx, *The Eighteenth* 75; emphases in original). At the same time, Gold's "Notes" would not be out of place within a politically catholic main line of renaissance criticism, in which dependence on white bourgeois patronage and racial discourse is found damaging to aims other than a Soviet America.

A second example of nuance and contradiction missed is found in Hutchinson's contention that Gold's critique "is integral with a vision of African American culture being in no essentials different from proletarian culture anywhere." Gold's aversion to "saxophone clowning" and his prediction of "Negro Tolstoys, Gorkys and Walt Whitmans" does little to blunt this contention; these aspects of his "Notes" indeed jibe with most of a 1926 letter he sent to *The Nation*, replying to Hughes's "The Negro Artist and the Racial Mountain" with the advice that it is impossible to "build up some special racial culture in this huge America." However, just as Gold's letter clouds this advice with talk of "Negro themes . . . enough for a lifetime of creative activity," his "Notes" follow the attack on cabaret compromise with an alternative canon of distinctly black culture heroes and forms. In a sentence that Hutchinson drops from his block quotation of the "Notes," Gold declares that "the 'spirituals' have promised" a great Negro art and literature; "the works of men like Frederick Douglass and Toussant [*sic*] L'Ouverture have shown the way" (3). Unless we discount all marks of black difference in the spirituals, Douglass, and L'Ouverture, it is tough to deny that the revolutionary Negro voice Gold expects to hear will be "racially" distinguishable from Beethoven and Wagner, if not essentially "different from proletarian culture everywhere." And jazz, the music in which Hutchinson anchors black distinction, would not always feature in Gold's Frankfurt School–style bestiary of mass culture. As I have previously suggested, his Savoy Ballroom spin led him to differentiate between the "cheap, stolen melodies" of Tin Pan Alley and the "jazz [that] belongs to the Negro race" ("Doing the Big Apple" 7).

This last reference to the swinging Gold of 1937 cannot unwrite his dismissal of jazz in 1930. But it points the way, I think, to the most serious flaw in the critical response to the "Notes": the confidence that they are the definitive word on Gold's Harlem Renaissance. Especially when the "Notes" are associated with an influential, bourgeois-abominating attack on the Harlem movement, this confidence deserves careful inspection. According to Hutchinson, 1930 marks the date when Gold's *New Masses* gave full reign to a crushing negative line on the renaissance, perfecting blows that would be thrown "throughout the rest of the history of commentary on the movement" (273). The journal's powerful harangue, Hutchinson maintains, "contrasts work songs of secular protest with the spirituals, scapegoats Carl Van Vechten for corrupting naïve young artists, takes the NAACP and Urban League to task as timid and bourgeois, and dismisses the Harlem Renaissance generally as irresponsible and 'inauthentic,' a show put on for decadent whites" (273). In fact, Gold's "Notes" present the spirituals as an impetus to the production of black proletarian art, but no matter. More meaningful is Gold's suggestion that Van Vechten's reign was not coterminous with the New Negroes' and thus not necessarily their defining moment: "I believe that Negro art and literature are only beginning. This cabaret obsession is but an infantile disease, a passing phase" ("Notes" 3). A raft of further commentary on the renaissance by Gold suggests that this belief was one he kept. Despite their prediction of later indictments of the Harlem movement, then, Gold's "Notes" did not usher in his final analysis.

Two of Gold's efforts from the late 1930s can tell the tale of revision. By the time of a 1936 piece echoing *The New Negro*'s call for a national Negro theater, Gold was confident that Harlem's renaissance was due to recover its health. "Negroes have given America all the truly native music it has thus far produced," he affirms, so it is rational to "believe that they can give us our first truly poetic theater" ("At Last" 18). Harlem, the "friendly soil" from which the "renaissance, as is well known, spread," would be this theater's natural American home (18). By 1938 Gold's estimation of renaissance man Langston Hughes had improved enough for him to write an introduction to the poet's *A New Song*, a book of verse Hughes dedicated to the International Workers Order. After retelling the anecdote of Hughes busing tables in the same "white man's hotel" in which Vachel Lindsay recited from *The Weary Blues*, Gold reiterates the *Crusaders'* wisdom that "most Negro intellectuals, at one time or another, eat the bitter bread of this economic slavery in which their race is kept in America" (7). The best African-American literature was thus a kind of volk-proletarian composite, both "a folk literature, close to the joys and sorrows of [black] people" and a voice for the freedom of black and white workers, "brothers in suffering and struggle" (7, 8). The Gold of *A New Song* had resolved that an heir of *The Liberator*'s class-conscious black renaissance again led the Harlem field.

As Barbara Foley reminds us, these changes of opinion in the late-1930s–model Gold were not unique among Communist cultural critics. Between 1930 and 1936 Van Vechten's presence on the "friendly soil" of Harlem had become less frequent, *Home to Harlem* had become a bad but dim memory, and Gold's ideas on black writing had absorbed the transition from the ultraleftist Comintern Third Period to the more inclusive Popular Front (Foley, *Radical* 183–93). Even during the Third Period's days of raging proletcult, however, Gold found it difficult to repress the sense that Harlem's literary upsurge had something to offer its proletarian kin. In 1929 Gold revisited his *Liberator* collaboration with McKay in a review of *Banjo*, praising his former coeditor as someone who "fought with all his friends, white and black," the better to avoid intellectual laxity ("Drunk" 17). Loudly and clearly, Gold targets the lack "of revolutionary feeling in [McKay's] novels" (17); the allegations against Van Vechten's "brood" are on their way. Never in doubt, however, is *Banjo*'s overall excellence or proletarian credentials. McKay's dialogue, judges Gold, "is the richest, freshest and most living . . . anyone is writing today" (17). Even better, it is pressed into the service of the genuine proletarian article: McKay "describe[s] Negro workers and migratories with the truthfulness and intimate sympathy of a proletarian writer," for "he is one of these workers" (17). The severity of Gold's 1930 "Notes" may thus be tied to a recognition that black "Van Vechtenites" such as McKay were like-minded practitioners of working-class realism, writers to whom self-described proletarians were related as much by similarity as by difference. In "Proletarian Realism," a manifesto published later in 1930 systematizing the views of "Towards Proletarian Art," Gold takes time to stipulate that "proletarian literature . . . portrays the life of the workers; not as do the . . . American jazzmaniacs, but with a clear revolutionary point; otherwise it is meaningless, merely a new frisson" (205–6).

Gold's enduring interest in the ties between Harlem Renaissance and proletarian fiction was to a great extent the product of his unusual collaboration with McKay at *The Liberator.* His authorial career answering his own calls for proletarian fiction was not far behind, however. In the late 1920s Gold may well have viewed himself as both a proletarian and a "black" writer struggling with what he tagged "Nordic Americanism" (*Hoboken* 598). *Jews Without Money* defined itself against "lurid articles in a Sunday newspaper" and "Ku Klux moralizers" (35, 37), in other words, against exoticizing and pathologizing accounts of a ghetto-dwelling "race apart" close to those with which Harlem writers were familiar. Like similar corrective work by these writers, Gold's novel was criticized by some on the left for excessive nationalistic passion and an attention deficit in the face of growing working-class consciousness. *Jews Without Money,* they complained, had failed to accent the unionization of Jewish garment workers (Rideout 152). Even more instructive about the discipline of African-American writing than this ghetto novel was a play Cruse and Hutchinson have company in ignoring, a little something Gold titled *Hoboken Blues; or, The Black Rip Van Winkle: A Modern Negro Fantasia on an Old American Theme.* One of the least principled reasons for Gold's assault on Van Vechten may have been that this three-act drama undertook the same trespass that *Nigger Heaven* had brought off so lucratively: to slip the bonds of whiteness and join, not merely advise, the Harlem Renaissance.

Hoboken Blues, or Minstrelsy in Reverse?

Though *Hoboken Blues* was selected for Van Wyck Brooks's *American Caravan* anthology in 1927, it was not produced until a year later. Initially rejected by the Provincetown Players, the drama found a home with the New Playwrights Theater,[13] an experimental company involving John Howard Lawson and John Dos Passos that Alexander Woollcott nicknamed "the revolting playwrights" (qtd. in Goldstein 26). Gold's play reflects the passion for the postrevolutionary Soviet stage that bit most of the New Playwrights. During a 1925 pilgrimage to the Soviet Union, Gold, like McKay before him, attended the Moscow theater of Vsevolod Meyerhold, the colleague of Sergei Eisenstein and Vladimir Mayakovsky who pledged to put the October Revolution into drama. In the interregnum before socialist realism, Meyerhold's promise to erase the gap between Soviet political achievements and dramatic developments prompted plays of agitprop content, constructivist designs meant to industrialize theatrical space, and actors who would "present" characters from a thoughtful and acrobatic distance (Hoover 100–101).

The published text of *Hoboken Blues* faithfully and ambitiously attempts to bolshevize the U.S. theater by fulfilling most of Meyerhold's program. Gold's agitprop subject is the revolutionary significance of an African-American stance toward labor under industrial capitalism. His recommendations for the stage set specify that "it would be a calamity to treat the scenes in the play realistically. They must be done by an intelligent futurist" (*Hoboken Blues* 548). Directions on the composition of the cast show Gold adapting Meyerhold's pre-Brechtian disruption of realistic characterization to satirize the insistent artificiality and crude stereotyping of "black" characters within blackface minstrelsy. Well before the dramatic whiteface inversions of Jean Genet's *The Blacks* (1958) and Douglas Turner Ward's *Day of Absence* (1965), Gold multiplies the ironies of his own authorial "racechange" with a peremptory note:[14] "No white men appear in this play. Where white men are indicated, they are played by Negroes in white caricature masks" (549). Suggestions for spirituals, blues, and jazz during and between the scenes are less indebted to Meyerhold than to the postwar revival of African-American theater. *Shuffle Along* (1921), featuring the songs of Eubie Blake and the voice of Florence Mills, was only the first of a string of black-produced Broadway musicals that showed no end as Gold wrote his own blues play. Ridgely Torrence's *Three Plays for the Negro Theatre* (1917), one acclaimed prelude to a postminstrel African-American drama, had before *Hoboken Blues* linked its parts with a singing orchestra performing spirituals.[15] This mixed bag of Afro-Soviet influences is further evidence that the margins of experimental modernism and literary proletarianism blurred in practice. Moreover, it is another sign that Gold's hopes for a syncretic proletarian–New Negro aesthetic outlived his contact with McKay at *The Liberator*.

The dramatis personae and crowded plot of *Hoboken Blues* owe their outline to the commonplace Harlem Renaissance theme of the rural migrant lost in the Negro Metropolis, to the Washington Irving tale invoked in the subtitle *The Black Rip Van Winkle*, and to the central play of Torrence's trilogy, *The Rider of Dreams*. Act I, set in an anachronistically black turn-of-the-century Harlem, introduces the protagonist Sam Pickens, propelled to New York by the southern lynch mob who murdered his brother. An analogue of both Irving's Rip and Torrence's impractical, guitar-playing Madison Sparrow, Sam prefers his farm cabin down home to his Manhattan apartment and his banjo to available wage labor. He is harassed on this score by his religious wife, Sally, a somewhat less shrewish

Dame Van Winkle. Sally convinces Sam that she will begin divorce proceedings if he breaks his word and fails to find a job in Hoboken, like Ha(a)rlem a locale with a Rip-appropriate Dutch past. Her husband's avoidance of the indignities of work in the white city, Sally protests, has come at her expense: "I gotta keep on washin' clothes and breakin' my back scrubbin' white folks' floors, so's yo' kin strut about saloons and poolrooms, playin' your banjo, singin', dancin', and talkin' " (581).

A progressively surreal act 2, flavored more by the blues than the spirituals, finds Sam job-hunting in New Jersey, even without a turnpike a far cry from the pastoral territory he had pictured. A position as a circus musician falls through when the ringmaster discovers that Sam can read and write: "Too civilized. We want savages. It pays" (589). A despondent Sam wanders into a public park, takes a cue from Rip, and sleeps for twenty-five years; in a pointed difference from Irving, the soporific is not alcohol but a billy club. Convicted of an informal statute against resting while black, Sam is beaten unconscious by four white police, the Keystone Cops gone feral:

> 1st Cop: Bust his arms and legs.
> 2nd Cop: Bust his skull and crown.
> 3rd Cop: Just a coal-black nigger.
> 4th Cop: Chase him out of town.   (591)

Sam's injuries at least allow him the comfort of utopian dreams. A beautiful black girl, looking "like Sally, Sam's wife, but much younger, serener," announces that she is "the Angel of Hoboken" and establishes Sam's rights to the city and to the appellation of artist (593, 594). Spartacus and Plato perform a pas de deux, with the philosopher suggesting that the Myth of the Cave could enlighten those shackled in industry. Sam then steps into a glowing city in which flowers bloom near factory gates and three hours on the assembly line are enough. His expert banjo playing cuts through prejudice and gets him elected president of something resembling an interracial Hoboken soviet. Sam's desire to work to his own rhythm and satisfaction, not for a "fat, nasty boss" (614), is finally fulfilled in this Land of Cockaigne plus electrification, Gold's industrial update of a communist future in which one would "hunt in the morning, fish in the afternoon, rear cattle in the evening, criticize after dinner" (Marx and Engels, *The German Ideology* 160).

Act 3 depicts Sam's inevitable awakening and return to the self-confident Harlem of the mid-1920s. "Harlem wuz a hawss-cah," thinks Sam, "but dis is a locomotive express train" (619). Gold's stage directions agree, indicating "the same cross-section of tenement and street as in the first act, but vastly more angular, confusing, colorful and jazzy; a composition of sharp, outrageous lines, an ensemble of militant statements by a drunken geometrician" (603). In the modernist Harlem of effortless speed and extemporaneous cubism, jazzers, students, and followers of Marcus Garvey compete with greedy cabaret owners (friends of Van Vechten?) to define the New Negro. Sam's excited description of "a place for de poor men, black and white, where birds sing sweet, and every house is full of music, and dere's sunflowers round de factory door" is initially mocked (626). The last word is his, however, along with the future symbolized by the marriage of his daughter to a studious young neighbor. Sam's scholarly son-in-law suggests that the old man's artistic talent, unappreciated in 1900, will be redeemed when the voice of "the black workers" is folded into Harlem's rebirth (610):

> Ethiopia is opening her heavy-lidded eyes; thousands of our young men and women are preparing a new renaissance; and I am one of them. No one can laugh at the Negro thinkers and artists any more—they fear and respect us—and we respect ourselves—for we are on the threshold of a new world! (610)

Sam closes the play leading a crowd of Harlemites in the singing of his composition "Hoboken Blues." Like Torrence's protagonist, Madison Sparrow, he reserves the right to dream; unlike his predecessor, Sam has convinced his community that dreaming is joyful and perhaps politically useful. Gold's hero, among the first contributions to the "veritable tradition of white radicals creating African-American protagonists to dramatize their views and concerns" (Wald 152), winds up a Harlem minister of socialist culture.

As Marcus Klein suggests, the oddball minstrel futurism of *Hoboken Blues* may have made it into *The American Caravan* because its folksy Rip Van Winkle intertext was in tune with the formula for new American writing favored by the anthology's main editor (241).[16] Van Wyck Brooks's recommendation that folk materials made the U.S. past more usable was similarly followed by Hart Crane, who in the same year that Gold completed *Hoboken Blues* began sketching a modern Rip who forgets "the office hours" in *The Bridge* (58). Gold's Rip-off is singular, however, in its attempt to hitch communism and what appears to be a stereotype of black laziness to Irving's myth of national origin and literary archetype for a U.S. canon of masculine retreat. With Sam dreaming of revolution's harvest, rather than dreaming through a revolution, *Hoboken Blues* proposes communism as Rip's proper politics and a worthy goal for a second American War of Independence. With Sam shirking his wife and labor according to Rip's directions, the play tweaks notions of black shiftlessness by investing a Harlem layabout with the Huckleberry values of American literature's classic boys' books, romances that tempt this investment by tracing a misogynous escape from white female morality into the arms of black male comrades.

Both sides of Sam's affinity with Rip shout yes to the banjo player's question "Ain't I American too?" (593). The text of *Hoboken Blues* aspires to undo minstrelsy's racializing oath of citizenship as it reverses the direction of the form's interracial transit. Nineteen twenty-seven, the year of both Gold's play and *The Jazz Singer*, the first talking picture, was perhaps the zenith of Jewish minstrelsy. Jewish entertainers such as Al Jolson, George Burns, and Fanny Brice had come to dominate the blackface stage by the early twentieth century. They found in burnt cork, argues Michael Rogin, what Gold detected in John Brown: a vehicle of Americanization. "Minstrelsy accepted ethnic difference by insisting on racial division," Rogin asserts. "It passed immigrants into Americans by differentiating them from [those] through whom they spoke," namely, black Americans kept outside the melting pot for reasons of uniquely unsmeltable "racial" difference (56). With *The Jazz Singer*, the Jewish magnates who made Hollywood delivered a "collective autobiography" in which the social wage of Jewish blackface—upwardly mobile Americanization—was confessed in brilliant sound (Rogin 84). Gold's drama is the work of a radical Jew without money hoping to quiet the jazz singer's voice with Sam's blues, the music of those whose full citizenship minstrelsy denied. The xenophobic nativism of the mid-1920s that Rogin sees as "*The Jazz Singer*'s invisible frame" (89) is impossible to miss in Gold's play, in which a white judge uses Sam's vagrancy to argue that "every foreigner in the country should be kicked out!" (598). Just as visible in *Hoboken Blues* is an antinativist response that refuses to forfeit the Americanness of blacks in the interest of imperiled Jewish assimilation. Not for nothing does Sam's son-in-law call him "Uncle Sam" (579).

Gold's resistance to minstrelsy's siren song of citizenship nevertheless comes at a high price. Crudely put, the left-wing Americanism of *Hoboken Blues* commandeers Rip to argue for a communism American-style, made by white and black men leagued against nativism, degraded labor, and demanding, conventional women. Sally, Gold's version of Dame Van Winkle, is distinguished from Irving's original in several respects. She enters Sam's Hoboken dream in the guise of a comforting angel, survives her husband's absence, and accepts his love after he returns, choosing Sam over a cabaret-owning stuffed shirt. Gold's plan of future freedom thus entails more than a band of brothers sharing the fruits of the factory. Yet his hero still manfully pioneers in creative work avoidance where other men lead in the realm of production: Sam dreams a path to communism in defiance of his wife. The compulsive masculinism of Gold's manifestoes for proletarian literature is thus largely undented by *Hoboken Blues*.

Neither does the play disdain all of minstrelsy's guilty white pleasures. Gold's dialogue often consists of the kind of distorted black dialect that McKay and James Weldon Johnson early identified as a cardinal enemy of the Harlem Renaissance. With lines like "Is we or isn't we going to git any more testifications?" (559), African-American speech becomes what Johnson denounced as a "mere mutilation of English spelling and pronunciation" (preface 41). The use of broad dialect is puzzling given Gold's later protests against the "vulgar" sounds the poet Archibald MacLeish put in the mouth of a character subtly named "Comrade Levine" (qtd. in Salzman and Wallenstein 238); when it hit home squarely, he seemed to register dialect's Othering force. Similarly, the play's comedy often relies on the minstrel staple of racial travesty. To take only one example, Gold relies on the innate humorousness of a character called Achilles McGregor, "a short, fat, jolly Negro in a big blue coat and driver's cap, with badge" (549). On the model of the blackface policemen and politicians who had wandered from the minstrel show to more respectable U.S. stage comedy by the 1920s, Achilles's classical name and unclassical physique are intended to emphasize a comic disparity between the black man and his station. The white Gold who imagined this overreaching black heel sampled the minstrel pleasure of "crossing boundaries to parody those who crossed boundaries" (Rogin 32). Knowing that Sterling Brown found "much hilarious comedy" in *Hoboken Blues* thus is not sufficient to quiet the judgment that Gold's parody of minstrelsy is at times not parodic enough (*Negro Poetry* 130). Knowing that Gold allowed the New Playwrights to violate his casting suggestions with a white company in blackface is enough to make us overlook any parody at all (Goldstein 19).

Ironically, *Hoboken Blues*'s most pronounced flirtation with racism derives not from its self-betraying debt to minstrelsy but from its faithfulness to an antiracist strategy common in Harlem Renaissance discourse: celebrating blackness by reversing the hierarchy of terms within white-authored white/black oppositions. The play's glorification of its hero's refusal of work threatens to sanction the racial binarism it recodes but does not displace, in this case, the opposition between white industriousness and black indolence. Sam's name alone evokes "Sambo" as much as Uncle Sam, the former the outstanding U.S. type of black male laziness whom Razaf imagined dancing with Lenin and Trotsky. What is most provocative about Gold's drama, however, is its care to insulate Sam from "-bo." From the title on, the play paints its hero as a descendant of Irving's Rip and thus indicates that his distaste for work may not be a racial trait. More critically, Gold repeatedly emphasizes that his hero does not reject work per se, only the paid work available to black southern migrants around Harlem. In act 1, Sam himself suggests that he "believe[s] in wuhk" (570) but that the positions offered in the North pervert the term. "When I wuz down south wid de fambly wuhkin' our little patch," he affirms, "I wuhked as hahd as anyboddy" (570). A pantomime at the start of act 2 reveals that self-hate is the main wage of the service jobs that are Sam's only alternatives to the factories he scorns and the circus he loves. He is shown kowtowing to detestable white-masked figures as a waiter in a restaurant, as a shoe shine, and as the live target in a carnival booth labeled "*Hit the Nigger and Get a Cigar*," the last presented as the logical fulfillment of the first two occupations (584–85; emphasis in original). When he resists complete humiliation in each of the three positions, he is fired and beaten. Sam's rejection of available work is associated with memories of sharecropping creatively recast as unregimented preindustrial labor and enabling dreams of such labor's dialectical reinvention on a higher level under communism. During his twenty-five-year siesta, his warm recollections of southern "sunflowers at yo' own cabin door" (570) are transmuted into a utopian Marxist vision of sunflowers at the entrance to a democratic factory.

Gold seems to have believed that the minstrel tastes of white workers were related to "the idea that blackness could be made permanently to embody the preindustrial past that they scorned and missed" (Roediger, *The Wages* 97). The blackface stage conventions established in the nineteenth century, David Roediger argues, were "the result of the desire to project onto Blacks the *specific* behaviors that brought such conflicted emotions to whites during the formation of the first American working class" (97; emphasis in original). As chapter 2 noted, Roediger draws on George Rawick to assert that white workers "cast Blacks as their former selves" when facing a new work ethos "that attacked holidays, spurned contact with nature, saved time, bridled sexuality, separated work from the rest of life and postponed gratification" (95). Temporarily donning burnt cork thus allowed this working class to indulge its affection and loathing for preindustrial ways both intimately and hygienically. *Hoboken Blues*, for all its flaws as published and performed, targets the debilitating linear history behind minstrelsy's equation of whiteness and industrial "working classness" and, by extension, the racist self-conception of minstrelsy's white working-class admirers. The play embraces the identification of African Americans with preindustrial values yet rejects the moment of censure and the imprisonment of these values within a rigidly racialized and rapidly fading arcadian memory. Sam's all-American slacking encourages the nation's entire proletariat to welcome the return of flexible, preindustrial work rhythms. More straightforwardly than Razaf's lyric-writing porter, he gives what Du Bois dubbed the gift of black labor: "the idea of toil as a necessary evil ministering to the pleasure of life" (*The Gift* 79). Gold's projection of this gift into America's communist future as well as its revolutionary past avoids bootless nostalgia and what Rogin describes as "a nationalist organicism [split] into a black past and a white future" (49). Sam is no historical exile, sealed within the archaic, but a representative of the preferable tomorrow in the preindustrial past, an exponent of a historically rooted prospective vision who matches the stage sets assigned to "an intelligent futurist." Even this oldest New Negro, Gold proposes, is a model of the true, dialectical movement of U.S. history toward the (re)liberation of work under communism.

Given Gold's often-quoted paeans to muscular youths who break from labor "in the lumber camps, coal mines, and steel mills" only to scribble out rough proletarian verses ("Go Left" 188), how can we account for *Hoboken Blues*'s glorification of a character who declines to proletarianize himself? Perhaps Gold was impressed by the dissenting, epicurean Marxism of Paul Lafargue's *The Right to Be Lazy*, an ebullient tract translated into English and published in New York in 1898. Taking cues from Charles Fourier and other socialists his father-in-law Karl Marx had rejected as unscientific, Lafargue prefigures Gold in affirming that the proletariat should recall the precapitalist past to prepare itself for the three-hour postcapitalist working day. The working class, instructs Lafargue, "must proclaim the Rights of Laziness, a thousand times more noble and more sacred than the anaemic Rights of Man concocted by the metaphysical lawyers of the bourgeois revolution. It must accustom itself to working but three hours a day, reserving the rest of the day and night for leisure and feasting" (19). It is also possible to attribute *Hoboken Blues*'s peculiarity to Gold's desire to pay respect to his own receding bohemianism, cultivated in the teens on the fringes of the Provincetown Players and *The Masses*. The play's salute to a nonworking member of the working class might then be interpreted as a reimagining of Gold's past stemming from a desire to keep the peace between departed bohemian and emergent supercommunist selves. Perhaps the Sam of 1900 is a younger, blacked-up Gold as envisioned by the Gold of 1927, with a taste for unalienated artistic labor elevated to a revolutionary virtue and bohemianism understood as an embryonic communism.

What is more likely and less dependent on speculation about Gold's library or personal mythology is that the hero of *Hoboken Blues* emerged at least in part in response to Claude McKay. In his dream discovery of the indissoluble interests of African Americans and the white working class, Sam reaffirms the interracial commitment of *The Liberator* that Gold shared with his coeditor when not worrying over the tolerance of white readers. In his embodiment of the idea that African Americans are disproportionately significant to U.S. Marxism, Sam is also a personification of McKay's "very acute angle" on the race question (letter to Max Eastman, 19 December 1934). Little wonder that McKay could suggest that Communists had shown him the sincerest form of flattery after his Soviet journey. Beneath its inadequately critical internal critique of minstrelsy, Gold's play advertises the "revolutionary attitude towards Negroes" that McKay demanded in his parting *Liberator* article ("Birthright" 73). *Hoboken Blues* certainly demonstrates that both the racial slander and interracial desire of blackface could infect the best-laid white radical plans to explode the form. The drama also qualifies, however, as Gold's belated tribute to McKay's position in the *Liberator* debates over "the race matter." McKay's simultaneous possession of the garlands of revolutionary and New Negro poetry is the standard of aesthetic achievement that Gold's play covets, a play that poses Sam's renaissance in Harlem as a lesson in proletarian revolution and a lesson to proletarian art.

The Gold Standard and the Logic of Modernism

In *The Hollow Men* (1941), a vindictive defense of the Depression-era height of literary proletarianism and the disastrous Hitler-Stalin pact, Gold claimed that it was African-American writers of the 1930s who finally succeeded in "lifting to human dignity . . . the Negro people as portrayed in literature" (48). The likes of Sterling Brown, Langston Hughes, and Richard Wright had shouldered the burden, though not without support from the "pioneers of proletarian literature" (48). Gold here offers slim indication that Van Vechten did not own the renaissance that had promised to do this "lifting to human dignity" in the 1920s, let alone that proletarian literature and the Harlem movement were confederate projects. He denounces the white Negro for providing the ugly pattern of the black hero that the renaissance followed, while approvingly quoting Eugene Clay's characterization of the New Negroes as a corps who "prided themselves on the fact that they could act, sing, paint and write as well as their white-skinned patrons" (qtd. on 47). Nowhere is there an admission that the careers of two out of Gold's three exemplars—Brown and Hughes— straddle the 1920s and 1930s, the heyday of the Harlem Renaissance and the heyday of U.S. proletarianism. The comments on African-American writing in *The Hollow Men* instead assemble a model of literary history in which the moment of the New Negro is confined to the 1920s and linked with a corrupting white patronage and the moment of an unshrinking black literature arrives with the 1930s and is linked with the inspiration of white proletarian forerunners. This model rests on and champions a series of stark conceptual divisions, divisions between African-American literatures under the auspices of the Harlem Renaissance and under proletarianism, between crippling and invigorating white influences on these literatures, and between the literary politics of two decades during which Gold had been writing in the name of proletarianism.

A very different perception of the relationship between the Harlem Renaissance and proletarian literature was sometimes voiced during the period of the latter's greatest influence on African-American writers. In a 1937 address to the Communist-sponsored Second National Negro Congress ("Resume"), Alain Locke himself emphasized "the considerable harmony . . . between the cultural racialism of the art philosophy of the 1920s and the class proletarian art creed of today's younger generation." The New Negroes had, "in theory at least, aimed at folk realism which is involved in and is not so different from social realism or even proletarian expression." Locke cites "Langston Hughes and Sterling Brown, who belong to both generations," as clear proof that "in the expression of Negro folk life," the writing of the 1920s and 1930s has "a common denominator." The noblest task of the Depression cohort of African-American writers was hence not to kill off their elders' renaissance but to extend and improve it, "to carry . . . motives of racial self-expression and folk interpretation out to sounder, fuller lengths." Locke's marching orders for the young were not issued in a void. Even Wright's "Blueprint for Negro Writing" (1937) admitted between attacks on debased Harlem primitivists that "the Negro has a folklore which embodies the memories and hopes of his struggle for freedom" and that any self-respecting African-American writing would enlarge "this folk tradition" (56).

Histories of U.S. modernism in black, white, and Red have ignored Locke's contention that the movement he volunteered to midwife harmonized and intersected with proletarian literature. If they agree with Gold and with each other on little else, they second Gold's 1941 opinion that the Harlem Renaissance and proletarianism are discontinuous; if related at all, related negatively.[17] Though it is now critical common sense, this design of gross fracture and opposition between the two bodies of writing had to be drawn up on the heels of their frequent mingling and shared disrespect for the ideology of the literary decade. Gold was composing and propagating what he called proletarian literature in the 1920s; Zora Neale Hurston was making her best use of renaissance topoi in the 1930s; and the texts of black bolsheviks as different as Razaf, McKay, Hughes, Brown, and Arna Bontemps indicate that it was possible during either decade to work within both schools or some hybrid. The very rhetoric of Gold's disassociation of New Negro and proletarian writing in *The Hollow Men* reveals the arduousness of the divisive operation. In praising proletarianized African-American writers of the 1930s for "lifting to human dignity . . . the Negro people as portrayed in literature," he draws on the metaphor of racial uplift employed by old guard proponents of the renaissance so often that it became an object of parody for younger New Negroes. Even in his effort to build opposition, Gold thus divulges the presence of the renaissance Other in a black literary discourse he claims is indebted rightfully only to proletarian pioneers. Such traces of the New Negro in the Newer Negro of the 1930s do not compel the conclusion that interwar African-American literature exists on a pure continuum, but they suggest that elements of renaissance writing—especially those molded by black bolshevism—fed smoothly into Depression-era black aesthetics. In place of the narrative of Harlem's renaissance giving way in toto before postcrash social realism, we might then envision the Depression-era reemergence of the position in the renaissance field that spliced New Negro and working-class insurrection, a position that took a low profile during the second half of the 1920s but never vanished chez Razaf, Hughes, and so on.

As this chapter has demonstrated, much of Gold's own thirty-year engagement with McKay and the larger Harlem Renaissance supports the notion of a "considerable harmony" between the movement's "cultural racialism" and "the class proletarian art creed." None of this is to minimize those episodes of white paternalism and unreconstructed racism in Gold's career to which the Cruse line draws attention; nor is it to wish away every barrier—racial and otherwise—between the renaissance and proletarianism, modernisms enticed by the manifestic declaration of dividing principles. It is rather to assert that the Harlem Renaissance lived and imagined by Gold, not just in 1941 but twenty years before and ten years later, gives the lie to both Cruse and *The Hollow Men*. Gold's aggregate response to the renaissance, in other words, denies the idea of the proletarian brain trust's intrinsic hostility to Harlem writing and the idea of a selfless proletarian redemption of spent New Negroism.

What are the implications of this conclusion? For one thing, it suggests that the U.S. proletarian literature that Gold symbolized and theorized should no longer be scorned by the maturing critical narrative of modernism's crossracial fascinations. Michael North, like other framers of this narrative, has no thought of proletarianism when maintaining that "linguistic mimicry and racial masquerade were not just shallow fads but strategies without which modernism could not have arisen" (preface n.p.). North's sketch of Gold as a McKay-bullying minstrel man works to charge white proletarians with a unique modernist crime (193): flattening the ambivalence of white desires for black forms and bodies into pure theft and horror. The most cursory look at Gold's *Life of John Brown*, *Hoboken Blues*, and *Jews Without Money* reveals, however, the familiar scramble of interracial attraction and aversion; in this respect, at least, Gold's proletarianism was a "normal" modernism. *Hoboken Blues*, we might even argue, is an impaired white plea to transform minstrelsy's "dialectical flickering of . . . moments of domination and moments of liberation" into a continuous beam of freedom (Lott, *Love* 18).

But a more significant implication of my final claim is this: numerous fictions and critical pieces by Gold suggest that his influential pronouncements on proletarian literature were formulated in conversation with Harlem's literary renaissance. Gold's thoughts on the relationship between the two schools ranged from near-identity to stiff competition, but a sense of proletarianism's special proximity to Harlem was constant. What Gold once described as the renaissance aim to "portray . . . the life of the workers" ("Proletarian" 205) stayed with him. From "Towards Proletarian Art" to *The Hollow Men*, he invoked the Harlem movement to shore up or point up the qualities of proletarian writing, the likeness and distinction between working-class and revolutionary literary perspectives. When Gold's *New Masses* begged the working class to "Write For Us!" it fittingly requested "revelations by rebel chambermaids and night club waiters," the mainstays of the renaissance's proletarian wing ("Write For Us!" 2). To adapt a conclusion from North, it seems right to declare that Gold's appointment with McKay and the Harlem Renaissance was not a shallow fad but an encounter without which U.S. proletarian literature would have risen more haltingly. The meeting of the New Negro and the Old Leftist at *The Liberator* may not have overridden U.S. proletarianism's response to

Soviet magnetism, but it fostered a national edition enlivened by the practice of African-American modernism. Even the Harlem star whom Cruse describes as Gold's nemesis might have approved of this concluding moral. Though he confessed he did not expect all literary leftists to see it, McKay considered his *Home to Harlem* an instructively "real proletarian novel" (qtd. in L. Lewis, *When* 227).

4 · Scottsboro Delimited: White Bait, Red Triangles, and Interracialism Between Men

White-black relationships were very close among the communists. . . . I thought it was pretty funny myself, being from the South. I found it strange that every couple, almost, was a mixed couple one way or the other. That was the age of unity.

> —Dizzy Gillespie, *To Be, or Not . . . to Bop: Memoirs* (1979)

Messin' white woman
Snake lyin' tale
Dat hang an' burn
An' jail wit' no bail

> —"Death House Blues," reprinted in *Proletarian Literature in the United States: An Anthology* (1935)

Surely, I said,
Now will the poets sing.
But they have raised no cry.

> —Countee Cullen, "Scottsboro, Too, Is Worth Its Song" (1935)

At the opening of the last chapter, I suggested that when the white Mike Gold jitterbugged with an African-American social worker at the Savoy Ballroom in 1937, he was hoping to discover vivid evidence of Communist humanity. I want to begin the present chapter by proposing that this dance of interracial partners also may have been fueled by in-house criticism of party interracialism. During the second half of the 1930s, years in which over two thousand black Harlemites spent time as party members (Naison 279), African-American women in the Harlem branch came to question an unplanned, uneven result of the Old Left's exceptional intolerance for segregation. By then, the Black Belt Nation thesis and the Depression's traumatic intensification of African-American poverty had directed five blacks aboard the U.S. party's Central Committee (Rampersad, *The Life* 217). Mandates against white chauvinism in lower-level Communist bodies had inspired *The Chicago Defender* to declare the party the sole institution in white America that practiced the egalitarianism it preached (Carter 89–90). Even the black bolsheviks' early hopes for a Communism unafraid of intimate social equality had been realized. But with lopsided effects: interracial heterosexuality in the scope of the party seemed to yield relationships between black men and white women but rarely the racial reverse. At benefits and house parties, black male comrades often danced with white women, while couples composed of black women and white men were harder to find. At the top of the Harlem party leadership, African-American men like Theodore Bassett, William Fitzgerald, and James W. Ford, the Communists' vice-presidential candidate in 1932 and 1936, contributed to the large majority of intermarriages then—as now—involving black men and white women (Naison 136–37). In 1935 a group of African-American women Communists first spoke openly of their opinion that this pattern of interracial romance had crossed the line between private preference and political danger. Overcoming a reluctance to be smeared as opponents of social equality, they asked for a ban on interracial marriages in party circles, 40 percent female at the height of the Popular Front (Naison 137; Foley, *Radical* 218). The tensions among civil rights workers kindled by the 1964 Freedom Summer coupling of white women and black men were previewed in full on the Old Left.[1]

Given the volatility of the subject, it is unsurprising that no self-generated record seems to remain of the black women's individual identities and general arguments against the imbalances of party interracialism. If these arguments matched those produced for a later, analogous resolution to the Comintern, however, they bore little trace of an unreflective resentment of "the white wife." Claude McKay's guidebook *Harlem: Negro Metropolis* (1940) recounts the author's 1938 visit with pioneering West Indian Communist Grace Campbell and a like-minded group of Harlem women who had assembled "to discuss the subject of all the Negro party leaders' being married to white women" (234). The gathering apparently resolved that these leaders' romantic lives condoned the U.S. creed of black women's subordination: "It was an insult to Negro womanhood that their radical leaders should take white wives, especially as the Negro woman is nationally regarded as being on a lower social and moral level than the white woman" (234). In a further instance of Harlem Communists anticipating Soviet authorization for their most radical overtures, Campbell forwarded their case "to Comrade Stalin and the Executive of the Communist International in Moscow" (234). At home in Communist New York, objections to interracial marriage were greeted with awkwardness. Abner Berry, the African-American community liaison who officially responded to the 1935 initiative, had an ungainly stake in the outcome. "The whole discussion, for me," he remarked, "was complicated by the fact that I had a white wife myself. . . . I was able to convince them that the Party couldn't outlaw such marriages, that it had to be left to the decision of each individual. We had to change the social conditions within and outside the Party so that the black woman could come into her rightful place" (qtd. in Naison 137). According to Mark Naison, the women's appeal did induce small alterations in those social conditions straightforwardly subject to the party's influence. Some black male Communists were inspired to launch "a 'movement back to the race,' breaking off relationships with white wives and girlfriends in order to find black women as partners" (Naison 137). Disregarding the comparative lack of concern over the affections of white men, Harlem organizers offered white male Communists dance lessons, reasoning (with no special sensitivity to rhythmic lore) that it would increase their willingness to break the ice with black women (Naison 137). We can thus perhaps set another incongruous image beside Joseph Freeman's official portrait of a cigar-chomping Mike Gold spitting in the studios of the rich (257): Gold learning a few steps from Harlem comrades before meeting the unnamed social worker who "could dance like a dream, and . . . was a Communist!" (Gold, "Doing the Big Apple" 7).

The Harlem party's internal frictions over interracial sexuality may already have reminded readers of what is probably U.S. anti-Communism's most American strain: its vision of the Communist camp as a laboratory of enthusiastic interbreeding. Robin D. G. Kelley notes that in the early-twentieth-century United States, Communism was subject to "a peculiar myth that linked [it] to sexual promiscuity and miscegenation. In the South the word *communism* itself (pronounced 'com-mune-ism,' according to W. J. Cash) had a curiously explicit sexual connotation derived from stereotyped visions of nineteenth-century utopian communal societies, which suggested that notions of 'free love' were integrally tied to communal living" (79). White southerners in particular feared that Communism's promised revolution would topple the racial-sexual moral order as it leveled economic differences. A 1934 strike wave in Birmingham, Alabama, was met with editorials against "Red literature preaching free love [and] inter-marriage" and a bulletin from the White Legion posing the routine segregationist question with a quaint addition: "How would you like to awaken one morning to find your wife or daughter attacked by a Negro or a Communist!" (qtd. in Kelley 79). For many whites in the South and elsewhere, the most frightening—and perhaps most titillating—aspect of sovietized free love was the prospect of open affection between black men and white women. Much as later civil rights leaders were defamed as chasers of the carrot of blonde beauty, black male Communists were said to be drawn to the party as an entrée to white womanhood. To "Coloured men," reckoned one worried commentator, "complete equality with the Whites, as proclaimed by Moscow, *means free possession of White women*" (qtd. in Kelley 79; emphasis in original). In such fantasies of Communism as the socialization of white male sexual property, white women comrades shone as the party's spoils. Even in less hysterical pockets of anti-Communism, white women were perceived as secret weapons in the party's battle for the heart, mind, and body of African-American manhood. Near the close of Ralph Ellison's *Invisible Man*, for example, Brotherhood bosses supervise white sirens who tempt the narrator to "confus[e] the class struggle with the ass struggle" (418), a rhyming phrase, incidentally, that Ellison borrowed from a well-circulated Harlem joke.[2] For her part, Zora Neale Hurston associated the party's use of white bait with its belief that black men equated U.S. citizenship with a right to white wives. One thing Communists never forgot, she suggested in 1951, was the Reconstruction-era absurdity "that the highest ambition of every Negro man was to have a white woman" (qtd. in Sollors, *Neither* 418). In anti-Communism's party world turned upside down, black men were invited left by white men as perverse as they were devious. Scrapping any jealous safekeeping of white women's sexuality, this twisted gang entertained a black male curiosity about white female flesh and an erotic shock troop lost enough to satisfy it. As Ellison's black male protagonist asks of the Brotherhood's white male management, "Why did they have to mix their women into everything? Between us and everything we wanted to change in the world they placed a woman: socially, politically, economically" (418).

Another black writer intrigued by the mythology of red date bait also "placed a woman" between black men and social change. Grafting the anti-intermarriage sentiments of Grace Campbell's group on to the notion "that the Communists get Negro men to join by seducing them with white women," Claude McKay from his late, antiparty slant observed that "the Communists, in trying to break down [the] taboo [against interracial sex], discover their most formidable enemy is the Negro woman. She remains the bulwark against the Communist penetration of the Negro minority"

(*Harlem* 233–34). In the fraught carnal rhetoric of this claim from *Harlem*, black women inside and outside the party somehow block the phallic advance of Communism into black America, an advance that black men are seemingly inclined to welcome as an infusion of sexual-political potency. McKay's own text and the most scrupulous histories of African Americans and Communism testify that his claim is as shaky as it is sexually loaded. At least two elements McKay himself discloses challenge his suggestion that Harlem party women endorsed anti-Communist charges of red seduction via white vamp: these women's sense that political responsibility for relationships between black men and white women rested with the former; and their expectation that Communism's final authorities would intervene against intermarriage. McKay's conclusion that the (singular) African-American woman was a "bulwark against the Communist penetration of the Negro minority" is disputed by recent social history revealing black women as bulwarks of African-American Communism. The party unit in early Depression Birmingham examined by Kelley was driven as much as staffed by a majority of black women "who often proved more militant than their male comrades" (33). The Harlem branch studied by Naison saw its largest affiliated union of the 1930s run by Rose Gaulden, a Harlem Hospital nurse; ex-Garveyite Bonita Williams led the party's Unemployed Councils; "Queen Mother" Audley Moore became one of the party's most visible street speakers and by 1942 secretary of the entire New York State division (259, 136). Despite all this, however, it is my view that the invidious gendering of some of the party's ordinary rhetoric of racial integration made it somewhat easier to produce anti-Communist caricatures of black male marks, white female lures, and black female interference. Well-meant party communications on the Negro Question could have encouraged black women to perceive a debarring from the channels and rewards of Communist interracialism.

Triangles in Tandem

Left-feminist literary critics Barbara Foley, Paula Rabinowitz, Deborah Rosenfelt, and the late Constance Coiner stress that the serious consideration paid to women's liberation on the Old Left was rivaled by an anxious masculinism that flowed between the party's political and cultural undertakings. Along with these critics, one may debate the extent to which sexist party iconography was rooted in Marxist productivism and whether Josephine Herbst, Meridel Le Sueur, Tillie Olsen, and other radical women writers eclipsed or enriched party and Marxist thought.[3] It is clear, however, that Communism's prevalent masculinization of its virtues extended to many representations of proletarian interracialism.

Admittedly, exceptions to the red literary rule that men in jeans instigate desegregation are not impossible to find. Some of the best-recalled proletarian fiction by white women, for example, regenders interracialism's avant-garde. Suzanne Sowinska observes that in Fielding Burke's *Call Home the Heart*, Grace Lumpkin's *To Make My Bread*, and Myra Page's *Gathering Storm*, three 1932 novels concerning the 1929 Gastonia, North Carolina, textile strike, "most of the 'Negro work' is, significantly, women's work. While the union drive provides the impetus for contact between the white and black workers, it is the [white] women workers who are depicted as the first to mingle with blacks on the picket lines" ("Writing" 125). Far more common among party-affiliated writers, however, are revelations of interracial brotherhood in the mode of another 1932 text, Langston Hughes's poem "Open Letter to the South," which climaxes with blacks and whites arm in arm and "Man to Man" (l. 68). As I have already discussed, the pages of *The Crusader* and *Hoboken Blues* likewise display black and white hands joining to defy unmanly disciplinarians of capital; the opposition of interracial laborers and feminized proprietors provides the gut-level rhetorical architecture. Yet the most interesting masculinist scenes in the discourse of Communist interracialism are knottier than these. Ironically parallel to the antimiscegenation strain in U.S. anti-Communism, they override binary designs to outline an interracial triangle, the geometrical form that has long synopsized the West's intellectual " 'commonsense' . . . [on] erotic relations" (Sedgwick 21).

In the case of this radical rhetorical triangle, we find what Eve Sedgwick would call an asymmetrical figure, one in which, contrary to Freud's oedipal family, the power differences attached to the gender and race of the three participants are fully known to affect the figure's contour and meaning (23–27). Here, black male and white male "rivals" are wed more strongly to each other than to the emotional object they hold in common: white women. In terms of Gayle Rubin's influential feminist essay "The Traffic in Women" (1975), these women become exchangeable commodities fusing relationships between males of different racial but identical class "families." In terms of Sedgwick's equally influential book *Between Men* (1985), the relationships thus cemented become types of interracial "male 'homosocial desire' " (1), Sedgwick's designation for a socially obscured range of male-male passions ranging from heterosexual male bonding to male homosexuality. The triangular rhetoric of Communist interracialism therefore casts crossracial alliance as a homosocial affair of white and black proletarians conducted by means of white women, who function locally as integration's conduits rather than as segregation's trip-wires. Through this rhetoric's three-way lens, black women appear to be either absent or distant, indistinct constituents of a racial minority gendered male or a remote fourth term awaiting the deliverance of male alliance making.

Thus far, my sketch of a radical rhetorical triangle may seem too abstract for comfort. Richard Wright's novel *Native Son* (1940), among the most cutting literary recreations of this triangle, will be discussed in chapter 6. The remainder of this chapter examines concrete textual products of the Communist effort to free the Scottsboro boys, a campaign that provoked numerous triangular variations as it helped to lift the party to its interwar height of African-Americanization. On the surface, the Scottsboro drive would seem to present an inapposite motive for triangular representations of interracialism. To the NAACP's dismay, the Communist defense of the nine young black men accused of raping two white women on an Alabama train in 1931 took aim at the whole edifice of southern legal lynching and consequently targeted a triangular mythography "in which the body of the white female [rape] victim mediates between the oppositional pairing of black beast and white protector" (Gunning 9). However, the rhetoric of the attack on the segregationist rape triangle early on assumed the shape of a second, shadowing interracial triangle, one in which distaste for the Scottsboro boys' accusers became the affiliative seal between black and white male worker-radicals. This antilynch triangle denied "always-already-sexual black male guilt" (duCille, "The Unbearable" 334) and revamped the nature of both male parties' "desire" for the white female term, yet a now-hostile libidinal attachment still glued a homosocial bond.[4] In effect, Communism's first wave of Scottsboro discourse built on a substitution of interracial triangles. With special reference to the writing of two African-American Communists, the well-known Langston Hughes and the unknown Louise Thompson, I will pursue several questions raised by this substitution: Could Communist attacks on the Scottsboro rape charges paradoxically have fostered anti-Communist myths of the traffic in red women, yet another specimen of triangular-homosocial logic? Did triangular-homosocial representations of Communist interracialism offer writerly agency to black male authors only at the cost of black female comrades, unaddressed in three-point promises of social and literary equality? How did black women connected with the party write their way around, through, or against these red triangles, common in Communist representations if not in Communist lives?

Scottsboro and the International Labor Defense

History's current verdict on the Scottsboro case—or cases (one defendant, Haywood Patterson, was tried four times)—is that nine African-American "boys" were falsely charged with rape for the true crime of winning fights with white men. On March 25, 1931, in the little town of Paint Rock, Alabama, nine black men under twenty were dragged off a freight train on which they had hitched rides in hope of finding work in Memphis. Once in Scottsboro, the county seat, they were initially booked for assaulting a smaller group of fellow hitchers who had asked them to leave a "white man's" car; after a few hours stewing in jail, they were charged with raping Ruby Bates and Victoria Price, young white women who had been riding the same train's rails. Several forces drove this escalation of charges. One was the inclination of white southern *men* to cry rape in response to black male truculence, to answer perceived challenges to their sovereignty in the language of violated sexual purity. In the words of Scottsboro historian James Goodman, Alabama prosecutors knew that all-male, all-white juries would see the defendants' fight with the white hoboes "as both precursor to the rape and proof that it had occurred" (222). Another force was Bates and Price's alarm at what it would cost in the coin of southern white womanhood to admit to friendly contact with indigent black men. Within weeks, the Scottsboro nine were found guilty, with the eight oldest sentenced to death. That the accused had actually outlived the three-day trial was a rarity that some white Alabamians hailed as a victory over lynch barbarism, personified by the mob who surrounded the Scottsboro jail with rope and kerosene. Less impressed was the International Labor Defense (ILD), a Communist legal aid auxiliary that Michael Denning dubs "the earliest Popular Front organization" (13). After jousting bitterly with the NAACP for control of the case, the ILD secured the trust of the defendants and their parents and took control of the appeal (Carter 3–136; Goodman 3–38).

The ILD's strategy—legal defense supported by mass action—at times looked to threaten danger to itself. On its left flank, the ILD would make the case an international Communist cause célèbre, a tack the NAACP worried could render the boys cannon fodder. Scottsboro would become a synonym for the system of rape paranoia and lynch terror that imprisoned the southern Black Belt Nation in sharecropping; it would demonstrate the necessity of mass antiracist protest and the Communists' Marxist-nationalist approach to African-American politics. "Precisely because the Scottsboro Case is an expression of the horrible national oppression of the Negro masses," *The Daily Worker* argued, "any real fight . . . must necessarily take the character of a struggle against the whole brutal system of landlord robbery and imperialist national oppression of the Negro people" (qtd. in Carter 137). On its right flank, and despite its final distrust of legalism, the ILD would retain some of the best lawyers in the country. With help from Walter Pollack, a distinguished constitutional attorney, the U.S. Supreme Court was persuaded to reverse the convictions of Ozie Powell and seven of the other defendants in the 1932 decision *Powell v. Alabama*. In 1933 the ILD hired Samuel Leibowitz, an undefeated New York criminal lawyer then mentioned as a successor to Clarence Darrow (and still sometimes remembered as a prototype for Bigger's attorney, Max, in *Native Son*). Beginning with the second trial of Haywood Patterson in Decatur, Alabama, Leibowitz conducted an exhaustive defense that kept the Scottsboro nine alive through an agonizing course of convictions, reviews, retrials, and prison violence. In 1937 the state dropped its charges against four of the defendants; four more were paroled in the 1940s; and the last, Patterson, escaped in 1950 to Michigan, whose governor refused Alabama's extradition request (Goodman 394–97).

It didn't take the release of the Scottsboro nine for the ILD to reap benefits for the party. Beginning in the early 1930s, Benjamin Davis and William Patterson, two politically savvy black Communist lawyers, skillfully managed the ILD's Scottsboro publicity drive. Naison's verdict that the Scottsboro campaign was the single action most responsible for the "Party's emergence as a force in Harlem life" (57) might be exported beyond black New York. An impressive cohort of black intellectuals had thrown their lot in with Bolshevism at the birth of a Harlem New Negro, but Scottsboro made Communism a household word in African-American clubs, beauty shops, and churches and added color to the party's rank and file throughout the United States. The Reverend Adam Clayton Powell, Jr., was not unique in his avid response to the ILD, proclaimed from pulpits as well as at Scottsboro rallies: "The day will come when being called a Communist will be the highest honor that can be paid an individual and that day is coming soon" (qtd. in Naison 87).

Scottsboro and Shakespeare in Harlem

Langston Hughes, the most public, productive—and prolifically red— African-American poet of the century, is often grouped with those persuaded to Communism by Scottsboro. Arnold Rampersad's biography cites a monumentalizing account of the bard of Harlem rushing to a Scottsboro symposium to cap the narrative of Hughes's conversion: "There is a tenseness, an agony in the Poet's face. It seems that his life depends on getting to that meeting in time. . . . The Poet talks passionately of the Scottsboro boys. They are innocent. They must go free" (qtd. in *The Life* 216–17). As Rampersad also notes, however, Hughes's introduction to the pro-black side of pro-Soviet politics came a decade before, courtesy of the Eastman-Gold-McKay *Liberator* (30). "I read every copy of that magazine I could get my hands on during my high school days," avowed Hughes, "I learned from it the revolutionary attitude toward Negroes. Was there not a Negro on its staff—and what other 'white' American magazine would have a colored editorial member?" (qtd. in Hutchinson 264). Hughes actually submitted his earliest poems to the journal, eventually placing a number in its immediate successor, *Workers Monthly* (Hutchinson 264). Later *Liberator* inheritor *The New Masses* accepted four of his contributions in 1926, three of which he included in *Fine Clothes to the Jew* (1927), a collection adopting the working-class metropolitan spotlight of what I've called Harlem Renaissance bolshevism. Even before Scottsboro, Hughes rounded out his literary leftism by assuming the presidency of the Communist League of Struggle for Negro Rights. It is somewhat facile, then, to conclude that Hughes's verse or politics was overhauled by the case; the settling on a Scottsboro conversion is one sign of the general desire to insulate the 1920s from the 1930s, Harlem's renaissance from the Depression "birth" of black proletarianism. Still, it would not be wrong to claim that Scottsboro melted Hughes's remaining resistance to imagining himself as a black bolshevik writer, one willing to produce for Communism's benefit.

Hughes is fittingly a solid, one-person rebuttal to Countee Cullen's 1935 poem "Scottsboro, Too, Is Worth Its Song," which takes fellow poets to task for failing to recognize "a cause divinely spun" (l. 16).[5] Hughes read and wrote poetry for the Scottsboro defendants, reciting his verse while visiting them on Kilby Prison's death row in 1931 and donating proceeds from the small volume *Scottsboro Limited* to their defense fund in 1932. With its composite of one resituated and four made-to-order pieces, this volume presents five ways of looking at the Scottsboro boys' innocence. The four-line poem "The Town of Scottsboro" is as truncated as its subject, the stunted legal and emotional growth of the "little place" where the boys were tried (l. 1): "Its court, too weak to stand against a mob, / Its people's heart, too small to hold a sob" (ll. 3–4). "Justice," which Hughes had first published in 1923, is similarly terse. In tune with its continued relevance in 1931, the poem proposes that African Americans have long recognized as sightlessness the official impartiality of U.S. law: "That Justice is a blind goddess / Is a thing to which we black are wise" (ll. 1–2). The loftier poem "Scottsboro," originally published in *The Crisis*, probably helped the NAACP decide that the Communists were banking on the deaths of the eight condemned. "[Eight] black boys and one white lie. / Is it much to die?" the speaker asks (ll. 3–4) and then answers with a procession of martyrs more vital than the living. "Deathless drums" (l. 7), which in *The Weary Blues* (1926) would mark the primitive beat of African-American blood, here pace a march of radical shades. Christ, John Brown, Nat Turner, and "Lenin with the flag blood red" all parade (l. 21). Unlike the first of these martyrs, "Who fought alone," the boys will have the solace of fighting and dying together, like "That mad mob / That tore the Bastille down / Stone by stone" (ll. 11, 13–15). The "8 black boys"—a number that supplied Alabama courts with a scenario of apocalyptic gang rape—invite Hughes to imagine a communal martyrdom appropriate to Communist times. With typical decency, he did not share the death-defying results with the Scottsboro defendants, choosing "mostly . . . humorous poems" to read in Kilby Prison (Hughes, *I Wonder* 61).

The major composition in *Scottsboro Limited*, the one-act verse play after which the collection is named, has few moments of humor but describes "Eight Black Boys" who decide precisely that it is much to die. With its directions for the simplest of stage sets ("One chair on a raised platform. No curtains or other effects needed" [18]), Hughes's text allies itself with the ambulatory aesthetic of 1930s workers' theater, realizable in union halls as well as formal playhouses. Thanks to this, and to the plans for a final union of audience and agitprop ("Audience: Fight! Fight! Fight! Fight!" [21]), the play reads like a model for Clifford Odets' better-remembered *Waiting for Lefty* (1935).[6] The proceedings begin with the Scottsboro boys in irons, walking deliberately through the center of the audience: "We come in our chains," one declares, "To show our pain" (18). This is too indefinite a show for "A White Man," who wants the boys to adopt an arch-proletarian plainness of expression: "Your pain! Stop talking poetry and talk sense" (18). Through the boys' consistently lucid, rhyming lines, Hughes points to poetry as the distillation of the sensible, demotic speech of black workers; for him, only the "Man" could want to disassociate poetic diction, black vernacular language, and a drama of black proletarian expression. This prosaic enemy of verse and Communism in fact never succeeds in squashing the boys' "talking poetry," a distant relation to the musical cookery of Razaf's "chefs of the Paradise" ("Kitchen Mechanic's"). The boys do reveal, though, that the Man's idea of justice had once convinced them that they would die in dishonor. In a simulation of their Scottsboro arrest and trial, a play within a "play for our misery" (18), they relive their descent to a condition in which they channeled the voices of the lynch mob; "Burn us in the chair! / The chair! The Chair! / Burn us in the chair!" (20). What saves them from this deadly internalization of hate is the intercession of "Red voices" and the metamorphosis of the "8th Boy," perhaps modeled on the most radical and outspoken, Haywood Patterson. With the cry "*I will not die!*" (20; emphasis in original) this character becomes nothing other than a "new Red Negro," an ideal of self-assertion for the other defendants and a conspicuous bridge between black bolshevism's New Negro discourses of the 1920s and 1930s:

> No chair!
> Too long have my hands been idle
> Too long have my brains been dumb.
> Now out of the darkness
> The new Red Negro will come:
> That's me!
> No death in the chair!
> *Boys:* (*Rising*) No death in the chair!   (20)

"Joining hands to build the right" (21), the Scottsboro boys act out the integrationist implications of their self-incorporation of red and New Negro identities. They and the (white-bodied) red voices meet onstage and close out the play clasping hands "in a row of alternating blacks and whites" (21). With the suggestion that "the *Internationale* may be sung and the red flag raised above the heads of the black and white workers together" (21), Hughes flaunts a marriage of black and white fighting New Crowds that the *Crusaders* would have toasted.

While the Birmingham White Legion managed to find a summons to heterosexual miscegenation within the comparable finale of "Open Letter to the South" (L. Thompson, "Southern" 328), the conclusion to Hughes's play is manifestly uninterested in male-female relations of any racial complexion. Its homosocial vocabulary of interracial touch, song, and struggle might be compared to veiled signs of same-sex desire elsewhere in Hughes's canon.[7] Yet on the intersecting levels of the play's narrative through-line and Communist polemic, the final dominance of this vocabulary is guaranteed by Hughes's recourse to the mainly homophobic trope of the antilynch triangle. "Two White Women"—and no black women—are featured in the drama (18). Even in the initial list of characters, the pair are interposed between the Eight Black Boys and the Eight Red/White Workers above whom the red flag will fly (18). Hughes's mediatrixes are effigies of the Scottsboro accusers Ruby Bates and Victoria Price, shorn of all distinction from each other by their lack of proper names and their uncanny teamwork. They "enter left, powdered and painted, but dressed in overalls" (19). Like their originals, they climb off the freight train denying the Sheriff's suggestion that "these black brutes been botherin' you" (19). They change their tune almost immediately, however, seduced by promises that "[they'll] get paid for testifying, and [their] pictures in the paper" (19). At the show trial, the two women slip into something more comfortable than speaking truth to sheriffs: a form of legal prostitution encouraged in Alabama courts. Before taking the stand, they remove "their overalls, displaying cheap loud dresses underneath, and powder their faces tittering" (19). In a "jazz tempo" that Hughes elsewhere rarely associated with real vice, they then exchange a sex story for limited fame and fortune: "They raped us in a box car underneath the sky" (19).

Beneath the overalls they share with the Scottsboro boys and thousands of virile workers in Communist cartoons, Hughes's Two White Women are as cheaply bought as the garish dresses and makeup he assigns them; their portion of the proletarian virtues is easily shed. In testifying to their untrue colors, they ease the way for the union of the drama's deserving pants wearers: the eight accused boys and the eight white-red voices. These white Reds carefully observe the trial from the audience and offer no objections to the boys' denial of white womanhood's veracity. An interracial male disbelief in and distaste for the Two White Women indeed looses climactic speech in a "murmur of Red voices": "We'll fight for you, boys. We'll fight for you. / The Reds will fight for you" (19). Mutual aversion to the pair, negatively libidinalized through their association with the sex trade, is thus a leading ingredient in the homosocial bond saluted in the final tableau. As in other appearances of the antilynch triangle, the jointly witnessed moral ruin of white women is, to adapt Sedgwick's formula, "just the right lubricant for an adjustment of differentials of power" between men of different races and class factions (76). Once more, those red voices belonging to women—white or black—must confine themselves to inaudible frequencies.

Hughes's drama in honor of the eight condemned scarcely refrains from asking the obtuse final question of his 1931 Scottsboro article "Southern Gentlemen, White Prostitutes, Mill-Owners, and Negroes": "And who ever heard of raping a prostitute?" (49). Such defenses of the Scottsboro defendants in the form of insults to the morality of their alleged victims were common in radical support circles, at least before Bates recanted her charges (more on this transformation later). During the first two years of the case, descriptions of Bates and Price as "notorious professional prostitutes" dotted Communist Party coverage. In April 1931 *The Daily Worker* broke word of an ILD investigation that uncovered allegations of previous lewdness with white and black men. A second ILD inquiry certified the women's bad reputation with numerous affidavits and the simple fact that they "admitted going to Chattanooga as hoboes and leaving as hoboes, on a train with a crowd of men in the night time" (qtd. in Goodman 187). Not all radical observers confused hoboes and whores, however. Occasionally, as in a casual line in Hughes's article, they took notice of the pitiful wages earned in the cotton mills where Bates and Price worked, and a few commentators seem to have realized that the sources of the ILD's affidavits "used the words *promiscuous* and *prostitute* synonymously" (Goodman 188). But outrage at the three thousand or more lynchings since Reconstruction did not allow much solicitude for the Two White Women. Neither did the vintage association of prostitution with capitalist venality, the latter sin just what Communists saw as the Scottsboro defendants' ultimate enemy.

In "Columbia," a 1933 poem written in the Soviet Union, Hughes's impression of Bates and Price's fraud explodes into an indictment of U.S. empire, capitalist venality's rising ambassador to the colonial world:

Columbia,
My dear girl,
You really haven't been a virgin for so long
It's ludicrous to keep up the pretext.
You're terribly involved in world assignations
And everybody knows it.
You've slept with all the big powers
In military uniforms,
And you've taken the sweet life
Of all the little brown fellows
In loin cloths and cotton trousers.
When they've resisted,
You've yelled, "Rape,"
At the top of your voice
And called the middies
To beat them up for not being gentlemen
And liking your crooked painted mouth.
(You must think the moons of Hawaii
Disguise your ugliness.)

. . . .

O, sweet mouth of India,
And Africa,
Manchuria, and Haiti.

Columbia,
You darling,
Don't shoot!
I'll kiss you!   (ll. 1–19, 31–37; emphasis in original)

Hughes's brash radical speaker, himself the possessor of a "sweet mouth" of color, would dispense the unvarnished truth to an aging, still-cruising America, her democratic innocence wasted by imperial vice. In harsh light, he reveals the "gem of the ocean" to be an international Scottsboro girl. Columbia's "crooked painted mouth" also falsely cries " 'Rape.' " Like Bates and Price's claims to virginity, hers are belied by multiple "assignations." As with prostitution in the Scottsboro courtroom, Columbia's streetwalking through imperial outposts is associated with bourgeois greed. Vampirically swelling with shanghaied labor value, she has "taken the sweet life / Of all the little brown fellows / In loin cloths and cotton trousers." In place of Alabama lawmen, "middies" and the rest of the trigger-happy U.S. military are poised to take revenge on the dark men who resist her charms: "Don't shoot! / I'll kiss you!" What vivifies Hughes's censure of Columbia is much the same as what animates his representation of Two White Women in *Scottsboro, Limited*: loathing for the linked errors of lynching, racism, and capitalism and a parallel, secondary disapproval of excessive/merchandised/deceiving feminine sexuality, not excluding the sexuality that fueled the national scandal of white women pursuing black men. The interracial red fraternity explicitly allied by these repulsions in Hughes's drama stands behind his colored speaker's assured debunking of One White Woman, her faux attractiveness and aggressive lack of virtue allied not so much with the erotics of the commodity as with the public hypocrisies of imperial rule.[8] In "Columbia," what Hughes viewed as the spectacle of Bates and Price's perjury expands into a way of seeing the corruptions of U.S. empire.

I don't pluck *Scottsboro, Limited* and "Columbia" from the mass of Hughes's collected works to negate his good reputation for *"genderracial"* resistance (Borden 333; emphasis in original) or to question the motives of his support for the ILD's courageous Scottsboro defense: the slim pleasure of anachronistic left one-upmanship is not my stake. I certainly don't linger over the texts to imply that Hughes's position as a probably bisexual male African-American radical specially impelled him toward literary misogyny: among assorted Communist others, his white, British-born friend Nancy Cunard wrote an equally disgusted Scottsboro poem about a white woman who cries rape when repulsed by a black worker ("Rape").[9] Neither do I wish to charge party writers of any sort with a greater-than-average dose of 1930s sexism. I select Hughes's two texts, and trace their interaction, to emphasize how deeply Communism's triangular Scottsboro rhetoric could penetrate, how flexible a literary attraction it could offer. Even the author of "The Negro Mother" validated this rhetoric's oversight of African-American women, thus mirroring the rape-lynch triangle, in which the negation of black women makes "possible the narrative casting of white women as prize and pawn" (Wiegman 102). Even Harlem's so-called poet lowrate, condemned in the 1920s for his placid representations of sexual commerce, adopted the rhetoric's disclosure of the repellent, lying prostitute behind the violated white lady. The odd power of this disclosure to confirm white southern fantasies of Communism's race-mixing sexual tumult is suggested in public rejoinders to Hughes's Scottsboro-era work, as much as in lynch threats against ILD officials for "blackening" the names of Price and Bates.[10] "If this bird thinks we are going to have social equality [read, "miscegenation"] in the South, he's crazy!" screamed a White Legion poster displaying Hughes's photo and poetry (qtd. in L. Thompson, "Southern," 328). Fears of miscegenationist "com-mune-ism" seem to have marinated equally well in anti-Communist broadsides depicting white women as sexual victims and in Communist ones casting them as sexually compromised victimizers.

That Hughes suspected this irony—and that the literary agency of black male Communists facing Scottsboro was not necessarily dependent on a homosocial triangle trade—is suggested by the 1931 poem "Christ in Alabama," the final text in the *Scottsboro Limited* collection:

Christ is a nigger,
Beaten and black:
Oh, bare your back!

Mary is His mother:
Mammy of the South,
Silence your mouth.

God is His father:
White Master above
Grant Him your love.

Most holy bastard
Of the bleeding mouth,
Nigger Christ
On the cross
Of the South.

Here, the stock emblem of the crucified lynch victim is draped over four stanzas framing an apocryphal Christian Trinity: a Scottsboro boy turned "Nigger Christ" with "bleeding," not blood-red painted, mouth; a black mother Mary enjoined to "silence," "Mammy" of this reviled son; and a white master/God-father without pity or love. The evident, iconoclastic political moral of the ensemble is that the South's champion miscegenationist—"White Master above"—has fingered his black sons for his own sins and chastised them in Scottsboro. Behind this, however, the poem's enterprise is to build a point-for-point alternative to the anti–rape-lynch triplet of Hughes's Scottsboro drama. "Christ in Alabama" describes an interracial triangle founded on the systematic sexual use of black women by white men, a triangle whose sheer southern pervasiveness was dimmed by the debate over lynching. It thus describes a figure that does not pivot on white women, banish black women, or even successfully triangulate among its three parties. Though a hushed black mother is placed between lines devoted to her white lover and her black son, she is no go-between. Unresolved tension clamps each member of the poem's trio into isolated stances and stanzas. Instead of a homosocial alliance clinched over white women scorned, we end with a black Christ on the cross and the three-way standoff of a frozen family romance, unable to speak its interracial name. The poem's silence on Scottsboro's Two White Women was probably not intended to mollify white southerners who objected to Communist reports of a frame-up by prostitutes; "Christ in Alabama" stops just short of picturing white southern Christians as a deicidal people. Its substitute triangle may instead have been aimed toward and by radical black women, one of whom—Louise Thompson—guided Hughes to the Soviet Union and passed him early information on the Scottsboro case.

Scottsboro and Madame Moscow

Even with the ongoing boom in scholarship on African-American women intellectuals, Louise Thompson is lamentably still recognized best for two temporary jobs as an artistic helpmeet.[11] In 1931 she was hired by Harlem

Renaissance Medici Charlotte Osgood Mason to provide secretarial services to two of her gifted "godchildren," Hughes and Zora Neale Hurston, as they collaborated on the play *Mule Bone*. For her trouble, Thompson received the third chair in one of the great unconsummated triangles in African-American literature. The fallout included her break with Masonic liberalism, a permanent disaffection between Hughes and Hurston, and the miring of their black vernacular theater in accusations of Hurston's plagiarism. In 1932 James Ford recruited Thompson to conduct a party of young African Americans to the Soviet Union to make the Communist protest film *Black and White*. Among her charges was Hughes, who, fearful of missing the expedition, had begged her to hold the boat to living socialism in New York harbor: "ITS AN ARK TO ME," he pleaded via telegram (qtd. in Rampersad, *The Life* 241). The film, like *Mule Bone* before it, was sacrificed to political infighting,[12] though travel through the Soviet republics convinced Thompson that she "preferred Russia to living in America" (qtd. in Naison 74). In Soviet Central Asia, she saw new colored "nations arising out of centuries of illiteracy, poverty and even nomad life" and proof of the wisdom of Communist ethnic policy ("With Langston" 157). Hughes and Thompson's political split with those skeptics in the *Black and White* party who dismissed her as "Madame Moscow" provides David Levering Lewis with his "ideograph" for the disintegration of the Harlem Renaissance alliance (*When Harlem* 291).

Beyond this reputation as a well-connected cultural midwife and fixer, a Harlem associate of Shari Benstock's modernist women of the Left Bank,[13] Thompson led one of the more significant careers in the twentieth-century African-American left. Born in Chicago in 1901, Thompson followed her parents, a cook and a domestic, through short stays in several isolated western towns. She was educated at Berkeley, particularly by a lecture from visitor W. E. B. Du Bois, in whose honor she accepted a teaching job in Pine Bluffs, Arkansas, and went at the uplift work of the talented tenth. In 1926 she relocated to the Hampton Institute, where she taught business administration and supported a student strike against the puritanical heritage of alumnus Booker T. Washington. Nineteen twenty-eight found Thompson fleeing the school along with its most energetic strikers. Confirming the idea that the black college rebellions of the era provided a talent reserve for the New Negro movement, she went straight to New York City. The Lockean side of renaissance Harlem welcomed her with some of its prime fellowships, from an Urban League sociology grant to a stipend from Charlotte Mason. This patron's presumptuous response to Thompson's part in the *Mule Bone* affair was a final political straw, however:

Thompson disowned Mason's support, helped convince Hughes to do the same, and launched a life's work in the institutions of the left. What she identified as a "distaste and hatred of white philanthropy" propelled her toward the party, a welcome escape from Negrophilist charity thanks to more than a decade of black Communist intervention (qtd. in Naison 43).

Starting with a relatively genteel post in the Congregational Education Society, Thompson rose from professional fellow traveler to party authority; by the mid-1930s, *The Crisis* could describe her as "*the leading colored woman in the Communist movement*" (Thompson, "Southern" 327; emphasis in original). In addition to shepherding the *Black and White* crew from New York to Moscow, she founded the Harlem chapter of the Friends of the Soviet Union and cofounded the party-supported Harlem Suitcase Theater, which produced Hughes's play *Don't You Want to Be Free?* She arranged Communist conferences on African-American women, more of whom she hoped would join her as party leaders (Sowinska, *American* 124–25). From 1933 to 1948 she was employed with the party-aligned International Workers Order, where she specialized in cultural outreach and union desegregation. Thompson spent some of her sparse spare time running the Vanguard, the most successful left-wing salon in 1930s Harlem, which sponsored dance, music, theater, and discussions of Marxist theory. She and her collaborator, sculptor Augusta Savage, offered parties along with dialectics in a Convent Avenue apartment and drew the likes of Romare Bearden and Aaron Douglas leftward (Naison 100). In the late 1960s Thompson was still organizing in Harlem, this time in support of another black Communist woman, Angela Davis (Kellner and Oppenheimer 353–55; Wilkerson 76–77, 81–84).

What was most responsible for winning Thompson the honorific of "*the leading colored woman in the Communist movement*" was Scottsboro. With onetime *Crusader* editor Richard B. Moore and lawyers Benjamin Davis and William Patterson (her husband after 1940), she was among the busiest Harlem presences in the ILD. One of the first large-scale Scottsboro benefits in Harlem, a 1932 dance at the Rockland Palace, featured a Thompson address between sets by Cab Calloway's orchestra (according to Denning, she helped to acquaint the Popular Front with the world of the big bands [333]). The *Black and White* journey saw her speaking to Scottsboro rallies in the Soviet Union. In 1933 she joined the National Conference for the Defense of Political Prisoners and helped to plan the "united front" march on Washington that ended with Scottsboro protesters demanding a meeting with President Roosevelt (Carter 248–49). Her work with the International Workers Order also entailed a harrowing visit to the Scottsboro case's Alabama home, which she wrote up in a 1934 *Crisis* article titled "Southern Terror." Stepping into author's shoes, Thompson here exchanged an intimate acquaintance with Birmingham jail cells for access to a reportorial genre near the top of the left's literary hierarchy.

Thompson and other African-American women writers have rarely been featured in histories of interwar radical literature, including, thus far, my own. Once unremarked, if not unfelt, their persistent absence has at least become the subject of apologetic explanatory footnotes in several of the best revisions of Depression-era literary proletarianism.[14] Suzanne Sowinska, whose doctoral work contains perhaps the fullest examination of modern African-American women writers and "radical agendas," proposes that "the reason for the omission is [a] complex but not . . . unfamiliar one, given the triple silences these writers faced as African-Americans, as radicals, leftists, or fellow-travelers, and as women" (*American* 108). Not all these silences were applied retroactively or only by enemies of the left. In the literary Communism of the red decade, Thompson and her peers could find ardent interest in African-American subjects and authorship, some precocious illuminations of black women's triple burden, and some stifling triangles in the manner of *Scottsboro, Limited*. This contradictory landscape may have figured in another reason why African-American women have been absent from histories of interwar radical literature: full-length works by black women versed in proletarian literature and/or the Communist movement did not begin appearing until the early 1940s.[15] As I will suggest in the next chapter, it was just conceivable during the 1930s to reinvent Zora Neale Hurston as an author of proletarian literature manqué (even as James Ford's *The Negro and the Democratic Front* [1938] commended someone named "Zora Neale Thurston" [qtd. in Foley, *Radical* 214 n. 1]). Yet a shelf of less-camouflaged left-informed books by black women only begins to accumulate in the following decade: Margaret Walker's *For My People* (1942); Gwendolyn Brooks's *A Street in Bronzeville* (1945); Ann Petry's *The Street* (1946). Tracing African-American women's writing within the interwar left thus involves pursuing texts in shorter forms, some of them still occasionally thought quasi-literary. Sowinska, Charlotte Nekola, and Paula Rabinowitz have led the way in this regard, uncovering and/or recontextualizing work by Marita Bonner, Edith Manuel Durham, and Ramona Lowe.[16] For the sake of my discussion of Thompson, Scottsboro, and Scottsboro's triangles, I want to emphasize the value of rediscovering black women's writing in a journalistic genre where brevity was a revolutionary credential.

If Thompson's article "Southern Terror" is not altogether literary, then neither is any other work of Depression-era reportage. According to Granville Hicks, Mike Gold, and the other editors of the anthology *Proletarian Literature in the United States* (1935), reportage was the most electric of the moment's exemplary literatures. Its status as a concise factual record, composed hurriedly for a deadline, suited it to the historical acceleration of "periods of revolution" and an impatient, potentially revolutionary public that "demands an answer—and . . . wants it today, this week, not a year hence" (Hicks et al. 212, 211). Its desire to induce action while recording it suited the demand for a literature of political incitement. Its conviction that who, what, when, where, and why are insufficient journalistic questions suited the longing of turbulent readers to "*experience* the event recorded. Reportage is three-dimensional reporting. The writer not only condenses reality; he must get his reader to see and feel the facts" (211; emphasis in original). This "he" is unusually significant. For the editors of *Proletarian Literature*, reportage lit a path from the intellectual-"feminine" activity of writing to the physical-"masculine" activity of proletarian labor, with its speed-ups, quotas, and bodily urgency. For many radical women, however, some of whose reportage these editors reprinted, the form also opened roads between "feminine" and "masculine" expression. Paula Rabinowitz traces the investment in the genre of figures such as Agnes Smedley and Meridel Le Sueur to its "direct rendering of (class) struggle through carefully detailed (individual) analysis" (2). By thus "link[ing] the genres of personal narrative and political economy . . . [reportage] connected traditionally feminine forms of writing to more conventionally masculine ones" (2). In Thompson's case, this connection seems to have invited literary self-cultivation and a special purchase on Scottsboro discourse. Her personal history, since the *Mule Bone* incident consciously immersed in Marxist politics, brimmed with possibilities for a confessional literature of class struggle. In particular, her own Scottsboro case, explored in "Southern Terror," warranted radical reportage in opposition to a triangular-homosocial rhetoric of working-class interracialism.

The first sections of this article locate Thompson in the wrong place at the wrong time—a Birmingham home during a police raid in 1934—and in the character of the innocent, resistant captive. More than a participant-observer of the deliberations of an Alabama court, she is their object and the controlling though not exclusive subject of her report. "Birmingham is a good place for good niggers—but a damn bad place for bad niggers" (327): so speaks city officialdom out of the blue in the article's first lines. Thompson reveals herself as the intended recipient of the advice—"in the course of my experience . . . I learned what [it] meant" (327)—but not before situating her reader as the unprepared butt of racial menace. The visceral experience effect valued by reportage is here served, as is the synecdoche of personal for class history, more fully drawn in the article's second half. Thompson goes on to reveal that she was arrested while entering the residence of a northern-born friend: "It so happened that the red squad was raiding her apartment at the time" (327). Despite her California ties, her political coloration makes her a generic northern interloper to the squad: "California, hell! You're one of those — yankee —, that's what you are!" (327). Loaded into the "black wagon," she is carted to the city jail without charge.

Though her article does not tell us so, Thompson's arrest was the consequence of the belief of Birmingham's police chief that Communists— outside agitator division—had masterminded over forty strikes by miners, textile workers, and longshoremen throughout the state that year. The party's role was in fact much humbler, but a large May Day demonstration and a surge in visiting radical writers such as Jack Conroy, Myra Page, and John Howard Lawson nurtured other conclusions on the ground. These writers' whirlwind tours of Birmingham, observes Robin Kelley, "resembled artists' sojourns to the front during the Spanish Civil War. They wanted to witness firsthand the heroism of Dixie's interracial vanguard, and those who experienced police repression or harassment wore their stripes proudly" (71). As represented in "Southern Terror," Thompson's encounter with local law enforcement was less thrilling: she was granted no lenient martyrdom. In the mind of the plainclothes squad, she indicates, her Communism put her beneath the racial underdog: "So you're one of those — reds what thinks you are going to get social equality for niggers down here in the South. Well, we think Communists are lower than niggers, down here—fact is, we don't even allow them to 'sociate with white folks, let alone have white folks 'sociating with niggers" (327). In Birmingham, Thompson goes on to suggest, all party women, not just white "lures," are suspected of free sexual association. "During the cross examination," she declares, "my questioners were inclined at first to make a joke of [her arrest], taunting me about 'my comrades,' slyly alluding to some intimate relationship with the men arrested with me" (327). It is her racial identity, however, that seems directly to prompt threats of physical/sexual violence. " 'What about turning this gal over to the Ku Klux Klan?,' " asks one policeman, " 'I reckon they know how to handle her kind' " (327). Others suggest tarring and feathering or "talking to her through the rubber tube" (a beating with a rubber hose or worse) (327). A judge remarks on her light brown skin and pretends to guess it is the result of another state's lax devotion to segregation: "Wonder where this gal is from? Looks like she came from Mississippi—that's the way they mix up down there" (328). More completely than male and "unmixed" visiting radicals, Thompson fulfilled the Birmingham police department's nightmare of Communism come to swallow the South. She was an advocate, probable practitioner, and seeming product of "social equality" and a disturber of the good news that black women could be counted on as "good niggers." Kept in custody for weeks, charged with two separate crimes, she was forced to prolong her sampling of local conditions. At the close of the firsthand sections of "Southern Terror," Thompson happily attributes her release to a national pool of radical workers.

In the remainder of the article, personal testimony shades into synoptic observation of the Birmingham scene and then Communist lesson taking. Reportage's "direct rendering of (class) struggle through carefully detailed (individual) analysis" here takes the form of two distinct narrative segments, the first accenting the facts of Thompson's individual ordeal, the second their class meaning and transcendence. On one level, this centrifugal attack allows Thompson to cash in her brutal experience of Birmingham for the profit of the party's African-American policy. In contrast to what she defines as "the voice of reaction in the midst of a people struggling for freedom" (328)—that is, the NAACP—Thompson has suffered and endured the attentions of the wardens of the Black Belt. Her article's concluding appeal for the party's working-class leadership is designed to ring with the authority of the Christ-like trials reported earlier: "Revolutionary leaders in the South are boldly defying all that the southern ruling class has striven to perpetuate, and terror and jail bars do not stop them" (328). This was a tactic the NAACP did not fail to notice, making certain that *The Crisis*'s introduction to the essay recalled the association's "*early days . . . in the South, when Secretary John R. Shilladay was beaten up as he stepped from a train in Austin, Tex[as]*" (327; emphasis in original). On another level, however, Thompson's move to tether personal to class narratives invites greater Communist recognition of the "southern Bourbon" violence faced by black women (328). The early account of her near-meeting with the Klan recalls the fact that black women were themselves sometimes lynched; the policemen's threats of "rubber hose" work and the bad jokes about intimacy with comrades hint at the white rape that fulfilled the myth of lascivious black womanhood.[17] Couched in the article's second half as proof of the party's gutsy African-American efforts, these details lose their gendered sting but not their inflection as exemplary ploys of the southern ruling class. Violence aimed against African-American women, Thompson suggests, is one arm of Black Belt counterrevolution and an injury to all its opponents.

The significance of such violence within Communist frames is reinforced by the most assertive maneuver in "Southern Terror": its shaping of Thompson's captivity narrative as her right to party Scottsboro discourse. Scottsboro is one of Thompson's repeated referents. When reflecting late in the piece on why southerners linked Communism and the Negro Question, she claims unexceptionally that "the International Labor Defense through the Scottsboro case has aroused the Negro people and rallied to their defense workers over the whole world" (328). Yet she is also sure to note in her confessional opening that her taunting by the plainclothes squad takes place in the same "Jefferson county courthouse where the Scottsboro boys are imprisoned" (327). By the time she reports on her release, her trial by southern terror is judged worthy of mention in the same breath with theirs. Indeed, she presents the conduct of the Scottsboro affair by the party and the state as a precedent for her own case. Her jailers' "experience with the Scottsboro case . . . made them cautious," she claims (328). Discovering "that the workers throughout the country were ready to apply their weapon of mass pressure against [her] arrest," the "Bourbon authorities" chose to set her free (328). "They wanted stronger grounds to prepare another frame-up against a Negro engaged in working class activity," she maintains (328).

Thompson here displays herself within the heart of Scottsboro's existential heart: inside the Jefferson County courthouse, inside the vulnerable body of its black prisoners under interrogation. She shows no envy of the eight Scottsboro death sentences but draws all possible attention to her own close shave with their legal authors. Black women as well as Scottsboro men, she demonstrates, are dragged before judge lynch. Their rescuing allies are not so much red male voices filtering through jailhouse doors as "workers throughout the country," among whose leaders are black women who have also seen the South from behind bars. The example of these leaders and the party's solution to the Negro Question, she submits, invite sustainable working-class interracialism, not the emotional sealant provided by variously desired white women. In these respects, Thompson's reportage takes up Barbara Christian's "persistent motif" in the literature of African-American women: "the illuminating of that which is perceived by others as not existing at all" (135). The specific darkness made visible in "Southern Terror" is the suppressed presence of black women within two interracial systems whose war was declared in Scottsboro: a southern practice of lynch discipline and a homosocial Communist rhetoric of black-white alliance. The first—deadly—system appropriately receives the harsher light, but neither goes unilluminated. For her part, then, Thompson wrote a way through Scottsboro's paired triangles against the exclusions of both the rape-lynch and the antilynch trios. To the most prominent African-American woman intellectual in 1930s Communism, the radical rhetoric of black male worker, white male worker, and white woman scorned was, like the Scottsboro defense in which it flourished, preparatory to swifter, wider calls to mass pressure.

Scottsboro Recantations

The way has been cleared, it seems, for two of the habitual conclusions of right-thinking, left-leaning cultural criticism: first, that would-be liberatory discourses—such as Marxism-Communism—militate against themselves by reposing on oppressive relations—such as gender-racial inequality—just beneath their radar and, second, that the keenest critics of this self-betrayal are the subjects of the snubbed relations—such as African-American women—drawing on self-made epistemic resources. It can indeed be concluded that Scottsboro's triangular-homosocial rhetoric of Communist interracialism was impaired by its mostly unexamined masculinist foundation. The rhetoric's success in fostering valuable African-American texts and rallying early support for the Scottsboro defendants—including support from black women[18]—was encumbered by less obvious weaknesses. Its mirroring of the rape-lynch triangle did little to counter anti-Communist figments that the party transacted its interracial business through immoral white women. Its indifference to black women did nothing to ease internal party tension over the sexual racisms of lived "social equality." Thompson's thorough rewriting of this rhetoric, it is equally just to conclude, derived in part from observing red triangles from the location of the African-American women they slighted. Another, older academic truism here springs to mind, however: it is more complicated than these conclusions have it.

For one thing, Thompson's dependence on and exposure of black women's insight in her revision of triangular-homosocial rhetoric did not preclude an equivalent dependence on party-approved genres and programs. Reportage, the form that "Southern Terror" visited to convert personal narrative into political prescription, was glamorized in *Proletarian Literature in the United States*, the closest thing in 1930s literary leftism to an authoritative anthology. Moreover, the article's case for its right to Scottsboro referents is tenaciously faithful to Black Belt–era party racial analysis. "And it is the Communist Party," Thompson devotedly declares near the conclusion, "which has analyzed the Negro question as that of an oppressed nation of people, defined the alignment of class forces for and against the Negro people's struggle for liberation, and begun the organization of white and Negro working masses together" (328). Thompson's redrafting of Scottsboro triangles, this is to say, did not hesitate to tap alternative narrative and political formulas available *within* Communism. Her ultimate concern was not to shatter the party line with irreconcilable knowledge but to have the party better acknowledge the African-American women already risking themselves in its southern strategy, already recognized, in fact, in selected literary performances such as "Christ in Alabama."[19]

By 1934, the year in which Thompson wrote her own "Letter from Birmingham Jail," fantastic upheavals in the Scottsboro case promised success for such reminders. In 1933 Ruby Bates, one of Scottsboro's supposed rape victims, astonished Reds and prosecutors by testifying for the defense. On the witness stand for Haywood Patterson's second trial, she repudiated her earlier testimony, denying she had ever been assaulted. Nancy Cunard, in the spirit of McKay's charge to white feminists in *The Negroes in America*, quickly praised her recantation as "the first great crack in the old Southern structure of white supremacy" (*Negro* 265).[20] Now it was Alabama's attorney general, not the Communists, who questioned the decorum of Bates's dress and accused her of selling herself. In one unexpected conversion, Bates's modified testimony left her prey to lynch threats; in another, she evolved into a party advocate. It was her labor in the textile mills, she thought, that allowed her to make sense of party theory: "All the people having to work so hard and getting practically nothing for it" (qtd. in Goodman 198). The hard-working mothers of the Scottsboro defendants, themselves new friends of Communism, embraced the radicalized Bates surprisingly quickly. As a team, she and the mothers orated, corresponded, and witnessed for the defense. With Viola Montgomery, Janie Patterson, and Mamie Williams, Bates presided over the Scottsboro march on Washington; Ada Wright and she published complementary statements on Scottsboro's class content in *Working Woman*, the party's magazine on women's issues (see Bates; Mother Ada Wright). Just months after the appearance of Hughes's "Columbia," all the connective points in Scottsboro's dueling triangles—and some outside—thus seemed to realign themselves toward the defense: one of the case's Two White Women had become a prized red voice, while the black women whose sons sat on death row welcomed this transformation and placed their own sympathetic pressure on radical Scottsboro rhetoric.

It would be edifying to declare that the combined forces of the Scottsboro mothers, Ruby Bates, and Louise Thompson broke the back of Communism's trade of interracial triangles. A more accurate assertion, however, is that these women forced Scottsboro's shifting legal terrain onto permanently contested representational territory. Their trials and radicalizations were flagrant rejoinders to radical dramas in which black women stand in the wings and white women only expedite Communist conversion. Embracing vocabularies within and without Communism, their public statements propelled expressions of red interracialism less subservient to the commerce between men (even Wright's *Native Son,* I will suggest later, might be submitted as evidence of this change). The first provisional conclusion of this chapter thus holds, but only with a caveat. Certainly, the triangular rhetoric of Communist interracialism was diminished by its homosocial foundation, too dense to render the changing shape of the Scottsboro case. Yet U.S. Communism's famous political expediency—in this case, its desire to win Scottsboro with aid from Bates and the defendants' mothers (and anyone else)—could lead it to revise its own early rhetorical investments and offer space on the page to less masculinist representations pledging Communist allegiance. For Thompson, an African-American woman immersed in labor organizing and the promise of the Nation thesis, this relief was enough. For Zora Neale Hurston, suspicious of driven talk about southern terror and the socialist future, it was much too little.

PHOTO INSERT

Men of Our Times

Andrea Paul Razafkeriefo, poet, song-writer and leading Afro-American humorist, whose poems and humorous articles monthly add to the joy of living for several hundred thousand people throughout the world, was born at Washington, D. C. on December 16, 1895 of native African and Afro-American parentage. He is a grandson of the late Captain John L. Waller, United States Consul to Madagascar, on his mother's side and a grandnephew of Ranavalona III, late queen of that island, on his father's side, who was a graduate of the

at least an hundred numbers of all sorts he has approached music publishers but twice, preferring to write for the amusement of himself and friends. In 1913, at which time he was but seventeen, his song, "Baltimo" was published by James Kendis Music Co., of New York, and was a sensational hit in Shubert's "Passing Show" of that year, at the Winter Garden. Not being wise to the tricks of the game he apparently did not derive from his song all the benefits that should have accured. For the past few years he has spent most of his time with poetry, contributing to local magazines and newspapers, mainly The Crusader and The Voice. He has, however recently written an immense song-hit, "The Fifteenth Infantry", which though just published is creating a great sensation throughout the country. He was happily married in 1915 to Miss Annabelle Geneva Miller of Charleston, S. C.

ANDRAE RAZAFKERIEFO

Royal Military Academy of France and fell in battle for Malagasy freedom, shortly before the birth of his son.

Mr. Razafkeriefo must have inherited his poetical ability from his mother, who is a poetess of great merit; and his musical talent from his father who was a great musician. He early began his communion with the Muses, writing his first verse "The Boys in Blue", at the age of nine. He began writing songs at the age of fifteen and though he has written

FIGURE I

Crusader feature praising Andy Razaf, March 1919.
(Courtesy of Garland Publishing, Inc.)

FIGURE 2
Martial cover of the March 1920 *Crusader.*
(Courtesy of Garland Publishing, Inc.)

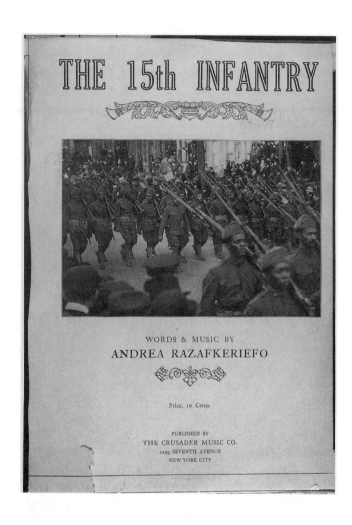

FIGURE 3

Sheet music for Razaf's composition "The 15th Infantry," published by the
Crusader Music Company, 1919.
*(Courtesy of the Manuscripts, Archives, and Rare Books Division of the Schomburg Center
for Research in Black Culture, The New York Public Library, Astor, Lenox,
and Tilden Foundations.)*

FIGURE 4

Claude McKay addresses the Fourth Congress of the Communist International
in the Kremlin's Throne Room, 1922.

(*From* Holding Aloft the Banner of Ethiopia: Caribbean Radicalism in Early Twentieth-
Century America *by Winston James ([New York: Verso Books, 1998].)*

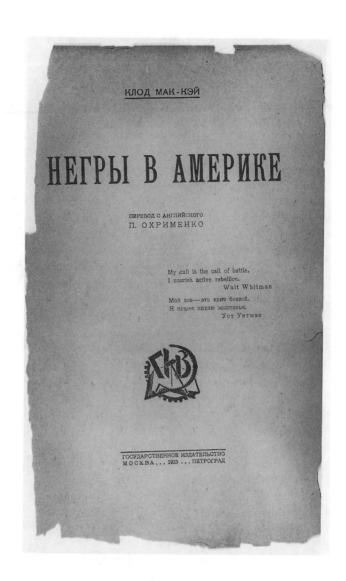

FIGURE 5

The title page of McKay's Soviet book *Negry v Amerike (The Negroes in America).*
(Courtesy of the Slavic and Baltic Division, The New York Public Library, Astor, Lenox,
and Tilden Foundations.)

FIGURE 6
Young Mike Gold as he appeared during the period of
Hoboken Blues, without cigar or sombrero.
(Courtesy of Alan Wald.)

Handwriting on photograph:
First newspaper photograph, U. & U. Syndicate
Day after "discovery" by Vachel Lindsay as a hotel.
Published with interview in Washington Star, Dec. 13, 1950.
Langston Hughes, Wardman Park Hotel, Washington, 1925

FIGURE 7
Langston Hughes as a lyric busboy, 1925.
*(Courtesy of the Yale Collection of American Literature, Beinecke Rare Book
and Manuscript Library.)*

FIGURE 8

The *Black and White* cast sailing toward the Soviet Union, 1932. Louise Thompson
sits on the deck to the left of the life preserver; Langston Hughes is third from the
right in the nearest standing row.

*(Courtesy of the Yale Collection of American Literature, Beinecke Rare Book
and Manuscript Library.)*

NEGROES
BEWARE
DO NOT ATTEND
COMMUNIST
MEETINGS

Paid organizers for the communists are only trying to get negroes in trouble. Alabama is a good place for good negroes to live in, but it is a bad place for negroes who believe in SOCIAL EQUALITY.

The Ku Klux Klan Is Watching You.
TAKE HEED

Tell the communist leaders to leave.
Report all communist meetings to the
Ku Klux Klan
Post Office Box 651, Birmingham, Alabama.

FIGURE 10 (FACING PAGE)

Ruby Bates and the Scottsboro mothers march on the White House, Mother's Day, 1934 (from left to right, Ida Norris, Janie Patterson, Ruby Bates, Mamie Williams, Viola Montgomery, with ex-*Crusader* Richard B. Moore of the ILD).
(Courtesy of AP/Wide World Photos.)

FIGURE 11

Birmingham Ku Klux Klan handbill warning against Communism, circa 1934.
(Courtesy of the Labor Defender *and the University of North Carolina Press.)*

FIGURE 12

Zora Neale Hurston around 1925, the time of her arrival in New York City.
*(Courtesy of the Yale Collection of American Literature, Beinecke Rare Book
and Manuscript Library.)*

FIGURE 13
Nelson Algren plays it cool well after *Somebody in Boots.*
*(Photograph by Stephen Deutch. Courtesy of the Department of Rare Books
and Manuscripts, Ohio State University Library.)*

FIGURE 14
Richard Wright plays it straight following *Native Son.*
(Courtesy of AP/Wide World Photos.)

5 · Black Belt/Black Folk: The End(s) of the Richard Wright– Zora Neale Hurston Debate

Farmers are bad medicine for Marxians.

—John Crowe Ransom, "The South Is a Bulwark" (1936)

Is it true what they say about Dixie?
Does the sun really shine all the time?
Do sweet magnolias blossom at everybody's door,
Do folks keep eating 'possum, till they can't eat no more?
Is it true what they say about Swanee?
Is a dream by that stream so sublime?
Do they laugh, do they love, like they say in ev'ry song? . . .
If it's true that's where I belong.

—Lyrics to "Is It True What They Say About Dixie?" (1936),
popular song written by Irving Caesar, Sammy Lerner, and
Gerald Marks, borrowed by Richard Wright for an epigraph
to *Uncle Tom's Children* (1938)

By now, the following story of literary conflict might as well be engraved on the sort of tablets featured in *Moses, Man of the Mountain*. In a 1938 piece at the back of *The Saturday Review*, Zora Neale Hurston administered a stern talking down to a younger, relatively obscure African-American writer who had panned *Their Eyes Were Watching God* (1937) in *The New Masses*, then U.S. Communism's cultural journal of record. While admitting that some of newcomer Richard Wright's "sentences had the shocking-power of a forty-four" ("Stories" 32), Hurston protested the heavy gunplay in his story collection *Uncle Tom's Children* (1938), named for the defiant offspring of Stowe's prototypical Old Negro. Wright had devoted his considerable talent to spectacular scenes of interracial violence rather than to the "fundamental phases of Negro life" and had thus fabricated "a book about hatreds" (32). "There is lavish killing," Hurston noted of one story, and the tally of virtuous black counterattacks throughout was "perhaps enough to satisfy all male black readers" (32). Despite this equal-opportunity blood and guts, evidence of the 1930s survival of the mold of the self-defending New Negro, Wright could not claim a brave self-direction while in Hurston's company. She alleged that *Uncle Tom's Children* was content to derive its tales of black-white warfare from "the picture of the South that the communists have been passing around of late," a lurid sketch of a "dismal, hopeless section ruled by brutish hatred and nothing else" (32). Hurston here implied that Wright's adoption of the party's red-colored glasses involved the same sort of minstrel technique he had detected in *Their Eyes*. Under the spell of a secondhand guide to the South, Wright took up the minstrel's burden of indulging a white racial fantasy, in this case, a proletarian Southern Gothic prepared by white Communists.

For a grievance against literary violence, Hurston's review was incongruously combative. Behind its toughness was not just the stringency of Wright's earlier attack but formidable intellectual disagreements now almost as deeply set in literary scholarship as their review-essay eruption. With its "lavish killing . . . to satisfy all male black readers," *Uncle Tom's Children* aggravated Hurston's frustration with social-protest machismo and the sociology of black cultural deprivation she saw as its running partner. Like W. E. B. Du Bois's "Of the Coming of John" (1903) and Jean Toomer's "Blood-Burning Moon" (1923), Wright's story "Long Black Song" supplemented Scottsboro-style interracial triangles, figuring southern race relations as a blood feud between white and black men fought over the bodies of black women. The remainder of his collection, describing a spectrum of uncringing black responses to white violence, could be read to assume that black life was "ruled by brutish hatred," a stony response to vicious white stimulus. *Uncle Tom's Children* thus likely ran afoul of Hurston's core conviction: her enabling faith in the health and self-regulation of African-American culture as studied through the spyglass of her atypical hometown, the black-governed village of Eatonville, Florida.

Whatever the precise mix of motivations behind Hurston's review, its rigor has not been lost on the post-1960s explosion of powerful black women's writing, an event for which the New Negro's long shadow has demanded the renaissance lexicon.[1] With the canonization of Hurston by those seeking maternal ancestry for this latest rebirth of black culture, her run-in with Wright has become the premier exchange within African-

American literary history. Few of the most influential reappraisals of Hurston fail to include an account of the debate attributing the clash to Wright's errors. In her introduction to Alice Walker's momentous Hurston anthology *I Love Myself When I Am Laughing* (1979), Mary Helen Washington explains the dispute in relationship to Wright's constricted view of the black quotidian: "Being black was such grimly serious business to Wright that he was incapable of judging Hurston's characters, who laugh and tease as well as suffer and who do not hate themselves or their blackness" (18). Barbara Johnson's "Metaphor, Metonymy, and Voice in *Their Eyes Were Watching God*" (1984), an effort to reconcile the once-hostile camps of deconstructive and African-American criticism, traces the gap between the two writers to something different but no less Wright's failing: his inability to acknowledge the black woman's overdetermined subject position (167). In *The Signifying Monkey* (1988), Henry Louis Gates, Jr.'s prize-winning theory of black literature drawn from the "text milieu" of this literature itself, the ante is upped by the claim that "no two authors in the tradition are more dissimilar than Hurston and Wright" (183). Their quarrel, and their contradictory theories of both black narrative and black subjectivity, Gates concludes, are markers of the "great divide in black literature" (182). Since Wright is seen to reject the same black vernacular legacy that Gates boosts from a critical subject to a signifying critical principle, this great divide compels the choice of Hurston's side. In the 1990s the Hurston-Wright breach and the preference for the contestant Alice Walker commemorated as "a native American genius" (foreword xiv) has repeatedly been rehearsed in extra-academic spaces, from Tina Brown's *New Yorker* to the editorial apparatus of commercial press reprints of Hurston's texts.[2]

As the differing emphases of Washington, Johnson, and Gates indicate, the proposition that Hurston/Wright names the formative division in the African-American literary tradition does a heap of cultural work. The notion of epic conflict between the two writers provides a ready answer to a gender-troubled literary-historical mystery: namely, how a female writer of Hurston's excellence and onetime fame was banished from the (androcentric, Wright-adoring) black canon of the 1940s to the 1960s. Within a broader feminist register, the vision of a Hurston/Wright divide underwrites genealogies of audacious black women's writing burdened by Wright's male line but boldly, dialogically responsive to it. At the same time, this vision dramatizes less intensely gendered oppositions undergirding the black modern within contemporary African-American criticism, oppositions such as race versus class, modernism versus naturalism,

Harlem Renaissance versus Chicago Renaissance, black nationalism versus Marxism, and so on. Often, the Hurston/Wright difference is shorthand and ballast for imagined dichotomies between black rural and urban selves and cultures and the affiliated binaries of South and North, folk and mass, all energized in the wake of the twentieth-century Great Migration. The abundant retellings of the great debate that readjudicate in favor of Hurston and the terms associated with her have indeed become staging points for an entire "ideology of the 'folk' " (Carby, "Ideologies" 126). According to this reconstruction of African-American cultural identity diagnosed by Hazel Carby, black Americans are most genuinely a rural, southern folk people; black culture is at bottom a rural, southern folk culture; and this culture's purest utterances are songs, tales, toasts, and other oral forms, which the finest black writing—Hurston's, not Wright's— inlays into literary discourse without pretense of elevation. During the 1980s the ideology of the "folk" was invigorated by sophisticated compounds of high black theory and "lowest down" folklorics and escorted by a new wave of black migrants returning to live in the American South.[3] For Carby, the decade's choice of Hurston over Wright was nonetheless a response to the unprecedented urban emergency of those who stayed put. At a historical juncture in which African-American urbanites were actually "under siege," she reasons, cultural critics required the assurance of *Their Eyes* "that, really, the black folk are happy and healthy" ("The Politics" 90).

Along with Carby and others wary of the vernacular-authenticity equation,[4] I can't help but agree that the ideology of the "folk" is just that: an ideology, a representation of the imaginary relationship of certain producers and auditors of African-American culture to certain real conditions of existence.[5] Yet my project in this chapter will not be to demonstrate (once more) that "folk" ideology is a reflexive stake of modern literary nationalisms touched by the West or an ironic desire dependent on the folk's actual disappearance within urban, (post)modern bad new days. I instead mean to dispute the negative ideology of Wright that the ideology of the "folk" typically yields, particularly when the latter is deployed in renarrations of the Hurston-Wright quarrel. Beginning with the impious attack of literary sons Ralph Ellison and James Baldwin, Wright's detractors have often posed him as the scourge of black folk, a figure whose work and personality were blighted by a denial of the black vernacular enforced by Communism.[6] In recent constructions of a Hurston-Wright championship bout, this depiction of "poor Richard" has only solidified, steering Wright to the fringes of folk-minded African-American canons and institutionalizing a scare story about the Old Left's violence to black writing's vernacular ingredient. My opposition to the dismissive ideology of Wright, especially its anti-Communist moral, will therefore take the form of a challenge to its major contemporary expression in the idea of an irresolvable Hurston/Wright difference.

Without seeking to minimize either Wright's masculinism or the immense value of Hurston's resurrection, I will argue that the participants in and explicators of the Hurston-Wright debate have blinded themselves to more-than-trivial points of contact between the two writers. In particular, nearly all have failed to grant that Wright as well as Hurston was attracted to a self-conscious version of black folk ideology following personal removal from its rural, southern footing and under the influence of northern, metropolitan instruction.[7] During the 1930s, both Hurston and Wright harnessed folk ideology to provide a symbolic countermeasure to a Great Migration that threatened to empty the population and cultural power of the southern Black Belt. Exploring this harmonic convergence between Hurston and Wright is a pragmatic deconstructive exercise, a means to reduce the unwieldy pile of antitheses now trailing their dispute. More fundamentally, it goes to show that the decade of Wright's closest involvement with the Old Left saw him least distant from Hurston and most favorably disposed to the literary merit of black folk. Depression-era Communism, I want to suggest, did not stand like a stone wall between folk ideology and the world's most celebrated black Communist author but instead offered him a temporary passport to Eatonville's environs.

Fictions and Disciplines of Automigration

The most significant relationship to the Great Migration shared by Hurston and Wright was their travel with it. Unlike most other major African-American writers of the period, the pair arrived in the metropolitan North of the 1920s after childhoods spent in the rural Deep South. Hurston's path took her from Eatonville, through contrasting educations with a touring theater company and at Howard University, to Manhattan in 1925. There, like the typical black migrant of historical accounts, she immediately sought assistance at the offices of the National Urban League. Wright conducted himself from Natchez, Mississippi, a town the WPA guidebook to the state would describe as "pastoral terrain" (qtd. in T. Davis, "Wright" 469), through a risky self-education in Memphis, to Chicago in 1927. His introduction to the Bronzeville of the South Side was eased by relatives, of which Hurston had none in Harlem.

Despite this common record of travel, Hurston's and Wright's autobiographies, both written in the early 1940s, imagine the meaning of their participation in the Great Migration in markedly different ways. Hurston's *Dust Tracks on a Road* (1942) addresses her shift to New York in just three compressed paragraphs, the most substantial of which skips from a description of immediate reasons for the move to a portrait of a new arrival bereft of external resources but otherwise untouched by the transition: "Being out of school for lack of funds, and wanting to be in New York, I decided to go there and try to get back in school in that city. So the first week of January, 1925, found me in New York with $1.50, no job, no friends and a lot of hope" (682). Despite the familiar list of the city neophyte's grounds for reinvention—"$1.50, no job, no friends and a lot of hope"—earlier jaunts with a light opera troupe and later folklore-collecting expeditions into Florida and the Caribbean are seen as more weighty migratory transformations. Her journey to the northern city is in fact not figured as part of a mass migration but as the product of a compulsive individual wanderlust whose contours are evident in a poetic childhood dream of "sitting astride of a fine horse . . . [and] riding off to look at the belly-band of the world" (584). Somewhat paradoxically, Hurston's cutting of bonds to the mass experience of the Great Migration preserves a conception of black community tied to the continued accessibility of rural southern folk. By casting her flight to New York as the outgrowth of an inborn desire to ramble and learn, not as a constituent of a large-scale labor migration thinning out the black South, she retains a view of the region's Eatonvilles as ripe for reconnections during which folklore and more private memories may be secured.

Wright's autobiography similarly poses his departure from the South as an episode of heroism, but unlike Hurston, he delineates a resistant northern landscape that frustrates hopes for easy self-making. In the opening of his memoir's Chicago portion, first published under the title *American Hunger* in 1977, urban impressions seem to have migrated directly from T. S. Eliot's collected poems. Like the mysterious, dismal cities of *Preludes* and *The Love Song of J. Alfred Prufrock* (1917), the "flat black stretches" of Wright's Chicago are "wreathed in palls of gray smoke" that signify shifting limits to perception and a kind of spiritual miasma, not just the presence of belching slaughterhouses (*Black Boy* 249). Like the London of *The Waste Land* (1922), this Chicago is "an unreal city" whose effects on the mind nevertheless cannot be evaded (249). "The din of the city entered my consciousness," Wright asserts, "entered to remain for years to come" (249). Wright's initial encounter with the Eliotic urban scenery is followed by a discussion of its effect on his aunt Maggie, a physical and psychological alteration measurable in the "frantic light in her eyes" (250). The entrance of the city's "din" into the consciousness of migrant Wright is thus not due to his special receptive capacity. With its troping of Chicago as alienating modernist wasteland and its insistence on the city's renovation of representatives of two generations of a black family, Wright's text drafts his arrival in the urban North as emblematic of a large-scale rift with the knowable territory of the rural South. Unlike Hurston's *Dust Tracks*, which privatizes northward migration and so maintains the aura of a stable southern folk community, his autobiography casts the trek north as a literal, transindividual remaking of looks and minds: the Great Migration has made it hard to go down home again, a place from which whole black families and their subjectivities have decamped.

It is tempting to speculate that the differences between Hurston's and Wright's representations of northern arrival are due to the different intellectual-disciplinary practices they encountered once settled: for Hurston, rural-disposed Boasian anthropology; for Wright, urban-disposed Chicago School sociology crossed with Communist Party theorizations of the Negro Question. In Hurston's case, work as an anthropologist and an anthropologically informed novelist may have made it necessary to deny that the Great Migration meant divorce with the rural South. The social-scientific discipline to which Hurston was introduced at New York's Columbia University initially involved her in anthropometric studies designed to explode the racial pseudoscience of the nineteenth century. Even while an undergraduate, she aided German-Jewish émigré Franz Boas's campaign to decapitate phrenology with its own statistics, carrying a pair of calipers to Harlem and buttonholing passersby for skull measurements. According to Robert Hemenway, this was "an act that many contemporaries felt only Zora Hurston, with her relaxed insouciance, could have gotten away with" (63). Hurston thought the act worth the expenditure of charm because she considered Boas anthropology's "King of Kings" (*Dust Tracks* 683). In his favor was the general antiracist punch of an explanation of human differences in terms of culture, not "racial genius." But Boas's culturalism could also stir specific, academically valuable self-knowledge in Hurston. Through a now-famous metaphor of self-disrobing, Hurston once explained that her Eatonville birth culture went unexamined until her contact with Boas's discipline: "It was fitting me like a tight chemise. I couldn't see it for wearing it. It was only when I was off in college, away from my native surroundings, that I could see myself like somebody else and stand off and look at my garment. Then I had to have the spy-glass of Anthropology to look through at that" (*Mules* 9). In 1927

Boas encouraged her to focus this spy-glass by going south in search of black folklore. Hurston seized the chance to return to her Florida birthplace, only the first of many visits during which she shuttled between the positions of field-worker and native informant and collected the material that would be worked up in nearly all her texts, ethnographic, literary, and hybrid. Her inseparable careers as anthropologist and imaginative writer thus came to depend on the same possibility of easy transit between rural South and urban North preserved in her autobiography's account of Manhattan arrival.

In Wright's case, however, the connection between intellectual training and autobiographical account of an introduction to the city is less clear-cut. The representation of the black migrant's separation from the rural South that opens the northern half of Wright's autobiography is succeeded by evidence that the purportedly antirural intellectual practices of Chicago School sociology and Communist theory pressed him to revalue his Mississippi past. Unlike Saul Bellow and James T. Farrell, novelists familiarized with the Chicago School while undergraduates at the University of Chicago, Wright was introduced to the first of these practices as an object of a social worker's ministration. Mary Wirth, the wife of the Chicago School's Louis Wirth, volunteered as Wright's case worker in early 1933 (Fabre, *The Unfinished* 93). Along with E. Franklin Frazier, Robert Redfield, and Chicago School founder Robert Park, the Wirths became Wright's own Boases, intellectual elders and admirers similar to Hurston's "Papa Franz" who taught how the dangerous absurdities of race thinking could be dismantled with scientific tools. The adjustment pains of black migrants to the northern city were not indices of racial dysfunction, advised Chicago School research, but conventional symptoms of a community undertaking the modernizing task of urbanization.

Wright's autobiography testifies that the Chicago School provided much of the intellectual foundation for his understanding of black urbanism, especially the "tragic toll that the urban environment exacted of the black peasant" (271). The use of the term "peasant," however, hints at the fact that the mountains of empirical material the school compiled on the South Side did not bury its fondness for black life outside city limits. Robert Park, for one, had been convinced that rural African Americans were the New World's own peasants during his years traveling the South as Booker T. Washington's emissary (Bone, "Richard Wright" 455). The mature Park's Darwinian scheme of modernization, a unidirectional narrative of "inexorable progression from simple to complex, homogeneous to heterogeneous, naive to sophisticated, rural to urban, agrarian to industrial, static to dynamic" (ibid.), did not deter an attachment to "doomed" peasant societies, supposedly marked by a preponderance of communal ties. Significantly, Park's muted fondness for the ways of peasant folk colors Wright's favorite Chicago School statement, Louis Wirth's "Urbanism as a Way of Life" (1938). Wirth's essay has been labeled the low point in the Chicago School's progressive oversimplification of Ferdinand Tönnies's classic typology of *Gemeinschaft* (community) and *Gesellschaft* (society). In "Urbanism as a Way of Life," two concepts that in Tönnies's hands had been coexisting orders of social negotiation are reduced to descriptions of two places, the country and the city (Bender 33). The latter of these places, the city, in which fragile, voluntary, "social" ties have supplanted the "communal" kinship relations of the rural, is now thought less the country's cousin than its gravedigger; for Wirth, the city has become the single evolutionary destination of modern society. Yet even he cannot repress the suspicion that the human costs of urbanization are exorbitant. "Urbanism as a Way of Life" ruefully admits that "the bonds of kinship, of neighborliness, and the sentiments arising out of living together for generations under a common folk tradition are likely to be absent, or, at best, relatively weak, in [a city] aggregate the members of which have such diverse origins and backgrounds" (70). As Carla Cappetti acutely observes, "having split country and city in order to foretell the urbanization of the world, the part that was suppressed, the rural world of community, intimacy, and being-at-home, continues to . . . haunt . . . under the guise of nostalgia" (69). Wright's best-loved Chicago School essay could not place the rural on the endangered list without intimating the need for preservation. The urban sociology that Wright discovered in Chicago—usually described as a major bone of contention with anthropologist Hurston[8]—was thus not immune to the sympathies inculcated in Hurston's more formal academic training. Recommendations to cherish the rural-communal hovered above Chicago School texts that saw the city as the end of modern history.

In the theory of the U.S. Communist Party, the second of the intellectual practices he came upon in Chicago, Wright confronted a body of knowledge and strategy struggling to politicize the interest in black folk culture that the Chicago School insinuated and Hurston actively pursued in the field. In her 1938 dressing-down of *Uncle Tom's Children*, Hurston numbered among Communism's fallacies the misconception that the South was "a dismal, hopeless section ruled by brutish hatred and nothing else" ("Stories" 32). It followed that Wright's account of the region was more a phantasm than a documentary, the necessary delusion of a party token whose prospects for political victory and pretensions to social real-

ism were hindered by the South's true colors as a bulwark against socialism. Yet Hurston's take on the party's position on the South was incomplete. She slighted the redemptive face of the Black Belt Nation thesis, the
controversial centerpiece of Communist policy on African America in the
1930s, up and running as Wright first entered the party's John Reed Literary Club in 1933. As explained in chapter 2, this break with Communist
slighting of racism, authored in part by McKay and other New Negro pilgrims, redefined the Negro Question as that of an oppressed nation.
Blacks remaining in the heavily African-American, largely rural Black Belt
stretching from Virginia to Mississippi were thought to have met all the
requirements of nationhood as defined by Stalin, comprising "*a historically evolved, stable community of language, territory, economic life, and psychological make-up manifested in a community of culture*" (Stalin 12; emphasis in original). "Both multiracial workers' solidarity *and* self-determination in the . . . Black Belt," Barbara Foley notes, were the politics called for
by this nation-in-waiting (*Radical* 174; emphasis in original). Both agricultural and factory laborers were to be rallied, in distinction to the *Crusaders'* renaissance focus on the service of the black urban proletariat. The
Depression-era party thus not only declared that African Americans possessed a "community of culture" whose locus was the rural South but formally accepted the possibility that this culture's stewards might choose
statehood on the (fancied) model of Soviet socialist republics.[9]

Wright himself indicated that a text distributed to honor the Black Belt
Nation thesis won him totally to Communism. His autobiography provides present-day readers with a heady experience of historical estrange-
ment as it praises Joseph Stalin's *The National and Colonial Question*, an
essay defending the doctrine of self-determination for oppressed nations
that Wright swears he "read with awe" (*Black Boy* 319). By delineating a
Soviet Union in which various "forgotten folk had been encouraged to
keep their old cultures, to see in their ancient customs meanings and satisfactions as deep as those contained in supposedly superior ways of living," Stalin inspired what Wright calls "the first total emotional commitment of my life" (319). Here was the promise that Communists respected
the rights of exploited people to organize autonomously, even to secede;
here was reassurance that the rights and cultures of minority national
groups did not contradict the rights and cultures of classes. At its core, the
essay impressed Wright as a revelation of "a new way of looking upon lost
and beaten peoples" (318). "How different this was from the way in which
Negroes were sneered at in America," Wright recalls exclaiming (319).

Wright's suggestion that Stalin pointed him toward a "new way of looking" at the "meanings and satisfactions" of African-American folk culture is likely to strike most present-day readers as gullible and unsavory, too removed to represent more than a dusty tableau in a gallery of 1930s excesses. Perhaps this is why Wright's critics generally do not mention his praise of *The National and Colonial Question* even when denouncing the high costs of Communism. But Wright's open enthusiasm for Stalin's theorizing cannot be written off to credulous Depression enthusiasms. Wright's appreciation was composed in 1943, in the dead center of his protracted separation from organized Communism (Fabre, *The Unfinished* 255). Later in the 1940s he elected to include it among the excerpts from his autobiography reprinted in *The God That Failed* (1950), Richard Crossman's famous anthology of memoirs by party defectors. Wright's enthusiasm for Stalin, as opposed to several of the outgrowths of the U.S. party's Stalinism, was longstanding. When some party intellectuals were lighting out for Trotskyism or more rightward destinations at the height of the Moscow Trials in 1938, Wright signed a statement in *The Daily Worker* agreeing that there was good evidence to convict Stalin's enemies (Fabre, *The Unfinished* 162–63). Wright would weather the Hitler-Stalin pact reached the following year, joining Ralph Ellison in the opinion that it expressed Marxist necessity (Fabre, "From *Native Son*" 202). Despite the perennial dream that Wright was expelled from the party for crimes of intellectual independence,[10] Michel Fabre's authorized biography confirms that he separated from the party under his own power—and without denouncing Stalin—between 1942 and 1944 (*The Unfinished* 239–56).

In Wright's eyes, Stalin deserved esteem not simply because he was the general secretary of the Communist Party of the Soviet Union, de facto leader of an embattled world socialism; he also had a reputation as the greatest protector of minority rights within the Communist pantheon. Stalin was himself a member of an ethnic minority group, a Georgian who at school had been instructed that his native language and literature were inferior to the Russian. The modern political calculus of self-representation, Soviet-style, ushered him into an early post as People's Commissar for Affairs of Nationalities; fully half of his published writing dealt with nationalism. His aid in drafting a Soviet constitution that forbade racism was better known abroad than his crushing of uncooperative nationalist movements, beginning with an uprising in his native Georgia (Munck 76–79). By the 1930s his Soviet Union was thus the focus of reveries of an ethnically and racially mixed nation free from prejudice, a kind of anthropological state headed by a brave radical ethnographer.

Wright was scarcely the sole African-American intellectual of the decade to picture Stalin's Soviet Union as a pluralist model for racist America. After the *Black and White* adventure, both Langston Hughes and Louise Thompson publicly praised Soviet assistance to the dark-skinned workers of the Central Asian socialist republics (Louise Thompson, "With Langston"; Hughes, *I Wonder* 101–89). Three decades after a 1934 pilgrimage, an unreconstructed Paul Robeson remembered how he had learned in the Soviet Union that "there was no such thing on earth as a backward people" (qtd. in Duberman 188). Like Wright, Robeson contrasted the situation of Soviet minorities with that of blacks in the United States, who were informed that their vernacular culture and language were "either dead or too primitive to develop" (qtd. on 211). In 1937 a homebound Alain Locke endorsed "the cultural minorities art programs being consistently and brilliantly developed in the Soviet Federation for the various racial and cultural folk traditions of that vast land" ("Resume"). Nearly sixty years before a succession of national independence movements dismantled the Soviet Union, the African-American left could see non-Russian Soviet republics in much the same way that Hurston saw Eatonville: as guarantors of the continued value of minority cultures in the midst of modernization.

Despite the glaring differences between Communism and anthropology, the former consequently presented Wright with what the latter had presented Zora Neale Hurston: a defamiliarizing second sight through which the culture of African-American folk could be seen as an intricate, functioning whole. Much as what Hurston dubbed the "spy-glass of Anthropology" allowed her to examine her Eatonville inheritance, Communism offered Wright what he called his "first full-bodied vision of Negro life in America" (qtd. in Naison 211), a complement to the "concrete vision of . . . the urban Negro's body and soul" provided by the Chicago School (introduction xvii). Both anthropology and Communism allowed a constructive sort of African-American double consciousness: an untorturous twoness allowing one to see birth cultures as both subject and object, thus ensuring that black difference could not be interpreted as black deficiency. Both anthropology and Communism confirmed black folk culture's status as something as worthy as supposedly more sophisticated systems. (The Black Belt Nation thesis, with its deflection of the nightmares and idylls of the primitive, indeed showed a specific debt to the anthropological concept of cultural relativism whose most effective popularizer was Hurston's "King of Kings.")[11] Finally, both anthropology and Communism conferred on African-American folk culture a compelling significance that nimbly and seductively leaped from the local to the global. The anthropological assurance that cultural difference ultimately proved a shared human creativity was matched by the Communist claim that the cultivation of minority cultures ultimately advanced the cause of world revolution.

The overwhelming bent of recent critics to favor Hurston's anthropology over Wright's Communism cannot rest on the premise that the latter demanded a peculiar compromise of folk blackness. For both Wright and Hurston, contact with a modern Western intellectual practice with claims to scientific authority and universality stoked a positively charged sense of African-American cultural difference. Werner Sollors's revisionist account of the making of ethnicity is illuminating in this connection. *Beyond Ethnicity* (1986) argues that the common perception of ethnic identity growing from "parochial beginnings to modernist assimilation" fails to notice "that ethnicity is continuously created anew and that assimilation and modernization take place in ethnic and even ethnocentric forms" (245). Even Garveyism, Sollors notes, can (and has) been read "as a 'trendy' ethnocentric movement which actually modernized its members" (245).[12] In the case of Hurston and Wright, the converse of Sollors's deconstructive formula for a modernizing ethnicity seems to apply: here, "ethnicization" takes place in the assimilating and modernizing forms of anthropology and Communism. Relativist ethnography, with its intimate defense of "premodern" societies, challenged the idea of beneficent Western modernization, but so did Communism after Lenin, with its harping on the violence of capital accumulation on a world scale and its calls for colonial revolution. Despite the Eurocentric factor within Marxist universalism, the object of Wright's political passion accordingly became a source for the recognition of African-American folk culture not unlike Hurston's Boasian spy-glass. More powerfully than the nostalgic edge of Chicago School sociology, Communism motivated radical reconstructions of Wright's South.

James Clifford and other postmodern critics of ethnographic authority have insisted that devotion to "the rural folk" and other supposed bearers of cultural purity, rootedness, and authenticity is born of modernity, in which mobility and cultural "inauthenticity"—the experience of being "caught between cultures, implicated in others"—are routine fates (Clifford 11). In the instance of the engagements with anthropology and sociology/Communism that the Great Migration extended Hurston and Wright, we find versions of African-American cultural belonging pivoting on the rural folk arising through intercultural contact in America's *echt* modern cities, contact that guaranteed some self-consciousness about the reciprocal nature of southern and northern, rural and urban, folk and mass identifications. Despite the dissimilarities between the scenes of city arrival in their autobiographies, both writers experienced displacement north as a process that provoked desires and provided directions for revisiting black southern folk culture, first denying this culture and then offering privileged intellectual access to it. For both Hurston and Wright, going up north introduced an alluring way to go down home as a professional author trained in the science of society, a career promising urban success by means of a clarifying double vision of the rural culture left behind.

Two "Stories of Conflict"

The compound perspective on the rural black South that Hurston and Wright developed in New York and Chicago is displayed in two kindred stories published in the 1930s: Hurston's "The Gilded Six-Bits," a 1933 text that led to the contract for her first novel, and Wright's "Long Black Song," a text first included in the original 1938 version of *Uncle Tom's Children*. With a symmetry absent from the writers' dueling book reviews, both of these stories represent the Black Belt as a soberly utopian counter to the antiutopian aspects of the Great Migration, increasingly obvious during the Great Depression. This is not to say that either text imagines the South as a pristine, conflict-free retreat from northern ghettos and urban unemployment. Instead, both present narratives of social antagonism in which the urge to migrate is a fatal temptation to be resisted. Both situate their narratives in the early years of the Great Migration yet cheat level-headed historicism by reinventing the moment as one in which the costs of the removal north can be seen as plainly as the potential gains. The final mission of Hurston and Wright's humble fantasy machinery is to propose imaginary alternatives to the Great Migration, to resupply its losses without assuming that the rural South and the urban North are related only by opposition.

Hurston's "Gilded Six-Bits" is a story of invasion, seduction, and the final victory of love, set in the Florida of the early 1920s and filled with the lyrical southern black dialect she was perhaps the first U.S. writer to stock in both dialogue and narration. The text begins with a sensual tableau of a black woman, a cabin, and natural surroundings that seem idyllic even in the shadow (and smelling range) of "the G and G Fertilizer works" (985). Missie May, young, strong, and pretty, bathes herself in a metal washtub. About her is a small, cheerful cabin, surrounded by honey flowers and chinaberry trees, within a black settlement supported by G and G's payroll. She eagerly awaits her husband, Joe, and the ritual with which they mark Saturdays: Joe will throw silver dollars he has earned at the plant through the door of the cabin and hurry to a hiding place where he waits until she discovers him and the candy kisses he has planted in his clothing. The game takes place as always, but Joe has news to report. A Mister Otis D. Slemmons from Chicago and other points north has come to town, a flashy entrepreneur who flaunts what Joe describes as "a five-dollar gold piece for a stick-pin and . . . a ten-dollar gold piece on his watch chain and [a] mouf . . . jes' crammed full of gold teethes" (989). Joe idolizes Slemmons as a black Rockefeller and an icon of city sophistication and insists that the couple visit the stranger's ice-cream parlor. After the trip, Missie May claims to be unimpressed. Slemmons's gold, she tells Joe, would "look a whole heap better on you" (990). A few weeks later, however, Joe's high opinion of his wife and Slemmons is shaken when he finds them together in bed. He rousts Slemmons out, in the process snatching the coin from his watch chain. Despite Missie May's regretful cry that "Ah love you so hard and Ah know you don't love *me* no mo'" (992; emphasis in original), time ticks by with Joe refusing to return to the marriage bed, clutching on to the gold as a sign of the household's depressed sexual economy and a moribund but threatening substitute for the phallus. "The yellow coin in his trousers," thinks Missie May, "was like a monster hiding in the cave of his pockets to destroy her" (993). Joe eventually relents, however, and leaves Slemmons's glitter behind in the sheets. After the lovemaking, Missie May fears that what was once a game with coins has become prostitution: "He had come home to buy from her," she worries, "as if she were any woman in the long house" (994). Yet she also discovers that Slemmons's coin is in truth just a gilded half-dollar and, soon enough, that she is pregnant. When Joe is assured that the baby is his, he travels to Orlando and trades Slemmons's trick money for an oversized bag of candy kisses. The story ends as Joe approaches Missie May back in Eatonville and inaugurates the ritual that signals the return of time as it was before Slemmons's arrival. "Joe Banks," Missie May calls out in the final lines, "Ah hear you chunkin' money in mah do'way" (996), happy to know that silver coins have taken the place of gilded ones and love the place of sex-for-cash.

The opening pages of Wright's "Long Black Song," a story set during the First World War and perhaps directly indebted to Hurston's, feed the appetite for southern pastoral that Wright saw as the lasting contribution of regional apologists such as Joel Chandler Harris. The text begins with a young black mother named Sarah singing a lullaby and nursing a baby in a farmhouse overlooking fields that "whispered a green prayer" (331–32).

This bucolic scene is soon spoiled by the appearance of a young and lecherous white salesman from Chicago peddling a combination clock-gramophone with a gilded edge, an item reminiscent of Hurston's gilded coins and one well chosen to symbolize urban-industrial time and urban-industrial leisure.[13] Sarah, shown to answer to solar rhythms in a number of interior monologues, is initially resistant to this commodity and the existential shift it represents. "We just don need no time, Mistah," she explains (334). Eventually, however, she surrenders to the object's temptations. Almost at once, the clock-gramophone's white salesman makes a sexual advance and inaugurates a scene that has become a touchstone of feminist rethinkings of Wright.[14] Sarah first resists and then responds to his hands and is seduced and/or raped. When Sarah's farmer husband, Silas, returns from selling crops in town and discovers signs of the salesman in their bed, he becomes violent with jealousy, smashing the clock-gramophone, whipping Sarah until she runs off, and vowing to meet the white intruder with gun in hand. On the following morning, the salesman is killed when he returns to collect a payment on his product, reduced in price from fifty to forty dollars after his liaison with Sarah. Within hours, Silas himself is cut down firing at a white posse as Sarah and the baby look on abstractly, as if watching a film.

On the plane of plot, at least, Hurston's and Wright's stories are closely joined. Both texts, Werner Sollors notes,

> contrast natural time with clocked time and focus on the intrusion of the capitalist ethos as a sexual seduction. Both imagine the seducer as a man from the outside (in both cases with a Chicago dimension), portray the female character as the more traditional one who yet yields to the temptation from the snake of the salesman of leisure (whether he be in the gramophone or ice-cream line), and show that the glitter of modern capitalism is not made of gold but merely gilded. ("Anthropological" 30–31)

Yet Sollors's perceptive reading of the parallels between the stories stops before it analogizes the seducers from the North with the seductions of the Great Migration. Both northerners arrive on the southern scene around World War I, the moment when the boll weevil invasion, the increasing dependency of the southern economy, a worsening of Jim Crow violence, and a labor shortage in the North combined to spark major out-migration (Marks 3). With their urban slickness, talents for promotion, and connections to Chicago—home of *The Defender*, the most powerful black propagandist for migration—the two invaders are allied with the agents sent south by northern industry. Admittedly, they are labor agents with a difference. Rather than courting male field hands, they direct their efforts toward home-working women, more firmly rooted in the southern soil while more attracted—suggest Hurston and Wright—to the new regime of consumption. Rather than guaranteeing train fare and lucrative wage work in the city, these agents promise the pleasures of eroticized mass leisure that such work could buy. Rather than collecting the reward a large head count of migrants could bring, they are left without a following when the price of their pleasures is magically disclosed before they can bring blacks north. As Joe exults near the end of "The Gilded Six-Bits," the northern seducer's lies are revealed as such before he can kidnap "folkses wives from home" (996).

Moreover, the agents are not so much salesmen of "the capitalist ethos," already arrived in the rural South, as flacks for a mass migration that jeopardizes those few remaining folk practices battling this ethos from within. The resistance to the temptations of migration that concludes both stories—tragic and violent in the case of Wright's—therefore does not restore an arcadian scene in which natural relationships rout money relationships. As mentioned above, the close of Hurston's "Gilded Six-Bits" sees Joe once again "chunkin' money in [Missie May's] do'way" (996). Even in its romance denouement, Hurston's story highlights the inescapability of the wage, something conspicuously absent from later black women's fiction conjuring the rural South as a precapitalist alternative (Willis 11).[15] Still, the full ritual of Hurston's couple does not conclude with the chucking of coins. The opening scenes suggest that Missie May will go on to search Joe's pockets for candy kisses, the freely chosen coin of love they win the luxury to employ after satirizing their dependence on the general equivalent: money. The resilience of Hurston's couple is thus indicated through their ability to restore an ironic game that reveals and defuses the mediation of their marriage by a wage-based industrial capitalist economy, monarch of the South before Slemmons. The imaginary alternative to the Great Migration offered in "The Gilded Six-Bits" is a restrained fantasy of a rural black folk whose freedom lies in an ability to resist the utter victory of the cash nexus that the migration threatens. Ironically, the very tokens of this freedom—candy kisses—are secured through work at G and G Fertilizer, which processes the funky, natural agricultural product of manure into a cash-convertible commodity, itself perhaps bound for the North.

The gory death of the salesman in Wright's "Long Black Song" likewise does not spell the defeat of a completely alien capitalist ethos. Sarah's reflections reveal Silas to be a would-be entrepreneur who intimately understands the relationship between the Protestant ethic and the spirit of capitalism, methodically saves his money to invest in land, and generally covets the status of a Slemmons (Sollors, "Anthropological" 38). Instead of capitalism per se, Wright's salesman peddles Chicago School–defined modernization, the grand transition from magical to scientific thinking, rural to urban social organization, agricultural to industrial production of which the Great Migration was a dramatic instrument. As Sollors proposes, Wright's introduction to *Black Metropolis* (1945), a sociological study of black Chicago by St. Clair Drake and Horace Cayton, suggests that the sociohistorical collisions articulated through the meeting of Sarah and the salesman are poached from Park and Wirth ("Anthropological" 36). "Holy days became holidays," notes Wright in a summary of Chicago School wisdom, "clocks replaced the sun as a symbolic measurement of time" (xxii). Mindful of the school's urban teleology, the alternative to migration offered in the sketch in "Long Black Song" of clocks replacing the sun is, if anything, more modest than that offered in Hurston's "Gilded Six-Bits." Wright's representative of the temptations of migration—in this case, a young white man—is, like Hurston's, successfully repelled before he lures "folkses wives from home," but at the cost of interracial murder and the meltdown of a black family. If there is signifying on Hurston's text in Wright's—an application of the vernacular-derived forms of repetition with a difference identified in Gates's *The Signifying Monkey*—then it consists in his rewriting of her comic conclusion as a bloody interracial clash. All the same, Wright's borrowing from the Chicago School's scheme of urbanizing modernization does not neglect the nostalgic rural underside. "Long Black Song" at once denies the school's conflation of the rural with the precapitalist and inflates its daydreams of doomed black peasants into scenes of a folk patriarch who takes up armed resistance to urbanizing agents. Like Hurston, Wright imposes a taxing defeat on the booster for migration in a rural southern setting that is familiar with capitalist relations yet shows the damages of the Great Migration in relief.

Moses on the Communist Road

Imaginary refusal of the Great Migration, rife in Hurston's work of the 1930s, is not confined to "Long Black Song" in Wright's. "Fire and Cloud," the story that follows "Long Black Song" in *Uncle Tom's Children* and concludes the first edition of that collection, rewrites Silas's isolated battle according to a communal design. Rather than beginning with a seductive scene of (temporary) pastoral fulfillment, the text opens with Depression suffering. The Reverend Dan Taylor hurries home, agonizing over how best to lead his rural black congregation through a time of hunger. He must choose between two frightening alternatives: instructing his church to trust in God and the good intentions of the town's white bosses or advising it to join in a demonstration organized by a pair of Communists, one black and one white, who have arrived from points north. As Taylor imagines it, he is a forsaken Moses expected to lead "his people out of the wilderness into the Promised Land," without the signs of fire and cloud which God provided the Israelites (357). In the absence of higher guidance, he is inclined to counsel acceptance but is troubled by what he sees around him as he makes his way home. Instead of barren fields, he passes acres of land on which "the grass was dark and green" (356). Not natural disaster but economic device has caused Taylor's community to starve. The market in its mystery has declared that crops cannot be sold, and the laws erected to protect it declare that blacks may not grow their own food on land on which they have worked all their lives. In an outburst steeped in the territorial imperative of the Black Nation thesis, Taylor informs God that the South has become an open-air prison for blacks dispossessed from the land: "The white folks say we cant raise nothin on Yo earth! They done put the lans of the worl in their pockets! They done fenced em off n nailed em down! Theys a-tryin t take Yo place, Lawd!" (364).

What Taylor decides is not to decide at all. After receiving a long-awaited sign during a night of testing by white thugs, he understands that the choice between the Communist road and the road of the black church is unnecessary. As he informs his son Jimmy, he has learned that the sins of Jim Crow can be erased only when the endemic faith of black Christianity is integrated with the imported faith of mass protest:

"Membah whut Ah tol yuh prayer wuz, son?"
    There was silence, then Jimmy answered slowly:
    "Yuh mean lettin Gawd be so real in yo life tha everything yuh do is cause of Im?"
    "Yeah, but its different now, son. Its the *people*! Theys the ones whut mus be real t us! Gawds wid the people! N the peoples gotta be real as Gawd t us! We cant hep ourselves er the people when wes erlone." (398; emphasis in original)

Like more than a few proletarian texts of the 1930s, "Fire and Cloud" ends with a strike scene. Taylor finds his calling as a new kind of Moses by joining the throng that marches to the heart of town demanding bread. Even when asked to speak with the town's white mayor up front, he refuses to leave its ranks, instead spontaneously reproducing Lenin's maxim that "*Freedom belongs t the strong!*" (406; emphasis in original). What is most arresting about the ending of "Fire and Cloud," however, is the absence of some of the recurring components of radical strike literature. Wright's setting is not a shop floor or city avenue but the center of a narrow southern town. His hero is not a newly radicalized factory hand or a previously vacillating middle-class intellectual but a sharecropper-preacher who learns that "Gawds wid the people!" The liberated social space prefigured by the moment of victory is not an egalitarian shop but a yeoman's paradise in the tradition of both Jeffersonian pastoralism and black folk ideology that should have made Hurston proud. As Taylor envisions it, Communism in action would look something like a farm and a folk culture of one's own:

> Lawd, we could make them ol fiels bloom ergin. We could make em feed us. Thas whut Gawd put em there fer. Plows could break and hoes could chop and hands could pick and arms could carry. . . . On and on that could happen and people could eat and feel as he had felt with the plow handles trembling in his hands, following old Bess, hearing the earth cracking and breaking because he wanted it to crack and break; because he willed it, because the earth was his. And they could sing as he had sung when he and May were first married; sing about picking cotton, fishing, hunting, about sun and rain. (358)

Like "The Gilded Six-Bits" and "Long Black Song," "Fire and Cloud" flaunts leaks in the rural/urban, South/North opposition: it is an interracial pair of northern, urban Communists that sparks rural blacks to draw on their own cultural resources and protect their southern place. Also like these texts, however, Wright's story diagrams a local alternative to the Great Migration: the black Christian conception of northward exodus as a "Flight out of Egypt" is rewritten as a southern march against conditions inspiring black flight. For a trek north, "Fire and Cloud" substitutes a southbound movement to synthesize northern Communism and black folk culture. Here, Wright tacitly counsels that the martyr's violence against migration represented in "Long Black Song" should give way to massive resistance. The placement of "Fire and Cloud" at the back of *Uncle Tom's Children* positions it at the end of the cycle of interracial homicide traced in the first three stories; it also situates it as the most complete solution to the dilemma of migration boiling throughout. Flipping from the opening story "Big Boy Leaves Home," to "Long Black Song," to "Fire and Cloud," readers move through several ideal-typical responses to Black Belt inequities. A vision of the Great Migration as a flight from lynching gives way to wish-fulfilling masculine defiance of migration's corrupt promoters and then to a blueprint for staying south with revolutionary intent. Only by isolating this progression's starting point—the sometimes separately anthologized story "Big Boy Leaves Home"—can *Uncle Tom's Children* clinch Wright's reputation as a Soviet-supplied Sherman laying waste to Hurston's Dixie.

When Wright remarks in his review of *Their Eyes* that Hurston is content to confine her folk within "a safe and narrow orbit which America likes" ("Between" 25), he is referring to the putative minstrelsy of her characters' emotional range. The metaphor of unthreatening enclosure also provides a key, however, to understanding Wright's more worthy misgivings over her intraracial focus. Moved by Communist hopes of combining southern black communities into a greater collectivity, Wright could imagine that widening the orbit of the folk to encompass the extent of the Black Belt was tantamount to black liberation. To his mind, Hurston's welcome challenge to pathologizing accounts of rural black communities thus needed to challenge the facts of rural white ownership, facts that at best hindered the flowering of black folk culture into black self-determination and at worst threatened the folk's existence by demanding removal north. When Reverend Taylor in "Fire and Cloud" chooses to reconcile black prophetic traditions and Communist tactics and act on his dreams of black land, he confesses Wright's desire to redeem folk ideology, to revise what he sees as a compensatory Eatonville of the mind into a spur to collective action. This ideology's symbolic resolutions to real social contradictions, Wright pleads, must themselves become real. It was this difference as to the political pitch and magnitude of folk ideology, rather than Wright's supposedly less organic connection to the folk, that created one of the few unbridgeable gaps between Wright and Hurston in the 1930s.

Fires and Clouds

It is telling, however, that the blueprint for the revision in "Fire and Cloud" of Hurston's folk could have been lifted from nobody but Hurston. In 1934 she published a very short story, "The Fire and the Cloud," in *Challenge* magazine, Dorothy West's major editorial project after returning from the *Black and White* trip. Wright knew West and her publication well; when the journal was revived as *New Challenge* in 1937, he thought enough of its past to accept the position of associate editor under West and fellow Chicagoan Marian Minus. It is more than likely, then, that Wright read Hurston's tale of a dead yet lucid Moses who evaluates his career leading the Israelites out of bondage while waiting to ascend from Mount Nebo.

The main business of "The Fire and the Cloud" is to demystify the Old Testament prophet as a god-man with some affinity for the culture of southern blacks, a concern that shows it to be the trigger for *Moses, Man of the Mountain*, the novel-length rewriting of Exodus Hurston published in 1939. Like the novel, the story aligns the Moses of scripture with the Moses of the folklore of the African diaspora. For a few of Africa's children, reports Hurston, "the stories of the miracles of Jesus [were] but Mosaic legends told again" (*Moses* 338); the Old Testament deliverer in whom European exegetes had seen a shadow of Jesus was given typological primacy. For others, Moses was both of this world and not of it, associated with significant historical events in the present as well as in the past. The folk Moses of "The Fire and the Cloud" is appropriately not without human weakness. The Old Testament's shining instrument of God becomes a blessed but weary old man whose divine mandate doesn't keep him from complaining that he gets no respect. "Look now upon the plain of Moab," he exclaims, "A great people! They shall rule over nations and dwell in cities they have not builded. Yet they have rebelled against me ever" ("The Fire" 999). Neither is this Moses above the occasional joke in informal diction that functions, as Hemenway notes of *Moses*, to puncture "the high seriousness of biblical rhetoric" (266). On one occasion, the prophet parodies his biblical tags of "nation-maker" and "law-giver" with the declaration that he is "Moses, The-drawn-out" (998). Though "The Fire and the Cloud" does not develop the transition from standard English to black dialect through which the novel's Moses manifests his increasing intimacy with the Afro-Israelites, the story's emancipator is also African-Americanized. His interlocutor on Mount Nebo is a chatty lizard inspired by the animal stories of black folklore, a creature reminiscent of the talking buzzards who make a surreal appearance in *Their Eyes*. Muttering to the reptile about the "stiff-necked race of people" he was commanded to lead (999), Moses adopts the "private wail" of intragroup frustration Hurston jokingly pronounced "sacred" to her race (*Dust Tracks* 773).

Oddly, the signifying network between Hurston's Moses story and Wright's has barely been traced. "Lines of Descent/Dissenting Lines," Deborah E. McDowell's introduction to a 1991 reprinting of *Moses, Man of the Mountain*, may be the single critical publication in which "The Fire and the Cloud" and "Fire and Cloud" are paired. McDowell maintains that Hurston's story "might be read as a short answer to Wright's version," in which she "liberates her pen from . . . the 'literary religion of socialist realism' " (x). It might well be read this way, but only with reference to some ideal order of texts: the publication of Hurston's "answer" predates the appearance of Wright's version by four years. More sound, if less creative, is to refrain from projecting Wright's current résumé as Hurston's true-believing disciplinarian back onto the 1930s and to read his variation on the Moses tale as a signifying response to hers. Wright, after all, knew "signifying" as a word and as a practice. Gates himself, while painting Wright's "naturalism" as the great given of twentieth-century black narrative—always the signifyee, never the signifier—admits that his apprentice novel, *Lawd Today*, contains "one of the earliest uses of the term *signifying*, ostensibly one year after . . . Hurston had used it in . . . *Mules and Men*" (*The Signifying* 97).

The title of Wright's story, "Fire and Cloud," is of course almost identical to Hurston's, as is its dusting of colloquial language to deflate the solemnity of Exodus. From Hurston's version, Wright seems to have learned that black Christianity's revision of the Moses story invited dissenting sermons on the meaning of black emancipation. Her portrait of the disaffection of Moses and the ungratefulness of the Afro-Israelites crystallizes the irony of turning to another to provide freedom for the self (Hemenway 268–69). Through Taylor's final decision to stand among the folk and embrace the "many-limbed, many-legged, many-handed crowd that was he" ("Fire" 405), Wright logs the complementary point that black leaders should reconceive their mandate as an obligation to aid the self-organization of their flocks. Even with its correction of Hurston's under-Communized construction of the black folk, Wright's "Fire and Cloud" thus appears to revise "The Fire and the Cloud" in an indebted and respectful style close to that associated with the black women writers who have explicitly claimed her as foremother. In this story, if not in his scathing review of *Their Eyes*, Wright renders a Hurston similar to the precursor created in the novels of later black women, "a literary forebear," declares Michael Awkward, "whose texts are celebrated even as they are revised, praised for their insights even when these insights are deemed inadequate" (8). Despite Wright's utter inability to register Hurston's feminism as a legitimate intellectual or political concern (not rare enough in interwar literary Communism), "Fire and Cloud" testifies that it was possible for him to appreciate—and appropriate—the literary results of her verdict that northward migration required southern reinvestment. In the imagination of this Wright text, Hurston was ripe for reconception as a proletarian author; to tailor

Blake's line on Milton, she was here judged a member of the Communist Party without knowing it.

After Entente: Bleakness and the "Blueprint"

By the end of the Depression, the covert entente between Hurston and Wright had disappeared along with overt airings of their disagreements. Hurston's elaboration of a resilient black folk survived the turn to the 1940s largely intact. Wright, however, appears to have marked this transition by abandoning hopes for an African-American folk Communism strong enough to battle the Great Migration. As Farah Jasmine Griffin notes, the black migrants to northern cities who dominate Wright's post-1930s fiction neither pine for the South nor resettle in it. *Native Son* (1940) concludes with Bigger greeting death in the Chicago that convicts him; the stranger-hero of the *The Outsider* (1953), Cross Damon, discovers an existential alternative to capitalist and Communist totalitarianisms in emigrating to Europe. Wright's historical text for *12 Million Black Voices* (1941), a WPA-style essay in documentary photography, is quiet on the prospects of the Black Belt Nation thesis, even as it culminates with a party-style display of black urbanites poised to assemble the future alongside white workers (Griffin 160–61).

Recent reconsiderations of the Hurston-Wright relationship deny that there were any affinities to fade in the 1940s. Casting dueling reviews as the fulcrum of a freighted set of critical oppositions, these reconsiderations install a historically undifferentiated sense of the writers' dealings, one that reads whole careers and whole tendencies in modern black literature in light of their trading of bad notices in 1937–38. Yet close comparison of Hurston's and Wright's fiction of the same period reveals a shared endeavor to protect the rural black folk from the worst of the Great Migration. Both authors ironically marked the decade of the public eruption of their rivalry by issuing texts imaginatively repelling black flight north. From the angle of these similarly restrained pastorals, employing the Hurston-Wright debate to pit Communism against the ideology of the "folk" looks exactly inappropriate.

What of other, later angles, however? What of the most infamous paragraphs in Wright's repertoire, the reflections in the autobiographical *Black Boy* (1945) on "the essential bleakness of black life in America"?:

> (After I had outlived the shocks of childhood, after the habit of reflection had been born in me, I used to mull over the strange absence of real kindness in Negroes, how unstable was our tenderness, how lacking in

genuine passion we were, how void of great hope, how timid our joy, how bare our traditions, how hollow our memories, how lacking we were in those intangible sentiments that bind man to man, and how shallow was even our despair. After I had learned other ways of life I used to brood upon the unconscious irony of those who felt that Negroes led so passional an existence! I saw that what had been taken for our emotional strength was our negative confusions, our flights, our fears, our frenzy under pressure.

(Whenever I thought of the essential bleakness of black life in America, I knew that Negroes had never been allowed to catch the full spirit of Western civilization, that they lived somehow in it but not of it. And when I brooded upon the cultural barrenness of black life, I wondered if clean, positive tenderness, love, honor, loyalty, and the capacity to remember were native with man. I asked myself if these human qualities were not fostered, won, struggled and suffered for, preserved in ritual from one generation to another.) (*Black Boy* 37)

There is much to offend and to question in this dismal catalog of black dread, numbness, and insufficiency, much more than the relentless alliteration of "our flights, our fears, our frenzy under pressure." The passage's incongruous academicism and self-conscious profundity nevertheless argue that it is no transparent recording of a definitive verdict. If we interpret Wright's arraignment according to its own pretenses, agreeing to take it as an unvarnished account of youthful meditations, we then accept that a teenager had independently arrived at the theory and terminology of Chicago School sociology and cultural anthropology, from the concept of "cultural barrenness" to the preservation of community through ritual. If we instead interpret the arraignment less naively and hear the voice of the cultivated 1940s Wright in the adolescent autobiographical subject, how do we assess the suggestion later in *Black Boy* that this subject's judgment was immature, flowing from early ignorance of African-American life? Understanding "the peasant mentality" of a black landlord and her daughter, Wright asserts in one of the final chapters, allowed him to discover "the full degree to which [his] life at home had cut [him] off, not only from white people but from Negroes as well" (205). One answer to the question above is that *Black Boy (American Hunger)*, read as Wright intended, describes a migrant life in which mature Communism helps to calm youthful disquiet over "the essential bleakness of black life in America." What the northern portion of Wright's autobiography terms "the first total emotional commitment of [its hero's] life"—his conversion to the cultural value of "forgotten folk" aroused by Stalin—actually follows the southern portion's mulling over black cultural absence. The memoir's turn from *Black Boy*'s "Southern Night" to *American Hunger*'s "Horror and . . . Glory" thus entails movement from fear to relative faith on the subject of African-American folk culture, movement fueled mainly by Communism. That Wright chose this arc for his memoir, composed even as his ties to the party were fraying, suggests the depth of his attachment to the folkisms of the left. This attachment would wither in the 1940s—witness *Native Son, The Outsider*, et cetera—but as a result of Communism's progressive weakness, not strength, in the Wright world system. Even his autobiography, a product of 1943 and reputedly the most folk-hostile text in the African-American canon, can't help painting Communism as a bridge between bleak and bright insight into black folks.

Back in 1937 one of the parties in the Hurston-Wright debate declared that an identifiably African-American "culture has stemmed mainly from two sources: 1) the Negro church; 2) and the folklore of the Negro people" (55). In the same outing, s/he recommended that black writers reveal the "revolutionary significance" of this culture's "nationalist tendencies" (59). It was Wright, laying down literary law in the manifesto "Blueprint for Negro Writing," published in the journal that succeeded the *Challenge* of "The Fire and the Cloud." Until we recognize that Wright approached the cultural value and literary use of black folk *through* Communism's sense of "revolutionary significance"—not despite it—we will misrecognize both the great debate with Hurston and the equally intricate relationship between African-American writers and the Old Left.

6 · Native Sons Divorce: A Conclusion

Let me give examples of how I began to develop the dim negative of Bigger. I met white writers who talked of their responses, who told me how whites reacted to this lurid American scene. And, as they talked, I'd translate what they said in terms of Bigger's life. But what was more important still, I read their novels. Here, for the first time, I found ways and techniques of gauging meaningfully the effects of American civilization upon the personalities of people.

—Richard Wright, "How 'Bigger' Was Born" (1940)

In the small-time vice-village of Matamoros I took a room in a hotel run by a woman who had entitled herself "The Mother of the Americans," though she didn't look like anyone's mother. There I wrote the first chapters of a novel I first called *Native Son.*

—Nelson Algren, 1965 preface to *Somebody in Boots* (1935)

Days after the first, March 1940 printing of his own novel entitled *Native Son,* Richard Wright mailed Nelson Algren a complimentary copy enhanced with a lavish inscription:

To—
My old friend
Nelson
Who I believe is still
the best writer of good
prose in the U.S.A.
—Dick.   (qtd. in Drew 121)

Algren, yet to become the celebrity underworld connoisseur of *The Man with the Golden Arm* (1949) and *A Walk on the Wild Side* (1956), received Wright's words as an inspiration and a summons, a confidence booster when facing publishers and a challenge at the writing desk. "Dear Dick," he quickly wrote in reply, "Native Son [*sic*] arrived this morning. I haven't begun it yet because I can't get past the autograph. I hope you meant it all the way, because it did something to me: I had a luncheon engagement with a man from Houghton-Mifflin and I guess before he was through he figured he was talking . . . to Emile Zola. . . . In short, I'm now hoping I can do something—just a little—toward earning that inscription" (qtd. in Drew 121). To Wright, at least, Algren already merited the inscription for years of literary camaraderie. Born just months apart, the two had been intimates since the early 1930s. When Algren's famous lover, Simone de Beauvoir, typed him as "that classic American species: self-made-leftist-writer" (327), she could have been classifying Wright; above all, the Algren-Wright friendship was sealed by concurrent self-making on the turf of Chicago's literary left. Nelson Ahlgren Abraham, the son of nonobservant Jews who settled in the stockyard city on the make, managed to obtain the B.A. that racism kept Wright from pursuing. All the same, graduating in the Depression year of 1931 with blond hair and a business card reading "editor . . . headline writer . . . et cetera" was no guarantee of upward mobility: before the economic crisis peaked, Algren would be arrested for stealing a typewriter (qtd. in Drew 32). Like Wright, Algren thus spent his early twenties drifting through a series of demeaning temporary jobs that fanned his desire to write and inclined him to Communism. Months of sobering adventure hoboing from New Orleans to the Southwest were followed by intense weeks of literary labor at his parent's Chicago home. In 1933, armed with an acceptance letter from *Story* magazine, he made his way to the John Reed Club in the downtown Loop, a party society open to younger artists willing to support "the revolutionary labor movement" and oppose "all forms of Negro discrimination" ("Draft Manifesto" 177).[1] There, Algren heard talks by the likes of James T. Farrell and threw himself into *The New Masses*, warring theories of proletarian literature, and the lives of other aspiring writers who shared his excitement over angry social description. "Dick" Wright, the club's rising star and most earnest member, became a particular accomplice.

Algren's college interest in sociology was rekindled by Wright's Chicago School contacts; his fuzzy comprehension of Marxism was focused by Wright's disciplined readings. The two shared what other Reed Club writers considered a suspect fascination with the lumpenproletariat, Marx and Engels' "social scum" hustling and intriguing beneath the history-bearing working class (*Manifesto* 482). Their common attraction to what became the slogans of existentialism—dread, existence, alienation—would later be confirmed by similar approval from de Beauvoir and Jean-Paul Sartre.[2] Some of the same non-Parisian mentors favored Algren and Wright: Jack Conroy, editor of the proudly midwestern *Anvil*, was both Wright's first publisher with a national reputation and a warm commentator on Algren's early stories (Wixson 361, 364–65). One Chicago acquaintance noted that Algren, usually diffident, "seemed especially good and kindly with Wright," and his friend reciprocated (Drew 103). After settling in New York in 1937, Wright led a visiting Algren on a grand tour of clubs in Greenwich Village and Harlem. When back in Illinois, Wright often stopped at Algren's rooms, once bringing along poet Margaret Walker, to whom Wright recommended Algren's advice while she completed *For My People* (Drew 103). As Wright was naming his first successful novel in 1939,[3] he had good reason to appreciate the continuing friendship; as the second epigraph to this chapter hints, Algren was the source of the tag "Native Son." *Somebody in Boots* (1935), Algren's own first novel and one of the first hundred books in Wright's private library (Fabre, *The World* 16), would have worn the name if not for a late shift: "The Native Son" slipped from Algren's title page to the title of part one. The "Mother of the Americans" under whose roof Algren wrote *Somebody in Boots* thus wound up nurturing Wright's *Native Son* by way of Algren's, two classic U.S. proletarian fictions in which righteous proletarians run scared.

Wright's novel took hints from *Somebody in Boots* greater than its working title. In one sense, Wright's inscription honoring his friend only returned the favor: Algren had deeply inscribed *Native Son*'s representation of a pure yet criminal product of America with as much native sympathy for fascism as Communism. Wright's novel's large and small resemblances to *Somebody in Boots*, seldom mentioned in the stacks of commentary on *Native Son*, provide the subject of this final chapter.[4] At its outset, I should confess my lack of interest in simply filling a gap in the study of Wright's sources or in recouping a simply inspiring case of interracial-intertextual bonding between literary Communists. What most impresses me about the congruence of the novels is its discordance with most convictions about the arrival of a post-Communist period in African-American letters. From the perspective of the Algren-Wright overlap, the timing and thoroughness of black writing's withdrawal from the Old Left looks somewhat less clear-cut, for the routine verdict that black literary Communism was entombed by *Native Son* seems less justifiable. Obviously, Wright's novel is no paean to easy integration on the Old Left; indeed, some party reviewers protested his hesitance to lead African-American protagonist Bigger Thomas into the light shined by white party defenders. Ironically, however, *Native Son*'s frustration of the fraternal plots of Communist interracialism fraternally reiterates that of *Somebody in Boots*, originally dedicated to "The Homeless Boys of America" (McCollum 10). Wright and Algren, Chicago confidants and comrades, joined the proletarian big leagues with allied antibuddy narratives. Both *Native Son* and *Somebody in Boots* consummate with the drama of a black-white male pair failing to bond despite the adhesive of Communism; both therefore cast doubt on the solidity of the New Negro–Old Left duo introduced during the Harlem Renaissance. Yet in the interracial interdependence of their challenge to the party's interracial imaginary, the novels together expose holes in the final chapters of prevailing cautionary accounts of African-American writing and Communism, accounts that Wright's subsequent memoirs and fictions did much to frame in the decades following *Native Son.*

Reading Wright's Slow Exit

As I suggested at the close of the last chapter, Wright's work in the busy years after *Uncle Tom's Children* disclosed the dimming of his hopes for a forceful African-American folk Communism. It was not that he disowned the party with the success of the collection, providing ammunition for the slur that the Old Left's cultural circles held only apprentices and mediocrities: he abandoned the party's Chicago branch in 1937, but he joined the staff of *The Daily Worker* and a Communist cell in his new home of New York City, where he basked in dozens of party events feting the book in 1938 and 1939. What Wright forfeited in the wake of *Uncle Tom's Children* was the certainty that the party's advocacy of African-American rights and culture allowed it to sound the depths of racialized identities inside and outside the Black Belt.

In "Bright and Morning Star," a story of a once-Christian black mother and her Communist son appended to the second, 1940 edition of *Uncle Tom's Children,* Wright reprises the theme of southern black Christianity shading into Marxist eschatology found in "Fire and Cloud." Fresh on the page, however, is the implication that black folk wisdom and Communist strategy are not yet smoothly commensurable. Despite the title referring at once to the Jesus of the spirituals and the red star of Communism, the finale hurls the reader back into the retrograde cycle of interracial violence traced in the opening stories. Aunt Sue's nagging suspicion that whites of any politics cannot be trusted is horrifically confirmed when she discovers that her son Johnny-Boy has been betrayed by a false comrade. She rushes through the woods with a revolver concealed in a winding sheet, only to watch her child die at the hands of white torturers who laugh at the idea that "niggers kin make a revolution. . . . A black republic" (435). Revenging Johnny-Boy with a bullet and her own noble death, Sue becomes one of the few gun-toting New Negro women in the literary martyrology indebted to Harlem Renaissance Marxism. Through her act of heroic self-immolation, Wright remedies boys-only readings of "If We Must Die" and his own stock of black women characters who "codify . . . the behavior of blacks according to the dictates of whites" (T. Davis, "Race" 433). But the blood-stained outcome of the text also jars the interracial Marxist faith early Harlem Marxists hoped to anneal through jointly witnessed radical martyrdom. The murder of Johnny-Boy, the black party organizer engaged to a poor white party woman, exists to be avenged because he "sees rich men n . . . po men," not "white n . . . black," a condition revealed as an inability to see part of the present (418).

Party-aligned critics were willing to pardon the ambivalence of "Bright and Morning Star." With the good notices for the original edition of *Uncle Tom's Children*, Wright had become one of the names to remember when Communism was accused of philistinism; his failure to place a rousing interracial conclusion on a story otherwise heroizing the makers of the southern black republic thus could be ignored or resourcefully embraced as a reminder that black nationalism was "not simply . . . a barrier to be superseded on the path to integrationist consciousness, but . . . a reality that cannot be readily dispelled and that must form part of the Communist movement's discourse and program" (Foley, *Radical* 209). Harder to swallow was the pronounced equivocation at the conclusion of Wright's *Native Son* (1940), the first Book-of-the-Month-Club selection written by an African American and the best-selling product of the black literary presence in interwar Communism. Despite prolonged instruction from Wright's sympathetic white party lawyer, Boris Max, Bigger Thomas—Uncle Tom's disrespectful grandchild—never agrees that his violent life finds authoritative meaning amid class history. In a final jail-cell conversation held as Bigger awaits execution, Max explains that the "owners of the buildings" suppress

> black people more than others because they say black people are inferior. But, Bigger, they say that *all* people who work are inferior. And the rich people don't want to change things; they'll lose too much. But deep down in them they feel like you feel, Bigger, and in order to keep what they've got, they make themselves believe that men who work are not quite human. . . . But on both sides men want to live; men are fighting for life. Who will win? Well, the side that feels life most, the side with the most humanity and the most men. That's why . . . y-you've got to b-believe in yourself, Bigger.   (*Native Son* 848; emphasis in original)

Bigger follows Max only part of the way from race to class to Marxian contest of feeling. While he laughingly assures his lawyer, "I reckon I believe in myself. . . . I ain't got nothing else" (848), he will not situate his faith within a grander existential rivalry between "rich people" and "men who work." What's more, he insists that his murders of girlfriend Bessie Mears and patronizing white party ally Mary Dalton lie at the heart of his self-validation. Audaciously signifying on Max's courtroom claim that his crimes "charged [his life] with a new meaning" (824), Bigger cries out, "I didn't want to kill! . . . But what I killed for, I *am*! It must've been pretty deep in me to make me kill! I must have felt it awful hard to murder. . . . What I killed for must've been good!" (849; emphasis in original). Max, who raises "his hand to touch Bigger, but [does] not," flees in despair, "grop[ing] for his hat like a blind man," unable to perceive the excellence in Bigger's creation through homicide (849). At the telling moment of fate in *Native Son*'s book of the same name, Wright's heir of both the Scottsboro defense and Hughes's black-embracing white hands fails a stringent upgrade of the "acid test of white friendship." In 1921 the Harlem Marxist journal *The Crusader* had proposed that this test be "simply whether [the white] person is willing to see the Negro defend himself with arms against aggression, and willing even to see Negroes killing his own (white) people in defense of Negro rights" ("The Acid Test" 9). In 1940 the ante was upped by Wright, now himself a Harlem-based Marxist: white radical friends must look squarely at his native son's elastic definition of self-defense and imperative violence, as well as the possibility that the meaning discovered there will not fulfill Marxist forecasts. As increasing numbers of readers have observed, Wright was far less forceful in imagining Bessie and Mary's sacrifice to Bigger's self-composition.

Not often noticed in *Native Son* is how Wright's concluding acid test for white radicals gains bite from the novel's earlier play with the kind of interracial triangles seen in early party Scottsboro discourse. Bigger murders first at the end of a night in which he is treated to unearned crossracial intimacy by Mary and her boyfriend, Jan Erlone, a more committed white Communist who samples soul food while declaring that African Americans have "got to be organized. They've got spirit. They'll give the Party something it needs" (517). As Mary and Jan make love in the back seat of the car that Bigger chauffeurs, he is "filled with a sense of them, [and] his muscles gr[o]w gradually taut" in response (518). Later, back at the Daltons' posh home, "the thought and conviction that Jan had had her a lot flash[es] through [Bigger's] mind" as he deposits a drunken Mary on her bed (524). His quickening desire and "her hips mov[ing] in a hard and veritable grind" seal Bigger's fear that he will be charged with rape, a terror that leads him to suffocate Mary when her blind mother enters the room unexpectedly (524). The possibility that Mary dies because Jan has "used Miss Dalton as bait" to lure Bigger to Communism is explicitly suggested by Buckley, Bigger's vicious prosecutor, and is thus associated with the worst of bargains between race- and red-baiting (743): *Native Son,* unlike *Invisible Man,* does not instruct that white party men deploy white temptresses to "confus[e] the class struggle with the ass struggle" (Ellison, *Invisible Man* 418).[5] Nonetheless, the scene of Jan's jailhouse visit to Bigger is orchestrated as the young Communist's unyielding attempt to secure an interracial male bond over Mary's passing. Even while mourning Mary and seething at Bigger—"I loved that girl you killed" (714)—Jan decides that "maybe in a certain sense, I'm the one who's really guilty" (713). He respectfully asks Bigger if he may "be on your side" against the white mob hungry to punish a rape that wasn't: "I can fight this thing with you, just like you've started it. I can come from all of those white people and stand here with you" (714). Yet Wright proceeds to deny the "traditional structure of male bonding that Sedgwick has defined," notes Robyn Wiegman, a framework "in which 'the spectacle of the ruin of a woman . . . is just the right lubricant for an adjustment of differentials of power [among men]' " (103; ellipses and editorial comment in original). Near the close of Jan's jailhouse visit, he stands not in Bigger's corner but "with white faces along the wall," the racial aspect of the vile Buckley and the sightless Mrs. Dalton blending into Jan's own; Bigger, from a distance, stares "feverishly and defiantly at [them all]" (722). Max's flight from Bigger's declaration of violent principles is thus preceded and burdened by Jan's incomplete extension of red fraternity, inadequately redeemed by Bigger's last-page request that Max "Tell Mister. . . . Tell Jan hello" (850). That the murder of a near-Communist gives occasion to this drive for brotherhood is evidence of Wright's confidence in the strength of party opposition to the myth of the black rapist. At the same time, the fact that Jan's effort builds on the destruction of Mary and Bessie and the sacrifice of his greatest love suggests that Wright saw prohibitive costs in combating the rape myth through triangular rhetorics.

Interestingly, prominent black party figures such as James W. Ford and Benjamin Davis were among the most vocal of Communists to object to *Native Son*'s seeming excess of "nationalist racial spirit" (qtd. in Fabre, *The Unfinished* 184). Davis, the International Labor Defense (ILD) authority responsible for the major review in *The Sunday Worker,* protested that Wright's exacting test of white friendship did not keep him from casting blacks as social casualties rather than as rebellious political actors. "Every single Negro character, including Bigger's own family," he objected, "is pretty much beaten and desperate—utterly devoid of the progressive developments among the Negro people, and in a city like Chicago where the Negroes are so politically articulate" (B. Davis 73–74). Where was evidence of "the great role which the Negroes play in the Party—from top to bottom—as the best instrument to fight for the full liberation of their people" (76)? Davis's evaluation demonstrates that African-American Communists, too, could read the post-1930s' Wright as a salesman of victimology, wary that his respect for the nationalism in party African-American policy had become destructively fettered to portraits in black dormancy and an inaccurately whitewashed Communism. For his part, however, Algren thought such criticism was parochial and ill-advised (Drew 125). So did Mike Gold, who jumped to the novel's defense in his *Daily Worker* column after first reporting only that "Dick Wright Gives America a Significant Picture in *Native Son*" (qtd. in Fabre, *The Unfinished* 184). Wright approached this change of heart in the seasoned arbiter of proletarian literature as an opportunity to vent frustration with intraparty hostility. In a lengthy private letter to Gold, he admitted that "until you spoke up in its defense, I'd all but given up hope that our movement could look deeper into the book, that we could doff our set of stock-reactions and think creatively about it" (qtd. in Fabre, *The Unfinished* 185). Wright proceeded to characterize his novel as a challenge to the tyranny of the "positive image," party-edition, and to the authoritative confidence that African Americans were on the verge of class war:

> There is [a] notion prevailing among ninety percent of all party members that all party comrades should be represented in fiction as white knights charging heroically into the enemy. Well, life just ain't that way; people just don't act that way. . . . I do not agree with Ben Davis when he implies that the majority of the Negroes are with the labor movement. Such an implication can become a tragedy as grave as that which the German working class made in estimating Hitler's chances for success. My aim in depicting Jan was to show that even for that great Party which has thrown down a challenge to America on the Negro Question such as has no other party, there is much, much to do, and, above all, to understand. . . . Despite all the heroic struggles the Party has put forward to win the Negro, it is still possible for a wave of nationalism to sweep the Negro people today.   (qtd. in Fabre, *The Unfinished* 185–86)

Wright's references to "our movement" and the "heroic struggles" of a "great Party" indicate that he believed that *Native Son*'s critique was in-house. His very impulse to inform Communism's senior literary umpire of his aims suggests that he hoped to win party exoneration. As I have noted, Wright did not break with Communism's "challenge . . . on the Negro Question" for two to four years after the Gold letter; to point up a single instance of basic loyalty, his displeasure with inflated self-estimations in the party did not deter him from accepting the vice-presidency of the American Peace Mobilization in late 1940, a Communist coalition against U.S. intervention in World War II demanded by Stalin's arrangement with Hitler. For most academic critics, however, *Native Son* flags the very moment when Wright's secession from the party became public or inevitable.

At one limit of this widespread understanding of the novel is the implication that Wright offers a thickly symbolic, brilliantly dramatic, anti-Communist screed. For example, the long close reading at the core of Joyce Ann Joyce's *Richard Wright's Art of Tragedy* (1986), the most consulted formalist study of *Native Son*,[6] concludes by suggesting that Wright paints the party that defends Bigger as no less racist than the parties who condemn him to death. In Joyce's appraisal, Max's eloquent defense "lead[s] us to believe that he is the one character in the novel capable of understanding" Wright's protagonist (111). Max's final alarm over Bigger's tragic epiphany, however, reveals that he and his party see Bigger as "a mere object" (116). Like State's Attorney Buckley, who emblemizes "mainstream America," Max, "representing the 'liberal' Communist party," employs his client "to enhance [his] political career" (116). Even granting Joyce's vision of Max's bigoted instrumentalism, however, it is hard to picture the career enrichment secured by his failed outing in the radical legal defense game; actual party attorney and Scottsboro veteran Benjamin Davis judged that "Max should have argued for Bigger's acquittal . . . , and should have helped stir the Negro and white masses to get that acquittal. From Max's whole conduct the first business of the Communist Party or of the I.L.D. would have been to chuck him out of the case" (76). Joyce's accent on the similarities between Max and Buckley nevertheless illuminates what can be called the *Invisible Man* reading of *Native Son*, the not-uncommon detection in Wright's text of an Ellisonian pattern of white institutional failures to glimpse blackness as presence that taints Communist brotherhood as much as its flag-waving enemies. More prevalent than this assessment of Bigger's sheer invisibility to the party, however, are interpretations that view him as the messenger of Wright's assured political conversion. Not for the last time, Donald B. Gibson's influential 1969 article on *Native Son* argues "that the thought processes leading to Wright's break with the Party were already in motion as early as 1939," the year Wright's final draft was set (104).

Max and his political company are not completely without recent academic defenders. Barbara Foley's work on "Race, Class, and the 'Negro Question' " in *Radical Representations* (1993) contends that "it is a mistake to conclude that the politics of *Native Son* diverge substantially from those of the CP or that the novel presages Wright's split with the party" (209). To start, Foley elaborates on Davis's unhappiness with the novel's lapses in documenting the make-up of Communism: "Wright's cynical reduction of the party to Jan, Max, and the wealthy fellow-traveler Mary Dalton gives a distorted representation of the composition of the Chicago CP, which by the late 1930s was an integrated organization rooted in the working class" (209). Yet her case against assertions of the party's irrelevance or hostility to Bigger rests on a sophisticated internal analysis of the novel's distinct narrative strata. Wright, she observes, did not confine himself "to focaliz[ing] the narrative through [Bigger's] consciousness," saturated with an "intense nationalism" (209). Instead, he overlaid Bigger's view with two "statements which insist that the reader contextualize Bigger's life and thoughts in a broader explanatory framework" (209–10): namely, Max's prolonged address to the court that tries Bigger and the 1940 essay "How 'Bigger' Was Born," which Wright included with every edition of *Native Son* after the first. Whatever the aesthetic justice of Max's lengthy speech, regretted nearly as often as the final chapters of *Huckleberry Finn,* Wright there addresses Bigger's crimes and fate in terms of Communism's Black Belt theory of African-American self-determination: "Bigger is a member of a nation within a nation; his existential nationalism is a reflection of this sociological fact" (210). The autocritique "How 'Bigger' Was Born," on the other hand, stresses "Bigger's symbolic status as an exemplar of class-based disaffection—possessed of '*snarled* and *confused* nationalist feelings' but nonetheless a product of a quintessentially capitalist social process" (211; emphasis in original).

Foley's argument for *Native Son*'s interlocutory Communism is compelling, not least because it unveils the dialogic complexity within the novel's notorious didacticism and accounts interestingly for Max's not-always-stimulating address. What remains to be explored, however, is the intraparty dialogue that shapes the most intensely nationalist of the novel's narrative levels, that focalized through Bigger's consciousness. The resistant awareness of Wright's protagonist, I want to argue, is filtered through the corresponding consciousness of Algren's protagonist in *Somebody in Boots,* not excluding those scenes of hindered red interracialism discussed above. Even the narrative layer presenting the greatest threat to Communist interracialism in *Native Son,* then, partakes of something of its target. This does not mean, of course, that Wright's over-all challenge is toothless, hypocritical, or unoriginal. Instead, it signals that Wright's critique—and *Native Son*—issues from within and funda-mentally addresses the Old Left's shifting theater of political contention and sometimes messy interracial exchange. I trust that this effort to uncover the dissonant Communism of Wright's novel is neither idle nor fussily doctrinaire. The nature and timing of Wright's literary farewell to the party has major consequences for cultural and political history, given Wright's onetime status as the world symbol of black writing and his con-tinuing reputation as the black Communist writer par excellence. Thanks to the proximate appearance of the Nazi-Soviet nonaggression pact, the after-Depression decade, and *Native Son*, 1939–40 has stood as the most common dating of black writing's withdrawal from the Old Left.[7] Despite the interwar span of my study, I hope that Wright's contribution to this eagerly post-Communist chronology will be less sure by the end of my conclusion.

The Other Bigger

Cass McKay, the "Texan-American" native son at the helm of Nelson Algren's *Somebody in Boots*, is a final descendant of "pioneer woodsmen" reduced to privation, illegality, and obsolescence well before the Great Depression (16). Among other business, the novel Cass dominates pro-poses that the "wild and hardy tribe that had given Jackson and Lincoln birth" (Preface 8) has degenerated into "white trash," that U.S. popula-tion created at the "confluence of white poverty and white criminality" (Newitz and Wray 175). In the absence of wilderness to subdue in the name of the nation, Algren's illiterate teenage hero reverses his ancestors' steps when fleeing his father's murderous temper, riding the rails north and east from his rural Texas home as the economic crisis of the 1930s deepens. Cass fades into the company of hoboes and, while never inured "to see[ing] the shadow of pain cross a human face" (*Somebody* 37), grows less sensitive to his own shame and hunger. On the best days on the road, he might ferret out "a head of lettuce the inner leaves of which were still fresh and green. That *was* luck" (109; emphasis in original). Only two locations—prison and Chicago—hold him long and concentrate Algren's rambling, picaresque narrative, often as frantically idle as the vagrant Cass. In the first resting place—prison—Algren's protagonist refines his judgment that "there were only two kinds of men wherever you went— the men who wore boots, and the men who ran" (55). Initially seen "cross[ing] . . . booted toes under him" (125), Nubby O'Neill, the toughest inmate in the El Paso County Jail, beats Cass into the recognition that some of the boot wearers do not "Own All" (83). In the second resting place—Chicago—Algren's hero discovers a talent for armed robbery and learns to love Norah Egan, a sweatshop seamstress turned prostitute. Cass, like Bigger after him, finds unprecedented strength and purpose in crime: "For the first time in his life he went toward danger without fear. . . . He had found something worth fighting for, and he was going to fight" (192). His confidence vanishes, however, when Norah abandons him during a botched store burglary. A heartbroken Cass returns from a second prison stay to a job in a burlesque house and to tutelage from a member of the city's large party contingent. Like Wright's Jan and Max, Algren's Communist teacher fails to transform his delinquent pupil's hatred for cruel "somebodies in boots" into a politicized opposition to the bourgeoisie, adamantly troped by Algren as shady pimps and "big-business scurve[s]" (237). Algren's antibildungsroman accordingly concludes with its hero having learned precious little—and certainly nothing lasting from Communism—in the transition from adolescence to adulthood. Despite all Cass's wandering, he ends within the same cramped horizon in which he began, his highest aspiration being to carve a "Hell-Blazer" tattoo on his chest (254).

In his exemplary literary history *The Radical Novel in the United States* (1956), Walter Rideout places *Somebody in Boots* within proletarianism's "bottom dogs" subgenre, a designation usurped from the title of a 1930 Edward Dahlberg novel. In distinction to narratives of strikes and proletarian conversions, Rideout's bottom-dogs books "ambush the reader with a relentlessly objective description of life in the lower depths" and do without "the assistance of slogans, resolutions, and other revolutionary gestures" (185). *Ambush* is the right word for Algren's assaultive figuration of the social violence of scrambling poverty. No fewer than four spectacles of decapitation involving dolls, beasts, and humans instruct Cass and the reader that the bodies of the hungry are condemned: "He was lying in an open lot that appeared to be chiefly a dumping ground. It smelled of dead flesh. The first thing he saw clearly was the head of a dog whose body was gone" (50). Still, Algren's scenes of dead dogs and punished boys at the bottom may be other than "objective" even according to the codes of literary naturalism. An epigraph from Charles Baudelaire—"*Harlots and Hunted*" (79; emphasis in original)—is only one trace of *Somebody's* brew of "reportage and nightmare, journalism and surrealism, sociology and poetry" (Cappetti 156). As Carla Cappetti remarks, Algren assumed "the poetic legacy of symbolism and surrealism" along with "the empirical legacy of the realist and naturalist traditions" (156), a double inheritance *Somebody's* infernal dogs share with *Native Son's* portentous rats and cats. Algren also assumed lower-depths gloom and grotesquery without disowning Marxist enrichment: here, too, *Somebody in Boots* parallels *Native Son* and fits somewhat awkwardly into the bottom-dogs prototype.

Like Wright, Algren combines a main narrative deferential to his protagonist's purblind vision with luminous alternative discourses aiming at superior explanatory power. Part 4 of *Somebody in Boots*, "One Spring in This City," counterposes disgusted, millenarian Marxian interpolations with Cass's obedient excitement over the "zigzag riot of fakery" at the Chicago World's Fair (235). "Be pure in your hearts," Algren's prophetic voice advises those who have duped Cass, "be proud yet a little while, wave your flags, sing your hymns, close your eyes, save your souls, go on grabbing. Get all you can while you may. For the red day will come for your kind, be assured" (238). Both part 3 and part 4 lead with clarifying epigraphs from *The Communist Manifesto*. Algren's jeremiad on "the red day" to come in the "One Spring in This City" section is anticipated by Marx and Engels' canonical guarantee that "in place of the old bourgeois society, . . . we shall have an association, in which the free development of each is the condition for the free development of all" (qtd. on 233). Part 3's epigraph features the *Manifesto's* less sanguine forecast for the lumpenproletariat, decaying in the face of capitalist industry: "The 'dangerous class,' the social scum . . . , that passively rotting mass thrown off by the lowest layers of the old society, may, here and there, be swept into the movement by a proletarian revolution; its conditions of life, however, prepare it far more for the part of a bribed tool of reactionary intrigue" (qtd. on 155). With this second *Manifesto* quotation, the likeness between Algren's and Wright's insertions of broadening discourses into protagonist-focused narratives becomes more than structural: "How 'Bigger' Was Born" also explains its hero's limitations with reference to the ideological ambivalence of Marx and Engels' lumpen. Portions of Wright's essay read like attempts to flesh out Algren's direct citation with the benefit of twentieth-century hindsight. Wright declares that the profoundly national Bigger could be captured by either revolution or reaction: "An American product, a native son of this land, [he] carried within him the potentialities of either Communism or Fascism" ("How 'Bigger' " 866). Complementing the lumpen of 1848, Bigger "is a dispossessed and disinherited man"; complementing Cass, "he is all of this, and he lives amid the greatest possible plenty on earth and he is looking and feeling for a way out" (866).[8]

The pedagogical program behind the pointed nativeness of Wright's lumpen hero is not identical to that behind the Americanism of Algren's native son, of course. *Somebody in Boots* luxuriates in the ideological contradictions that emerge as Cass, a free, white, and youthful heir of officially honored frontier yeomen, is dismantled by an American "CENTURY OF PROGRESS" (238); *Native Son*, on the other hand, relishes the indigenous manufacture of an urbanized, post–Great Migration incarnation of the "bad nigger," just a twentieth-century wrinkle on America's officially dishonored nightmare Other. Both these ventures, however, draw on the founders of Communism to elucidate a native son unaligned with either side of the bourgeois/proletariat and fascist/Communist divides; in the process, both challenge revolutionary certitude while exalting the revolutionary classics. The unassailably American bloodlines of Wright and Algren's criminal heroes thus query U.S. party optimism, grounded in patriotism with the 1935–39 Popular Front, even as they satirize 1920s' nativist efforts "to transform American identity from the sort of thing that could be acquired (through naturalization) into the sort of thing that had to be inherited (from one's parents)" (Michaels 8).

When layed out as directly as this, the partnership between *Somebody in Boots* and *Native Son* seems overt and unextraordinary. Even so, several generations' worth of criticism has snubbed *Native Son's* relationship to the novel where it found a name. Algren's evaporating U.S. status as an author of serious fiction is one reason why. Beginning his career as the "Proust of the Proletariat" (Wright's phrase) and going on to win the first National Book Award for 1949's *The Man with the Golden Arm*, Algren lived long enough to see his politicized symbolist-naturalist style stricken from the record of the literary (qtd. in Drew 129). As late as 1960 Wright was willing to include Algren alongside Twain, Proust, Dreiser, Dostoevsky, and the like on a list of "the great novelists I reread with the greatest pleasure" (qtd. in Fabre, *The World* 15). Non-American readers seemed to agree with Wright's estimate, snapping up Sartre's translation of *Never Come Morning* in France and a dozen other foreign-language renderings from Brazil to Japan (Cappetti 147). By then, however, U.S. cold war critics were making a habit of disciplining the proletarian old days via Algren's reputation. In a 1956 review, for example, Leslie Fiedler dismissed him as "the bard of the stumblebum," a marketeer of "sentimentality pretending to be politics" (qtd. in Cappetti 149). Relegating Algren to an inert radical past, the eventual author of *Love and Death in the American Novel* (1960) dubbed him a "museum piece, the last of the Proletarian Writers" (qtd. on 149). Robert Bone and other early advocates of African-American fiction in white academia were understandably reluctant to impede progress "Toward an [aesthetically] Autonomous Negro Art" by associating the African-American tradition's paramount author with such a relic (Bone, *The Negro Novel* 249).[9]

Yet Algren's declining fortune is probably not the strongest reason for the lack of studies pairing *Native Son*'s Bigger and *Somebody*'s Cass. For all the similarities to Wright's hero, Algren's protagonist is the sort of restive white racist who might join the mob clamoring for Bigger's execution. Whenever toughness is required, Cass fills his speech with "shines" and "niggers"; falling in with a bunch of hoboes led by Jones, a coolly vicious white northerner, he participates in the gang rape of a black woman drifter whose husband has been killed by a lynch mob. "White! White! Mah Joe you burnt!" she cries, as Cass and his peers prepare to carry out the interracial sexual brutality in whose name Joe was punished (93). To Algren's uprooted southwesterner, blacks representing the law of the boot wearers replace Indians and cattle-rustling badmen as preferred emblems of evil. Lounging in a lakefront park near the spot where the 1919 Chicago race riot began, Cass vows "to get me a couple o' them nigger cops out in Englewood, with both guns a-blazin' like Wild Bill Hickok's" (178). Cass's lover, Norah, is similarly inclined: "I hate Nigger kids," she thinks, disgustedly spotting children who could be Bigger's young brother and sister (166). Cass and Norah's racism is cast throughout as the dangerous refuge of a white lumpen blasted by the Depression, a last fund of rank and explanation from which to assemble an identity more dignified than Marx and Engels' "social scum" (Marxism's "white trash"?). However destructive of selves and necessary affiliations, this racism authorizes Cass to explain unemployment in Chicago without recourse to scenarios of personal moral failing: "In Texas it's Mexes an' up here it's shokes. Say, didn't I see twenty nigger cops out in Englewood? Didn't ah see twenty dinges with mailbags draggin' letters all over the derned post-office one day?" (212).

What distinguishes Algren's early analysis of this compensatory racism is the proposition that it is experienced as compensatory—even as counterfeit—by those to whom it pledges the comforts of whiteness. For example, Cass must consciously remind himself of his black hating as he finds himself drawn to Matches, an African-American "match," or double, in the form of a fellow vagrant of his own age and height. "Ah'd better shake this shine," Cass is forced to "caution . . . himself" (119), discovering that he empathizes enough to adjust the shoe on Matches' swollen, scaled-over foot. Nubby O'Neill's most precious point of honor—his hostility to "everything not white and American"—is a "highly-feigned hatred" (125), no less affected than his favorite tattoo. "Texas Kid. His Best Arm," it reads, though he is in fact "from South Chicago" and his hand has been amputated after an industrial accident (128). The white desire for blackface transformation, Eric Lott speculates, emerges "when the lines of 'race' appear both intractable and obstructive" ("White" 475); Algren alternatively suggests that during periods in which economic suffering and homelessness obviously become no respecters of color, these lines appear far too permeable and destructive of privilege, making a white application of "whiteface" both more necessary and more laborious than ever. Early in his travels on the bum, Cass indeed discovers that one is not born a white but must act to become one; as Nubby puts it, there are "things . . . a man got to learn before he's a *real* white man" (169; emphasis in original). Roaming through a city park in El Paso with Matches, Cass is shocked to hear a white cop address him as "nigger":

> Cass cocked his head, half-unable to believe what he had just heard. Slowly then he understood: a white man who walked with a "nigger" was a "nigger" too. He recognized the park bull as the other bull took his arm, and he said, "Ah'm not no nigger," but the bull made no reply.
>
> Cass wasn't afraid, somehow. . . . Going to jail was all a part of this life; no one escaped it for very long and he'd been pretty lucky for a long time now. What he didn't like, what got him by the short hairs, was that crack about being a nigger. . . .
>
> "Ah'm not no nigger," he repeated; but the cop didn't seem to hear. (122)

What stops a white man in training from "walk[ing] with" and becoming a "nigger," Cass discovers, is something less forgiving than a private decision to arrest the racial Other inside him (an internal Other, in Cass's case, much more expressive of "excessive" human compassion than of the usual indulgence in "exotic food, strange and noisy music, outlandish bodily exhibitions, or unremitting sexual appetite" [Lott, "White" 480]). A sweeping system of social coercion, fonder of punishment than discipline and not confined to park police, also enforces Cass's will to whiteness. The periods in which he fails to recall his hatred of African Americans invariably end in confinement and pain imposed by "real white m[e]n" with better memories. Tending to Matches, for instance, wins Cass not just a jail term but a beating by fellow prisoner Nubby, who finds the new inmate guilty of being a "nigger lover . . . , very strong on anythin' black" (126–27). Algren's protagonist initially manages to avoid the physical penalty for this crime by sobbing out the assurance "Ah *hates* them ugly black sonabitches" (127; emphasis in original). When he fails to thrash a new Mexican prisoner with convincing enjoyment, however, he is forced to take the victim's place, once more learning that a white man loses any special protection from lawbreaking when coming to the aid of his racial "inferiors." In the minutes during which Nubby's thick belt lands on his backside, "pain taught Cass that he must never again treat a black man or a brown as he would a white" (140). With such scenes seeking objective correlatives for the social policing of whiteness, Algren suggests that the frontiers of "blanchitude" (Wynter 150) are not merely unself-evident but patrolled by anxious white troopers, some themselves imprisoned by the racial state. Outstripping much of the most radical recent academic work on whiteness, *Somebody in Boots* insists that the enforcement of racial boundaries takes the form of white-on-white as well as interracial violence. In discussing *Native Son*, Virginia Whatley Smith comments that Bigger's entrapment in "a carceral society" can be seen in his suffocating ghetto "freedom" as well as in his official imprisonment (97); in Algren's novel, Cass's time inside and outside jail entails a similarly expansive incarceration by whiteness's putative benefits.

Ironically, what may have most deterred explorations of the common terrain of *Somebody in Boots* and *Native Son*—the former's preoccupation with the white casualties of white racism—is close to the heart of Algren's most significant anticipation of Wright's novel. The force that restrains Cass from the organized left is not a real or imagined stake in the market: he is fully capable of recognizing "The Owners' " opinion that "this is our world, louser. We do not claim you, you have no right here" (83). Rather, Cass's political discernment is dulled by the demands of racial supremacy, a birthright he must earn. Though this supremacy is lived painfully and precariously, suggests Algren, it qualifies as the highest obstacle between bitterly impoverished whites and effective opposition to their authentic adversaries. Five years before *Native Son*, *Somebody in Boots* accordingly figures Communism and antiracism as imperatively synonymous. Just as Bigger does not often distinguish between the party and a program to dissolve "that white looming mountain of hate" (*Native Son* 782–83), Cass and friends cannot seem to think of Reds without visualizing black and white together. The initial thematization of Communist activity in Algren's novel occurs when Cass and Norah are awakened by a party demonstration against eviction. "Reds puttin' on their act," as Norah sees it, means "Niggers an' white guys listenin' to a nigger talkin' from a car, an a whole gang of sheenies runnin' up an' downstairs draggin' furniture into a house" (198).[10] Before he returns to deep political sleep, Cass himself views a Communist rally as a more inviting interracial spectacle: "The heads were black or the heads were white; flood-beams lit fair hair or hair that was kinky. It was night in the park, and these were the people" (243). When closest to an intimation of Communism's promise, Cass senses that blacks are gingerly approaching vanguard knowledge: "Sometimes [he] had had the feeling that Negroes, everywhere, were listening to some strange new thought, sometimes half-unwillingly, sometimes eagerly. They were hearing strange words, yet half-feared to look where the speaker stood" (243).

Appropriately, the most alluring bearer of the "strange new thought" of Communism encountered by Algren's hero is an African American. Much as Bigger's head tutor in party antiracism is one of the the first whites who becomes recognizably human to him, Cass's instructor is one of the first blacks whose companionship "it did not occur to him to refuse . . . because [he] was a Negro" (240). The character who plays Max to Cass's Bigger is Chicagoan Dill Doak. In part, Dill embodies the Harlem Marxist template of the poised, militant New Negro socialist as refurbished by Algren. He never addresses "a white man with servility, and he could not be patronized" (240). He counsels active resistance, escape from religion's opiate, and complete social transformation: "These ministers use religion to stabilize things—and things are so rotten they ought to be dumped in the nearest garbage-can, 'stead of being perfumed. To hell with humility, meekness—I believe in fightin' " (242). He shares with the Communist lawyer of *Native Son* an incisive intelligence trained by Marxist theory into a taste for global analysis. Along with Max and other party theoreticians, Dill conceives of the U.S. Negro Problem as one component of the international dilemma of capitalism. Cass thus often finds him "brooding over the foreign-news page of a daily paper. . . . Daily he sought to prove to Cass, with newspaper clippings, that in South America the United States was at war with England 'by proxy' " (240). In the style of Bigger, who appreciates Max's efforts and intentions but does not completely grasp his speech at his trial, "Cass [doesn't] know what 'by proxy' meant; but nevertheless he listened to Doak, and sometimes read the clippings. Cass felt a need of companionship that was almost like a hunger; inwardly he felt grateful to Doak for even speaking to him" (240). Dill's offers of friendship and knowledge to Cass do not end with this short course in imperialism. Again like Max, Doak hopes to unmask his pupil's fatalism as mere ideology, on one occasion meeting Cass's opinion that prostitution was "everywhere an' likely al'ays will be" with the classic historicizing reply, "It hasn't always been, and it won't always will be, and it isn't all over. In Russia this is already a thing of the past. We must change the order of things here too" (242). It is Dill who chaperones Cass to several Communist rallies, where both can hear political debate between black Marxists and black nationalists and watch "fists sho[o]t upward into light—black fists, white, and brown" (243).

The analogies between Wright's Max and Algren's Dill end abruptly, however, when it comes to their respective employments. Rather than serving as a senior attorney with the "Labor Defenders," Wrightspeak for the ILD, Dill makes ends meet as a performer in the "colored company" of the cheap burlesque house where Cass works a barker (227). A kind of proletarian Robeson in voice as well as politics, Dill possesses a booming basso that "flickered the gas flames behind the exit signs when he sang *Asleep in the Deep*" (227). At least temporarily consigned to a strip club in the Loop, Dill is compelled to supplement his musicianship with the basics of minstrel-inspired entertainment. While "offstage he spoke and acted in a way in which Cass had never seen or heard a Negro speak or act before," Dill "on the stage . . . was a light-footed, dance-loving, song-loving, rubber-limbed mappet [*sic*], full of a rich, black belly-laughter" (227). Despite his smarts, dignity, and conscientious teaching of the fundamentals of class struggle, Algren's Chicago Lenin-to-be thus acts the darky for his pay.

Why does Algren present Cass's Communist tutor as a New Negro artist-intellectual confined to employment in a Chicago burlesque house during the very years in which burlesque dedicated itself to "the true strip," a "last-ditch and ultimately unsuccessful strategy to stay alive" (R. Allen 244)? Perhaps it is to suggest that cagey proletarian revolutionaries should take guidance from everyday African-American resistance and wear the mask until the red day arrives, thus augmenting Gold's advice in salvaging the New Old Negro Sam. Perhaps it is to challenge the assumption, detectable in Wright's 1930s' work, that the greatest black contribution to Communism would emerge from the rural southern folk and their culture. Model party militant Dill is thoroughly urbanized, and his "cultural production" before transitory, anonymous audiences is just as thoroughly noncommunal and nonorganic. Perhaps Dill's onstage behavior makes the less party-directed point that socially defined blackness, as much as its white counterpart, relies on the willed enactment of stereotype. In any case, Dill's performance and Cass's response lay open the libidinal energy within the homosocial discourse of black-white radical brotherhood launched in early renaissance Harlem. Before Cass learns to respect his tutor's knowledge, he is impressed by Dill's vigor and physique. Watching the black company perform several times a day, Cass's eyes are drawn to this "veritable dynamo of a man" (227). Dill's muscularity intrigues, as does his "bullet-headed" form, his skin "as black as the ace of spades," and his electrifying, "limitless energy" (227), all of this inside a theater now devoted to full sexual display. Scarcely seeing the white and black female strippers "after a while" (227), Cass chooses Dill as the focus of what Eric Lott—with due apologies to Laura Mulvey—has termed the "pale gaze" (*Love* 153). Lott notes that in the context of nineteenth-century blackface minstrelsy, this gaze entailed "a ferocious investment in demystifying and domesticating black power in white fantasy by projecting vulgar black types as spectacular objects of white men's looking. This looking always took place in relation to an objectified and sexualized black body, and it was often conjoined to a sense of terror" (ibid.). In the radical burlesque context of Algren's novel, however, Cass's look is a prelude to the estranging, subjectifying recognition that Dill's power is not confined to a strong, erotic body. As the phonetic similarity of the weird name Dill Doak and the word *dildo* implies, any vision of Dill as the unthinking, "bullet-headed" black phallus of white reverie is an artificial expedient. Dill's very physical energy, Algren notes, "amounted to an intelligence in itself" (*Somebody* 227), and his more properly political brilliance wins him the chance to alter Cass's pale gaze into a red one. Again reminiscent of Gold's Hoboken hero, Sam, Dill's bodily fulfillment of minstrel stereotype is designed as an invitation to Communist schooling.

During the final Chicago sequences of *Somebody in Boots*, Algren aligns Dill's fraternal tutelage of Cass with the tradition of Harlem Marxist rhetoric pitting black and white male New Crowd brothers against Old Crowd capitalist fathers. The two halves of Algren's interracial pair may be mismatched in intellect and education, but they share the same generation, exploitation under the same older male boss (the suitably pitiless Herman Hauser), and the possibility of an equal interest in overcoming such owner-patriarchs through interracial radicalism. Together, the young bachelors share a trip to the World's Fair, walks home from work many nights while talking "of many things" (241), and more than a few "park forums" on Communism (245). It is fitting, then, that a reassertion of the law of the father clinches Cass's withdrawal from Dill's instruction: Nubby O'Neill, the sadistic El Paso jail trusty and itinerant professor of whiteness, returns to declare himself Cass's true "papa" (172).

Even prior to Nubby's return, Cass's interest in Communism wavers: like Bigger, he respects his tutor perhaps more than his tutor's subject, complaining that party orators "talk sech lawng words that it don't all make sense" (245). Yet Cass's final separation from Dill and his forums comes only with the reappearance of Nubby's brand of racial enforcement. Heading for bed after a stroll with Dill, Cass is lured into a doorway and reintroduced to the wages of "nigger-loving." In an echo of the punishment meted out to Cass for walking beside Matches, an earlier black brother figure, Nubby batters his wayward son for "five times in two weeks . . . walkin' with a nigger so black he looks like a raincloud comin' down the street" (247). "How come you doin' me this way, son?" wonders an anguished Nubby, "How come you ferget how I slap hell out o' you once fer messin' with them ugly black sons-abitches? You fergit 'most everythin' a body tries to learn ya, don't ya?" (247). Algren gives every indication that Nubby will never again need to worry over such amnesia. Cass quickly chooses the cruel father's instruction in whiteness over Dill's in Communism. The party rallies that Cass and Dill attended rapidly become "the merest fly-speck in [Cass's] memory" (248). Unlike Wright's Max, Dill does not even get the chance to take leave of his recalcitrant pupil: on Nubby's command, "Cass never walked with Dill Doak again" (248). In the novel's denouement, Cass is broken by another betrayal by Norah and left to swallow Nubby's decision that he is not yet white enough to deserve a name besides "son" (254). Despite the crude sign of white racism's impotence in Nubby's "castrated," handless arm, the "Texas Kid" thus registers an Old Crowd victory over Dill's offer of New Negro alliance, assuming the despotic place of Cass's homicidal biological father, the suspiciously named "Stubby" McKay. Algren's native son begins and ends in the throes of an oedipal whiteness only temporarily relieved by Communism's society of brothers.

With its many steps to ensure that readers digest the tragedy of Cass's immobility, *Somebody in Boots* qualifies as one of the most thoroughly antiracist texts in the proletarian inventory. Its bleak scrutiny of the debits of whiteness might have been even richer had James T. Farrell, author of a critical reader's report for the Vanguard Press, not requested the whitening of Cass's lover in the first draft, a mulatto prostitute named Val. An interracial affair, thought Farrell, could not be represented "as if it were not an extraordinary union which would have effects different from the mating of two people from the same race" (qtd. in Drew 83). No better was the affair's evidence that Algren was "putting in the party line" (qtd. on 83). This last comment reflects the intensity with which the Depression-era party was identified with interracialism; backhandedly, it compliments the cultural power of texts by white as well as African-American Communists "looking to people of color as symbols of resistance" (Wald 153). To the limited extent that the "party line" can be identified with the certainty that racism would drown in history's wake, however, Algren's novel can be seen as a grievance against Communist faith. Nubby's triumph over Dill signals the frustration and possible defeat of the party not just by pure products of lumpen America but by the native production of mandatory whiteness. *Somebody in Boots* preaches both the necessity of color-blind Communism and the warning that the red day would never arrive unless the party acknowledged that competing lessons in white racism, doled out without respect to skin, were reinforced by prodigious violence.

Yet with just this preaching, Algren creates the preconditions for one of the most impressive acts of literary interracialism in interwar Communism. When searching for the "dim negative of Bigger," Wright reports in "How 'Bigger' Was Born," he "met white writers who talked of their responses, who told me how whites reacted to this lurid American scene. . . . But what was more important still, I read their novels" (862). *Native Son's* title, politically divergent narrative strata, and infatuation with lumpen indigenousness bear witness that *Somebody in Boots* was high on Wright's reading list; the eerie likeness between Bigger's and Cass's stanchings of red interracialism shows Algren's influence where it is least suspected (or inspected): at the resistant core of Bigger's dominantly nationalist consciousness. Communism guarantees interracialism in neither novel; each projects into an uncertain future the sturdy alliance between black and white New Crowds the Harlem Marxists had once thought imminent. But in the common outlines of their antibuddy narratives, Algren's and Wright's texts fulfill some of the Harlem Marxists' original design for a mutually beneficial interracial radicalism. That *Native Son's* inside critique of the Old Left is indebted to *Somebody in Boots*, a prime example of this left's preferred literature, underlines the achievements as well as the failures of the black-white interchange the Harlem Marxists had instigated. Even in representing hindrances to this interchange, Wright enters its history to revise Algren's earlier, mirroring representation. Wright's *Native Son*, then, can be declared foreign to the Old Left only if Algren's native son is deported from its cultural territory.

The End That Failed

Wright did eventually leave the party behind; in 1944 he began bidding it a tortured good-bye in a string of autobiographical excerpts that some black radical authors never forgave (Foley, "The Rhetoric" 538). As Alan Wald, Bill Mullen, and others have lately argued, it is a major simplification, if not an unvarnished case of anti-Communist wish fulfillment, to believe that African-American writing as a whole dutifully followed Wright's lead. The difference-leveling "Age of Wright" was not declared until after his passing; Old Left–linked figures such as Arna Bontemps, Lloyd Brown, Alice Childress, Shirley Graham Du Bois, John O. Killens, and Willard Motley continued to yield work showing black Marxist coordinates. Among the small crowd of African-American literary communists specifically considered in this book, tales of disaffection are not universal and few separations replicate Wright's pattern. Ellison, an enthusiastic public salesman of the serpentine Communist line on World War II (Foley, "The Rhetoric" 540), does seem eventually to have endorsed Wright's last straws: namely, an irritation with Communist critics of *Native Son* and a disappointment with the party's decision to support Roosevelt's war presidency over antidiscrimination measures (Fabre, "From *Native Son*" 200–202). Claude McKay, however, had moved with his editor, Max Eastman, toward a precocious anti-Stalinism—a course few black leftists pursued—just in time to miss the powerful leg up enjoyed by Wright, Ellison, and other party-allied writers in late-1930s' Harlem (McKay, *Harlem* 181–262). *Crusaders* Cyril Briggs and Richard B. Moore were expelled from the party in 1942, caught on the wrong side of a charge of overindulgent black nationalism prosecuted by other Harlem party leaders (W. James 288–89). Later, both were invited to reinstate membership, Briggs returning when the winds of African-American policy shifted back to his Marxist nationalism. *Crusader* poet Andy Razaf, meanwhile, had anticipated many veterans of the radical 1930s in applying himself to the better wages and progressive possibilities in the mass culture industry (Wald 104), reemerging in the late 1940s and 1950s as a less clandestine anti-anti-Communist. Thompson and Hughes were no less typical in avoiding any blunt rift with Communism, the latter even after his face-saving appearance before the McCarthy committee in 1953. African-American literary communists thus exited the Old Left much as they entered it, for compound reasons and at numerous moments but with a common obligation to the promise of interracial struggle and disclosure and their own and their racial community's self-direction. In his mammoth survey of Caribbean radicalism in the United States, *Holding Aloft the Banner of Ethiopia* (1998), historian Winston James reviews the actions of Briggs, Otto Huiswoud, McKay, and Moore and concludes that "all the evidence suggests that Caribbeans were among the most outspoken members of the Communist Party, including on racism and on the 'Negro Question' "

(286). Let the record show that these vocal, adopted Harlemites, products of a special black diaspora linking the West Indies, uptown New York, and Soviet Moscow, also helped to initiate a practice of African-American literature as outspoken as any, stamped but not fully contained by the years between the wars, productive of a race-radical modernism that was not black alone.

Notes

Introduction

1. Throughout this study, "Communist" with a capital "C" will be used to refer to individuals and movements directly tied to the Third (Communist) International established by the Soviet Bolsheviks in 1919. Like Michael Denning, I will use the word "communist," with a small "c," to refer to individuals and movements that "thought of themselves as generic 'communists,' . . . the way earlier and later generations thought of themselves as generic 'socialists,' 'feminists,' or 'radicals' " (xviii).

2. Though McKay's party membership is still often mistakenly denied (see Dietrich 47), he spoke freely of it in the early 1920s. In December 1921, for example, McKay informed distant acquaintance Charles J. Scully "that he [was] still a [Party] member" and added that he "intend[ed] rejoining the I.W.W. because he owe[d] about one year's dues" (United States, 16 December 1921). Unknown to McKay, Scully was an informant for the Bureau of Investigation, the predecessor to the FBI. For this and other such details, I owe thanks to Tyrone Tillery, who shared with me his copy of McKay's FBI file, patiently obtained under a Freedom of Information Act request.

3. With help from newly declassified sources, Taylor Branch's *Pillar of Fire* details how both the FBI and state-based segregationist groups presumed that the civil rights movement was just another face of Communist conspiracy.

4. Barbara Foley sifts the binary anti-Communist logic of Ellison's "whitewash" of the party in the recent essay "The Rhetoric of Anticommunism in *Invisible Man*."

5. I treat specific aspects of Cruse's argument in chapters 1 and 3. *Black Aesthetic* editor Addison Gayle, Jr.'s history of the African-American novel, *The Way of the New World* (1975), also articulates a nationalist anti-Communism.

6. See, for example, the approaches to the Hurston-Wright debate in Henry Louis Gates, Jr.'s *The Signifying Monkey* (1988) and Deborah E. McDowell's "Lines of Descent/Dissenting Lines" (1991). In chapter 5, I focus on the relationship between recent readjudications of this debate and anti-Communist habits of perception.

7. Such studies would include George Hutchinson's *The Harlem Renaissance in Black and White* (1995), Walter Kalaidjian's *American Culture Between the Wars* (1993), and Michael North's *The Dialect of Modernism* (1994). I consider Hutchinson's view of the cultural field of the Harlem Renaissance at length in chapter 1, whereas Kalaidjian and North enter the conversation in chapter 3. Sieglinde Lemke's *Primitivist Modernism* (1998) might also be added to the list above; Nancy Cunard's pro-Communist *Negro* (1934) anthology becomes Lemke's prime example of the very worst in white modernism's incorporation of black forms: "[Cunard's] alleged solidarity with the black race is consistently undermined by her primitivist and communist orthodoxy; in the end, Cunard's is an antiracist racism" (138). I steal the formulation "love and theft" from the title of Eric Lott's captivating study of blackface minstrelsy, where it names the popular form's "mixed erotic economy of celebration and exploitation" (*Love* 6). Lott himself offers a traditional excursus into the cautionary history of African-American writers and Communism in the 1994 essay "Cornel West in the Hour of Chaos." Here, Cruse's *Crisis of the Negro Intellectual* is cited en route to the conclusion that "black self-subsumption to the organized white left can be fairly well demonstrated to have had disastrous effects on innovative black cultural thinking . . . and political organization" (45).

8. Much recent revisionist work on U.S. proletarian literature has taken on the bugaboo of Soviet mastery. In particular, Barbara Foley's *Radical Representations* (1993) convincingly disproves "the thesis that the American [literary] Marxists simply attempted to clone themselves off the Soviet example" (63).

9. My conclusion that the U.S. party's Stalinism is beyond a flaw is prompted in part by Alan M. Wald's *Writing from the Left* and by the cumulative impact of the new evidence (not always the timeworn conclusions) offered by volumes in the ongoing Annals of Communism series of the Yale University Press (see Klehr, Haynes, and Firsov; and Klehr, Haynes, and Anderson).

10. The work connected with all these *post*s is nearly as copious as it is significant. Shelley Fisher Fishkin's review essay "Interrogating 'Whiteness,' Complicating 'Blackness' " offers a useful annotated bibliography of both postessentialist explorations in racial theory and postsegregationist criticism of U.S. literatures. Of pronounced value to my project have been the integrationist literary histories mentioned in note 7, above, and analyses of U.S. and Black Atlantic racial cultures by Hazel Carby, Henry Louis Gates, Jr., Paul Gilroy, Stuart Hall, Eric Lott, Michael Rogin, and David Roediger. The continuing renaissance of scholarship on the culture of U.S. leftism, particularly on the literature of the Old Left, has been an inspiring stimulus. I am especially obliged to recent full-length studies by James D. Bloom, Constance Coiner, Michael Denning, Barbara Foley, Cary Nelson, Paula Rabinowitz, and Alan Wald. Forthcoming books by Bill Mullen, James Smethurst, and Suzanne Sowinska have also been highly valuable.

11. See Barbara Foley's chapter "Race, Class, and the 'Negro Question' " in *Radical Representations*; James A. Miller's "African-American Writing of the 1930s: A Prologue" and his entry "Communism" in *The Oxford Companion to African American Literature*; and many of the essays collected in Alan M. Wald's *Writing from the Left*.

12. See Robin D. G. Kelley's *Hammer and Hoe: Alabama Communists During the*

Great Depression (1990) and Mark Naison's *Communists in Harlem During the Depression* (1983).

13. It should be noted, however, that James A. Miller has asserted that "the relationships between African American writers and Communism span several decades" and first arose in "the years immediately following World War I" ("Communism" 166).

14. Barbara Foley finds successful unity of these "contradictory elements in the CP's analysis of the 'Negro question'" in the texts of William Attaway and Richard Wright, whom she regards as the major black contributors to the proletarian novel (*Radical* 203).

15. Paul Gilroy's *Black Atlantic* stands behind my juxtaposition of Marxism and the black vernacular arts as countercultures of modernity, and my conception of these arts' utopian politics (38).

1. Kitchen Mechanics and Parlor Nationalists

1. Barry Singer's groundbreaking biography notes the persistence of this interpretation of the song and asserts that "Razaf's lyric stripped bare essences of racial discontent that had rarely if ever been addressed by any African American musically until Razaf wrote them down in 1929" (219). Given the oscillating religious and secular meanings of the freedom sought in the spirituals, this assertion should probably be more modest. "Black and Blue," it seems fair to say, has a lyric featuring one of the earliest outbursts of explicit antiracism in black-authored popular music intended for an interracial audience. Yet it is not *the* earliest. Decades before Razaf produced his rejoinder to Dutch Schultz, African Americans Bob Cole and Billy Johnson had slipped "No Coons Allowed," a "coon song" that directly criticized Jim Crow, into the 1898 New York show *A Trip to Coontown*. In 1928 Razaf himself had published the similar "Ole Jim Crow," with music by C. J. Johnson.

2. There is a good chance that forgetting the author of the lyrics of "Black and Blue"—the least mediated trace of Armstrong's performance that Ellison can reproduce—will be less common in the future. Eric J. Sundquist's useful guidebook *Cultural Contexts for Ralph Ellison's* Invisible Man (1995) acknowledges Razaf's authorship and reproduces the song's words in full, as does the section entitled "The Vernacular Tradition" in *The Norton Anthology of African American Literature* (1997).

3. Gloria Hull discusses the tyranny visited on women writers by conventional periodizations of the renaissance in *Color, Sex, and Poetry: Three Women Writers of the Harlem Renaissance* (1987); Cheryl A. Wall quotes Hull and offers the example of Fauset and the women poets in *Women of the Harlem Renaissance* (1995), a synoptic study of the movement's female prose writers (10).

4. The most successful effort of the brothers Johnson was "Under the Bamboo Tree" (1902), now best known to literary types as an intertext in *Sweeney Agonistes*, T. S. Eliot's unfinished, minstrel-indebted "Fragment . . . of an Aristophanic Melodrama" (74).

5. A wide selection of Razaf's lyrics as sung by artists from Bing Crosby to Sarah Vaughan can be heard on a terrific 1994 disc issued by the Smithsonian; see *Waller/Razaf: American Songbook Series*. Bobby Short's 1987 tribute album to Razaf, *Guess Who's in Town*, is well-intentioned but musically flat archivism.

6. Razaf is granted a short listing in *The Harlem Renaissance: A Historical Dictionary for the Era* (1984), edited by Bruce Kellner; he is swiftly treated as a "successful and brilliant lyricist" (106) in the essay collection *Black Music in the Harlem Renaissance* (1990), edited by Samuel A. Floyd, Jr.; and he has a very small but featured role in discussions of the renaissance in *Terrible Honesty* (1995), Ann Douglas's account of New York's "mongrel" modernist culture of the 1920s. Eric J. Sundquist's review essay of recent renaissance criticism, "Red, White, Black and Blue" (1996), mentions Razaf's poetry for *The Negro World*, borrows part of its title from Razaf and Waller's song of racial protest, and briefly submits "Black and Blue" as evidence of the need to take jazz and stage performance seriously when exploring the "intersection of black and white culture through which modernism evolved" (114). Ted Vincent's *Keep Cool: The Black Activists Who Built the Jazz Age* (1995), a work that deserves greater attention in the United States, considers Razaf at more length, construing him, as I do, as a link between New Negro radicalism and the world of early jazz. Yet Razaf remains absent from the main lines— and big books—of renaissance criticism. Even Barry Singer's biography of Razaf, *Black and Blue* (1992), a text explicitly dedicated to the work of recovery and redemption, places its subject "well outside the Harlem Renaissance mainstream" (177).

7. A particularly concrete instance of the liking for affective geography in Harlem Renaissance criticism is provided by Steven Watson's *The Harlem Renaissance: Hub of African-American Culture* (1995). Watson devotes two facing pages to a street map of "The Heart of Harlem," on which the relative location of renaissance brand names such as the Dunbar Apartments, "Niggerati Manor," and the Cotton Club is noted (132–33). Recovering the movement's history here becomes the business of a walking tour, one to which I hope to add *The Crusader* offices as a necessary stop.

8. Labor historian David Roediger offers a bold, empirically dense account of the formation of this identity in *The Wages of Whiteness: Race and the Making of the American Working Class* (1991). Eric Lott's *Love and Theft: Blackface Minstrelsy and the American Working Class* (1993) examines this identity's construction with greater psychological and theoretical elaboration, as well as privileged reference to blackface performance.

9. In one of the few admissions that a significant portion of the staff of the literary renaissance was not safely ensconced in nationalist parlors "far beyond the menial labor and poverty of Harlem's vast working class," Sidney H. Bremer notes that "Claude McKay worked as a railroad steward while he wrote the clarion poem for the New Negro, 'If We Must Die' (1919); Hughes was waiting on tables—having just returned from one of his several stints as a messboy at sea—when *The Weary Blues* (1925) was going to press" (138). Countee Cullen, who joined the Communist Party in the 1930s, had early work experience as a busboy, while Zora Neale Hurston labored as a maid and manicurist as well as "a popular novelist's secretary and chauffeur" (138).

10. Sociologist Arlie Russell Hochschild has examined this emotional form of service labor alienation in the case of flight attendants; see *The Managed Heart: Commercialization of Human Feeling*.

11. I am partly indebted to Sidney Bremer's insightful chapter on the renaissance in *Urban Intersections* (132–64) for these thoughts on the relationship between Harlem service labor and the anxiety of renaissance patronage.

12. Other verse evidence of Razaf's early class radicalism can be found in "Social-ism," a poem from the late teens or early twenties that he clipped and pasted in his own scrapbook. "Some fear our talk / As children fear the thunder," Razaf's socialist speaker complains, "For we stand for the people's cause / And not for theirs—of plun-der" (ll. 10–12). A later poem in the same collection condemns the use of "Commu-nist" as an all-purpose slur: "Whenever you don't like a guy / There's one way, safer than your fist / For you to give him a black eye / Just label him a 'Communist' " ("Communist" ll. 1–4).

13. George Hutchinson argues persuasively of the need to attend to "the actual institutional context in which" formally traditional poets such as Cullen and McKay operated (24). Without such attention, the notion of the mastery of form threatens to become a free-floating, allegorical key for black interpretation.

14. To take just four influential revisions of the renaissance that leave Locke's dom-inance largely unchallenged, Houston Baker's *Modernism and the Harlem Renaissance* (1987), a new historicist assault on both positivist literary history and debates over the renaissance's putative failure, lauds *The New Negro* as the movement's "seminal dis-cursive act" (72) and a "sounding gesture of national significance" (73); Gloria Hull's *Color, Sex, and Poetry* (1987), a study of the neglected women renaissance poets Angelina Weld Grimké, Alice Dunbar-Nelson, and Georgia Douglas Johnson, indicts Locke's misogyny and male-only nepotism but claims that he "gave definitive shape to the 'New Negro' in his 1925 anthology of that name" (7); Walter Kalaidjian's *Amer-ican Culture Between the Wars* (1993), a refutation of "scholarship on high modernism [that] has largely silenced the century's complex and contentious social context" (2), recasts the renaissance as a full-fledged modernist avant-garde yet still declares *The New Negro* its "foundational text" (84); and George Hutchinson's *The Harlem Renais-sance in Black and White* (1995) culminates with a lengthy reading of Locke's anthol-ogy, couched as the movement's intellectual fulfillment and "most comprehensive sin-gle text" (387).

15. See, for example, Hutchinson's revealing discussions of Locke, pragmatism, and Boas in *The Harlem Renaissance in Black and White* (especially 91–92, 425–28). By con-trast, Bernard W. Bell's still useful pamphlet-book *The Folk Roots of Contemporary Afro-American Poetry* (1974) stresses Locke's connections to Herder (20–31).

16. For that fraction, see the songs "Ole Jim Crow" (1928), discussed in the first note to this chapter, and "Dusky Stevedore" (1928), which manages to fulfill every cliché about tuneful black muscle on the levee while accentuating the economic com-pulsion that moves it.

17. Paul R. Gorman discusses the related issue of the Lost Generation's maturation "in the age of modern urban entertainments" in *Left Intellectuals and Popular Culture in Twentieth-Century America* (127–28).

18. Briggs's athleticism was also noticed by the Bureau of Investigation agents assigned to trail him, who warned each other that he was a "fast walker" (qtd. in Korn-weibel 152).

19. Ted Vincent documents in detail *The Crusader*'s love affair with the blues; see *Keep Cool: The Black Activists Who Built the Jazz Age* (152–60). For firsthand examples of the journal's enthusiasm for the music, see the piece entitled "A Successful Business

Man" (on W. C. Handy) and the illustrated article "Mamie Smith and Her Jazz Hounds"; see also the publicity photo for Lucille Hegamin and the Blue Flame Syncopaters in the April 1921 issue (6) and the advertisement for songs by "THE BEST COLORED WRITERS" published by the Handy Brothers Music Company in December 1921 (inside cover).

20. Both Barry Singer's biography (239) and Eric Sundquist's *Cultural Contexts for Ralph Ellison's* Invisible Man (115–16) proceed as if the song mocks only African-American infatuation with Communism. For an interesting parallel with the tune's fond importing of U.S. stereotype into the Soviet Union, see Langston Hughes's chapter on "The Mammy of Moscow" in *I Wonder as I Wander: An Autobiographical Journey* (82–86).

21. Unlike the rest of *A Kitchen Mechanic's Review*, this song's constitutive mix of Razaf's lyric and Johnson's music is documented in a recent reissue of recordings by Fats Waller and His Rhythm.

22. Razaf also invests wage work with desire in "Machinery," a song written for Connie's *Hot Chocolates of 1935*, a sequel to *A Kitchen Mechanic's Revue*. The ill effect on labor of the automation of service work is the subject of this Depression lyric: "Automatic elevators, automats instead of waiters, / Ev'ry day inventin' something new. / I wish they would in-vent, something to pre-vent / A jobless man from feelin' like I do."

23. Recently adapted by Paul Gilroy in *The Black Atlantic: Modernity and Double Consciousness*, the term "counter-culture of modernity" was introduced by Zygmunt Bauman to describe the Western Left's immanent, surprisingly respectful critique of modern capitalist democracy and rationality; see Bauman's "The Left as the Counter-Culture of Modernity."

24. Paul Gilroy contends that any convergence of Marxism and the black vernacular critique of modernity is "undercut by the simple fact that in the critical thought of blacks in the West, social self-creation through labor is not the centre-piece of emancipatory hopes. For the descendants of slaves, work signifies only servitude, misery and subordination. Artistic expression, expanded beyond recognition from the grudging gifts offered by the masters as a token substitute for freedom from bondage, therefore becomes the means towards both individual self-fashioning and communal liberation" (*The Black Atlantic* 40). I would argue that Razaf's artistic expression opens the possibility of black self-creation through labor—and thus eases the convergence of black critical thought and Marxism—by means of a reverie of work as art and art as work.

2. Home to Moscow

1. For a look at the interpretive failings of *The Secret World of American Communism* from the perspective of a leading "new historian" of the American party, see Maurice Isserman's "Notes From Underground."

2. Contrary to Klehr, Haynes, and Anderson, even the arguable superiority of Soviet influence does not make it a diversionary "commonplace" to "maintain that the American Communist party made its decisions as a result of a complex interaction between local events and conditions, on the one hand, and international super-

vision, on the other" (4–5). Both less and more powerful elements of an interaction, of course, may determine its result. In addition to studies by Mark Naison and Robin D. G. Kelley, a short list of influential "new historical" works on U.S. Communism would include Maurice Isserman's *Which Side Were You On?*, Roger Keeran's *The Communist Party and the Auto Workers Unions*, and Paul Lyons's *Philadelphia Communists, 1936–1956*. Michael E. Brown's 1993 essay "The History of the History of U.S. Communism" assesses the contributions of the new historians, connecting their unprecedented ability "to reflect on the historical significance of the party to American life" with a new, quasi-sociological emphasis on the complexities of organizations (21). Theodore Draper, dean of the old historians, replied at length to younger radical challengers in *The New York Review of Books* of May 9 and 30, 1985; this response is reprinted as the afterword to the 1986 edition of his important history *American Communism and Soviet Russia*. In 1994's "The Life of the Party," Draper indicts Brown in particular and anti-anti-Communist history in general while reviewing a collection of new historical essays, *New Studies in the Politics and Culture of U.S. Communism*.

3. The fullest prior examination of *The Negroes in America* that I know of can be found in Wayne F. Cooper's biography *Claude McKay: Rebel Sojourner in the Harlem Renaissance* (185–89), an indispensable resource for all McKay questions. Cooper does not seriously explore McKay's engagement with Marxist theory, however. *The Negroes'* status as something of a well-kept secret is signaled by Geta LeSeur's article "Claude McKay's Marxism," which mistakenly asserts that the book was commissioned but never completed—in any language (228–29).

4. Clarence Walker's historiographic survey "The American Negro as Historical Outsider, 1836–1935" casts Du Bois's *Black Reconstruction* as the terminator of "black historians' emphasis on ideas as the motivating force of American historical change" (106).

5. Carter Woodson's long career as an entrepreneur of black history is discussed in August Meier and Elliott Rudwick's *Black History and the Historical Profession* (1–71); his methodology as a practicing historian can be sampled in the frequently revised textbook *The Negro in Our History*, written with Charles H. Wesley. Minister, politician, and historical autodidact George Washington Williams's *History of the Negro Race in America from 1619 to 1880* (1882) is sometimes labeled "the first scholarly account of the history of black Americans" (Meier and Rudwick 3). Clarence Walker's "The American Negro as Historical Outsider, 1836–1935" argues that the attribution of historical agency to African Americans is the overriding interest of early black history (92–93).

6. The derivation of Du Bois's radical view on Reconstruction is pursued in David Levering Lewis's introduction to the 1992 reprint of *Black Reconstruction in America*. Lewis notes that in a December 1909 paper for the American Historical Association, "Reconstruction and Its Benefits," Du Bois began rehearsing the case "that the Reconstruction experiment had given to the defeated South democratic government, free public schools, and progressive social legislation" (vii).

7. The Dunning School of Reconstruction history is treated in Eric Foner's Du Boisian *Reconstruction: America's Unfinished Revolution, 1863–1877* (xix–xxi). The

school's ur-text is Dunning's 1907 study *Reconstruction, Political and Economic, 1865–1877*.

8. The "postrevisionist" history of the 1970s and 1980s, illuminating Reconstruction as anything but a radical episode, is also usefully reviewed in Foner's *Reconstruction* (xxii–xxiii).

9. The socialist *Messenger*'s understanding of the strategic position of African-American labor was even more precise and pointed. In a 1920 article entitled "Organized Labor and Negro Workers," the journal contended that "Negro cotton workers produce nearly 60 per cent. [*sic*] of the cotton of the entire world" (6). If they formed a union and struck, they could undermine the "great banks in New York, London, Paris and Berlin [that] depend for their existence upon the sweat and toil of the Southern Negro cotton pickers" (6).

10. Stuart Hall's much-quoted redefinition of race as "the modality in which class is 'lived' " is contained in the 1980 essay "Race, Articulation, and Societies Structured in Dominance" (55).

11. Robyn Wiegman interestingly discusses such racial-sexual displacements in *American Anatomies: Theorizing Race and Gender* (81–113).

12. My claim of McKay's primacy on this count takes issue with David Roediger, who describes Du Bois's *Black Reconstruction*, published over a decade after *The Negroes*, in the same terms (*Black* 14).

13. The best of this tradition of black thought on whiteness would include several of the essays in Ralph Ellison's *Shadow and Act* (1966); James Baldwin's *The Price of the Ticket* (1985); Toni Morrison's *Playing in the Dark* (1992); and W. E. B. Du Bois's *Black Reconstruction* (1935), which speaks of "a sort of public and psychological wage" extended to white workers of the South (700). As the Du Boisian title of Roediger's *The Wages of Whiteness* indicates, he has not been shy of recognizing "acute African-American students of the 'white problem' " (12). His 1998 collection *Black and White: Black Writers on What It Means to Be White* is a well-constructed introduction and sampling.

14. Hazel Carby's *Reconstructing Womanhood: The Emergence of the Afro-American Woman Novelist* illuminates Ida B. Wells's thought and protest against lynching during the turn-of-century black "women's era" (108–16).

15. The January 5, 1923, edition of the English-language *International Press Correspondence* reprints a version of the "Negro Theses" in the midst of a report by a "Comrade Billings" (14–16); this version ends on the same page that the text of McKay's report to the Comintern begins. Harry Haywood, who knew Huiswoud for decades, identifies Billings as a Huiswoud pseudonym in *Black Bolshevik* (225).

16. Where Wayne Cooper sees the influence on the Negro Commission of "West Indians . . . simultaneously much more nationalistic, class conscious, and international-minded than . . . American-born blacks" (180–81), I see a 1922 Comintern impressed by West Indian–born blacks trained in an internationally focused Harlem Marxism. Cooper's passing comment on the black impact on "the official stance of the Comintern regarding blacks" is nevertheless a rare encouragement (180).

17. The context of Briggs's September 1917 call for a separate black nation on U.S. soil is treated in detail in Robert Hill's introduction to the facsimile edition of *The*

Crusader. While I will keep myself from pursuing the controversy over Briggs's possible invention for Marxism of the thesis that U.S. blacks composed an oppressed nation, I will remark that the autobiography of Harry Haywood, the ex-ABB member who helped to initiate the 1928 Black Belt Nation line, qualifies its author's greatest claim to theoretical preeminence as follows: "I was the first American [Communist] (with perhaps the exception of Briggs) to support the thesis that U.S. blacks constituted an oppressed nation" (230).

18. For the course of Haywood's career in the United States and the Soviet Union, see his *Black Bolshevik: Autobiography of an Afro-American Communist.*

19. It is notable, however, that McKay's anti-Communist turn entailed the mistaken claim that "the plan of a Negro nation within the nation, carved out of the black belts of the South" was the brainchild of "James S. Allen, the white Communist expert on Negro affairs" (*Harlem* 222–23).

20. Only the balance of Lenin's and Stalin's great influences on the Nation thesis can be debated. Theodore Draper presents a minimalist view of Lenin's importance in *American Communism and Soviet Russia*, detecting "Stalin's voice" above all others in the final chorus (335–45), whereas Cedric Robinson draws a more equitable portrait of Lenin (the outfit's brains) as "the theoretical and ideological midwife" (309) and Stalin (its dangerous brawn) as "the authority through which the Comintern and the American Party had come to recognize Blacks as an oppressed nation" (311). Robinson nonetheless recognizes the debt of the thesis to Harlem radicalism: "In the background were the UNIA [Garvey's organization] and the Brotherhood [ABB]. They had established the political and ideological preconditions for the Party's policies and successes" (311). I can only agree with Robinson here; without the motivation of his *Black Marxism*, this chapter might not have been conceived. I would add, however, that *The Negroes in America* places the ABB much closer to the foreground of the thesis than Robinson allows. At the conclusion of a detailed article on McKay's Soviet hajj that appeared only after this chapter was written, Aribert Schroeder similarly suggests that "both Huiswoud and McKay . . . must be credited for the fact that from 1922 onward absolute racial equality became obligatory for Communist parties worldwide" (15). Alan Wald more generally notes that Communist thinking on African America "was initiated in the Third International with input from US Black Marxists" (219).

21. My comment on the Black Atlantic's stretch into Moscow is inspired by Gary Holcomb's suggestive work on McKay's erotic and political "diaspora cruising" and by David Chioni Moore's article "Local Color, Global 'Color': Langston Hughes, the Black Atlantic, and Soviet Central Asia, 1932." Moore contends that Hughes's writing about his 1932 visit to Soviet Central Asia "test[s] the borders of even the expansive, quatro-continental and archipelagic Black Atlantic formulation" of Paul Gilroy (50).

3. The Proletarian as New Negro

1. For an example of Lewis's unfavorable evaluation of Communists and their writing in 1937, see S. Lewis (37).

2. Jazz historian Marshall Stearns reports that Dizzy Gillespie had just joined Teddy Hill's big band when it began working at the Savoy Ballroom in 1937 (233).

3. Hasia Diner identifies these conventions in *In the Almost Promised Land*, a his-

tory of the roots of Jewish support for African-American causes. Diner's introduction traces visions of compromised interracialism to recent black critics of the feel-good approach to Jewish participation in civil rights struggles (xi). Her work goes on to demonstrate, however, that such misgivings are more than the present's projection.

4. Kalaidjian paints Gold as a proletcult ideologue who responded to the renaissance's "younger generation of outspoken black talent" with "telling conservatism" (86). The critique of Gold's dismissal of this generation concentrates on a single Gold effort, a 1926 letter to the editor of *The Nation* written under the influence of his own outspoken black vernacular play *Hoboken Blues*. I examine North's treatment of Gold at some length in the review essay "Black and White, Unite and Write," which challenges the idea that white literary proletarians were exceptions to the rules of crossracial investment on the modernist scene.

5. McKay's *Negroes in America* reprints the Maverick article in full with the explanation that *The Liberator* ran it "under the name of its author—a woman. But when it appeared in print the author, who was afraid of the consequences, sent a note to the magazine to the effect that it had been composed by a group of people, that she alone was not the author, and therefore she protested against the appearance of her name in the magazine" (83).

6. Evans's well-known Black Arts poem is now accessible in *The Heath Anthology of American Literature*. McKay thought enough of Randle's "Lament" to reprint it whole in *The Negroes in America*, couching it as an example of New Negro creativity. In its transcendence of dialect and its "intimate and subjective character," not avoiding notes of racial protest, the poem emblematized his early conception of a black literary renaissance touched by "a new spirit among the Negro masses" (73).

7. This analogy between the two violences can be compared to later efforts in the same vein discussed in Nelson (119–22).

8. The valuable checklist that Wayne Cooper includes in the McKay anthology *The Passion of Claude McKay* misses McKay's *Liberator* review of Charlie Chaplin's *My Trip Abroad*.

9. Cruse mysteriously invokes a critique of McKay that Gold did not write to claim that "the Communists and Gold" disliked "If We Must Die" (49).

10. A suggestive consideration of how political poets in the first decades of the century manipulated and reinvested traditional poetic forms is contained in Cary Nelson's *Repression and Recovery* (22–24, 41–43). George Hutchinson's *The Harlem Renaissance in Black and White* informatively discusses Max Eastman's aesthetic theory (255–57) and uses this discussion to demonstrate why "McKay was precisely Eastman's type of poet" (255).

11. The links between radical labor and proslavery are foregrounded in David Roediger's *The Wages of Whiteness* (76).

12. For an analysis of the enigmatic racial identity of the Confidence Man in the Melville novel of the same name, see Karcher (186–257).

13. Marcus Klein suggests that the Provincetown Players rejected *Hoboken Blues* on "political grounds" (240) but does not clearly describe these grounds or provide supporting evidence for his claim. In 1926 Gold did send a manuscript of the play to Provincetown's Eugene O'Neill, who praised the first act—"corking, amusing new

stuff!"—but found the rest "somehow terribly scrambled in form" ("To Michael Gold" 206). Perhaps unsurprisingly, the author of *The Emperor Jones* had nothing bad to say about the racial politics of *Hoboken Blues*. The first act he found so fresh is the most obliged to conventional blackface comedy.

14. The term *racechange* is borrowed from Susan Gubar's *Racechanges: White Skin, Black Face in American Culture*, which coins the word as an economical synonym for crossracial mimicry.

15. For an account of the music used in Ridgely Torrence's *Three Plays for the Negro Theatre*, see Clum (101).

16. That Gold's *Modern Negro Fantasia on an Old American Theme* was embraced by the cultural nationalists of *The New Caravan* complicates Hutchinson's portrait of the *Masses-Liberator-New Masses* group, in which Gold is painted as an enforcer of enmity between New Negro–positive U.S. nationalism and antirenaissance proletarian internationalism (268–75). Turning to a different aspect of Gold's *Fantasia* on Irving, the play's representation of a black Rip also tips its hat to the Afro-Dutch folklore of New York and New Jersey. Folklorist David Steven Cohen argues that the descendants of Dutch slaves in the region, while relatively weak in numbers, forged a distinct strong culture. For example, by grafting African survivals "onto the Dutch celebration of Pinkster," or Pentecost, they created a transgressive holiday akin to carnival in New Orleans, similarly celebrated by both blacks and whites (40).

17. Naturally, there are a few near-exceptions to this literary-historical rule. Hutchinson, while avoiding the proletarian label, suggests "that more institutional, aesthetic, and ideological continuities exist than have so far been recognized between the Harlem Renaissance and later African American social realism, between Langston Hughes's 'I, too, sing America' and Richard Wright's *Native Son*" (277). I agree in full and hope that this book reveals several of them. In an essay that provides an illuminating corollary to my own work on McKay, James A. Miller declares that "as African-American writers drifted toward the Left during the 1930s . . . they encountered in Marxist thought echoes of and reverberations from the debates of an earlier era" ("African-American" 88). Neither Hutchinson nor Miller, however, pursues the interaction of the Harlem and proletarian renaissances per se.

4. Scottsboro Delimited

1. In *Mixed Blood: Intermarriage and Ethnic Identity in Twentieth-Century America*, Paul R. Spickard describes the anxieties raised by interracial relationships within the civil rights movement of the mid-1960s. More than a few contemporary observers, he notes, "pointed to a special set of tensions operating around the coupling of Black men and White women" (281). *Meridian* (1976), Alice Walker's postmodern historical novel of the civil rights generation, represents these tensions and their overcoming by means of a decade-long interracial erotic triangle among three artist-activists.

2. Mark Naison identifies the ass struggle/class struggle gag as one of numerous jokes in Depression Harlem concerning the party and interracial sexuality (281).

3. Constance Coiner's (sadly) final work on Tillie Olsen and Meridel Le Sueur, U.S. feminism, and the Old Left, is gathered in *Better Red* (1995). Barbara Foley's exhaustive revisionist history of proletarian literature, *Radical Representations* (1993),

contains a pointed chapter entitled "Women and the Left in the 1930s." Paula Rabinowitz's less intensively Marxian *Labor and Desire* (1991) looks at the reshaping of proletarian literature by narratives of gender, maternity, and feminine sexuality and
argues for a reading of women's revolutionary novels as a distinct genre, or "secondary
zone," within proletarianism (64). Deborah Rosenfelt's relatively early exploration of
the intersection of U.S. women's literature and class radicalism can be found in "From
the Thirties: Tillie Olsen and the Radical Tradition" (1981) and "Getting into the
Game: American Women Writers and the Radical Tradition" (1986). Foley emphasizes several differences between her political-critical position and that of Coiner and
Rabinowitz, contending that "the best framework for assessing the disparities between
[female literary radicals'] discourse and that of the movement as a whole is not one
that counterposes Marxism with women's emancipation but one that theorizes the
historical weaknesses and strengths of the Marxism of the 1930s left" (Radical 243).

4. I use the word *desire* here in much the same way that Eve Sedgwick's *Between
Men* employs it: as a name "not for a particular affective state or emotion, but for the
affective or social force, the glue, even when its manifestation is hostility or hatred or
something less emotively charged, that shapes an important relationship" (2).

5. Hugh T. Murray demonstrates that Cullen's Scottsboro summons was answered
by a number of poets, "as well as others who may not have earned the title" (82). In
"Changing America and the Changing Image of Scottsboro," Murray offers a registry
of forty years of Scottsboro-related work by black and white authors, charting alterations in the delineation of the case in relationship to broader historical shifts.

6. Not everyone forgets Hughes's play, the text of which is still difficult to obtain
without access to a large university or public library. Amiri Baraka revived the drama
with the Anti-Imperialist Cultural Union in 1977. For this and other aspects of his
allegiance to interwar black bolshevism, see the Baraka interview "Restaging Langston
Hughes's *Scottsboro Limited.*"

7. The growing, still mostly unpublished body of work on gay-positive and homo-
erotic representations in Hughes's canon can be sampled in Anne Borden's "Heroic
'Hussies' and 'Brilliant Queers': Genderracial Resistance in the Works of Langston
Hughes." As its title suggests, Isaac Julien's film *Looking for Langston* (1989) employs
Hughes's verse and moving image as springboards to a lyrical meditation on black gay
identity in the Harlem Renaissance and after. On the larger intersection between the
Harlem Renaissance and an emerging urban African-American homosexual subcul-
ture, see Eric Garber's "A Spectacle in Color," the chapter "Building Gay Neighbor-
hood Enclaves" in George Chauncey's *Gay New York*, and the chapter "Slumming" in
Kevin J. Mumford's *Interzones*.

8. In discussing Gail Finney's analysis of modernity and the representation of
female psychology, Rita Felski remarks on the readiness of modern texts to associate
the female prostitute with a capitalist "culture increasingly structured around the
erotics and aesthetics of the commodity" (4). In one sense, Hughes imports this association into the public sphere of imperialist commodity traffic.

9. Cunard's interest in and for Scottsboro, Communism, and interracial sexuality
goes well beyond the scope of this half-sentence. Her *Negro* anthology, featuring an
entire section on the Scottsboro case, was dedicated to her first African-American

friend and lover, jazz pianist Henry Crowder. In a *Negro* contribution entitled "The American Moron and the American of Sense—Letters on the Negro," Cunard bravely reproduced excerpts from the violently obscene letters she received from KKK admirers while staying in Harlem. "Any interest [in African America] manifested by a white person, even a foreigner to America (such as myself)," she theorized, "is immediately transformed into a sex 'scandal' " (197). Her public campaign against this conversion of red interest into sexual infamy, conducted even as she publicly commemorated her love for Crowder, is a significant moment in the history of more than one radicalism. For the complexity of the binds among Cunard's erotic life, black advocacy, and Communist partisanship, see Jane Marcus's "Bonding and Bondage: Nancy Cunard and the Making of the *Negro* Anthology."

10. Several of historian James Goodman's Scottsboro stories reveal the resentment of white southerners over defense questioning of Bates and Price's character. See, in particular, "What Better Evidence Was Ever Put Up to a Jury" (136–46).

11. Thompson will be better recognized on her own terms should the memoir she began with Margaret B. Wilkerson be published. Wilkerson's 1990 article "Excavating Our History," meanwhile, remains among the fullest biographical accounts of Thompson.

12. Dissension between *Mule Bone*'s coauthors kept the play from production until 1991, when it was played at New York's Lincoln Center with additions (and bowdlerizations) by the late George Bass. The tale of *Black and White*'s shipwreck—the film was canceled by its Soviet backers—has been told often and with varying political spins. For a first-hand account from the left, see Thompson's "With Langston Hughes in the U.S.S.R." David Levering Lewis's *When Harlem Was in Vogue* describes events from a liberal distance (288–91).

13. Benstock's term for these practitioners of "literary midwifery" (21) is also the name of her influential feminist revision of modernist literary history, *Women of the Left Bank*.

14. See, for example, the first note to Rabinowitz's preface to *Labor and Desire* (183) and the first note in the chapter "Women and the Left in the 1930s" in Foley's *Radical Representations* (213).

15. Foley's research leads her to conclude that Margaret Walker's *Jubilee* (1966), drafts of which date to the mid-1930s, "is the only full-length work of prose fiction by a black woman writer in any way associated with the proletarian movement" (*Radical* 213 n. 1).

16. Charlotte Nekola and Paula Rabinowitz's anthology *Writing Red* reprints poems, short stories, and reportage by Marita Bonner, Edith Manuel Durham, and Ramona Lowe. Thompson's work is not included, though Sowinska discusses her role as a party intellectual in *American Women Writers and the Radical Agenda, 1925–1940* (123–25).

17. According to a 1974 statement by a Kentucky-based organization of socialist feminists, "even at the strongest time of the civil rights movement in Birmingham, young activists often stated that nothing could protect Black women from being raped by Birmingham police" (Group of Socialist Women 5).

18. Angela Davis's biographical portrait of black Communist Claudia Jones sug-

gests that the early movement to free the Scottsboro nine was instrumental in usher-
ing some black women into the party. See *Women, Race and Class* (167–71).

19. These claims regarding Thompson's relationship to party resources themselves
draw on the work of Barbara Foley, who stresses "the conscious commitment of
women leftists to the Communist-led movement" (*Radical* 241) and argues that
"female literary radicals did not—covertly, unconsciously, or otherwise—espouse a
different political line [from the party's]" (242).

20. Bates's blow to "the old Southern structure of white supremacy" was in fact
preceded by the 1930 formation of the Association of Southern [white] Women for the
Prevention of Lynching. Black women were at the forefront of the modern anti-
lynching movement, of course, from Ida B. Wells, author of *Southern Horrors* (1892)
and *A Red Record* (1895), to Mary Talbert, first president of the Anti-Lynching Crusaders, founded in 1922 (A. Davis 191–96).

5. Black Belt/Black Folk

1. The vocabulary of renaissance is common in discussions of recent writing by
African-American women. One clear-cut example is offered in the subtitle to the 1990
anthology *Wild Women in the Whirlwind: Afra-American Culture and the Contemporary Literary Renaissance*, edited by Joanne M. Braxton and Andrée Nicola McLaughlin.

2. See Claudia Roth Pierpont's *New Yorker* article "A Society of One: Zora Neale
Hurston, American Contrarian" and Henry Louis Gates's afterword and Mary Helen
Washington's foreword to the Harper Perennial reissue of *Their Eyes*.

3. The best available accounts of the black migration to the South that began in the
mid-1970s are John Cromartie and Carol B. Stack's "Reinterpretation of Black Return
and Nonreturn Migration to the South, 1975–1980" and Stack's less conventionally
scholarly *Call to Home*.

4. These others would certainly include Ann duCille in *The Coupling Convention*,
particularly her chapters 4 and 5.

5. In an earlier published version of this chapter, I suggested that Carby's understanding of folk ideology as a "discursive displacement of contemporary [urban] conflict and cultural transformation" problematically grasps this ideology as a sheer inversion of real (urban) history (Carby, "The Politics" 89); see William J. Maxwell, " 'Is It
True What They Say About Dixie?' " My own definition of folk ideology is obviously
indebted to the Louis Althusser warhorse "Ideology and Ideological State Apparatuses
(Notes Towards an Investigation)."

6. In "The World and the Jug" (1963–64), Ellison claims that Wright "could not
for ideological [read "Communist"] reasons depict a Negro as intelligent, as creative
or as dedicated as himself" (127). "How awful," Ellison laments, "that Wright found
the facile answers of Marxism before he learned to use literature as a means for discovering the forms of American Negro humanity" (126). By setting at odds Wright's
leftism and the possibility of unshrouding the plural excellence of African-American
culture, the post-*Invisible* Ellison creates a rationale to recast his former mentor as a
black writer in color only, an arrogant isolato whose denial of his own cancels any
debts owed by literary relatives. It is essential to remark, however, that the Ellison of

twenty years before was prepared to attack fellow Marxists for associating Wright with the idea that "Negroes have no capacity for culture" ("Richard" 103). In the 1945 essay "Richard Wright's Blues," the same paragraphs of *Black Boy* that "The World and the Jug" cites as evidence of Wright's disbelief in high black humanity are read as the "strongest affirmation" of the contrary (103). Prior to his graduation from Communism, Ellison could attribute the strength of Wright's autobiography to its unforced mastery of the black vernacular code of the blues, "the specific folk-art form which helped shape the writer's attitude toward his life" (90). Wright's "lyrical prose . . . singing lustily as he probes his own grievous wound," reminds Ellison of Bessie Smith and indeed spurs his famous definition of the blues form as "an autobiographical chronicle of personal catastrophe expressed lyrically" (90). Oedipal burnout and intensifying anti-Communism were required to foster Ellison's conversion to the Wright-versus-black-folk line. James Baldwin, a native son of Wright who had less of a paper trail in *The New Masses* to explain, brilliantly developed this line in a trio of essays: "Everybody's Protest Novel" (1949), "Many Thousands Gone" (1951), and "Alas, Poor Richard" (1961).

7. Nearly all, because Gunter Lenz plays down certain perceived differences among Wright, Hurston, and the folk tradition in "Southern Exposures." Werner Sollors's "Anthropological and Sociological Tendencies" and Carla Cappetti's *Writing Chicago*—studies that inform this chapter in a host of ways—invite more nuanced, less faultfinding accounts of the Hurston-Wright dispute, though neither focuses on the relationship between Communism and folk ideology.

8. See Gunter Lenz, "Southern Exposures"; Robert Bone, "Richard Wright and the Chicago Renaissance"; Werner Sollors, "Anthropological and Sociological Tendencies"; and Carla Cappetti, *Writing Chicago*.

9. The party's emphasis on the Black Nation thesis shifted in relationship to policy changes during the 1930s, especially the adoption of the Popular Front. As Barbara Foley demonstrates, however, the thesis was unusual in its longevity and its consistent ability to channel party literary and political work (*Radical* 181). Wright's "Bright and Morning Star," for one, a story written in 1938, continues to invoke a southern "black republic" by name (435).

10. A recent articulation of this dream can be found in a essay by Arnold Rampersad, editor of the welcome Library of America edition of Wright. Its title tells all: "Too Honest for His Own Time."

11. In conversation with Paul Robeson, film director Sergei Eisenstein, no less, suggested that the Soviet phrase "national minorities" was conceived as an antidote to the punishing term "primitive" (Duberman 187).

12. When speaking of Garveyism as a "trendy" modernizing movement, Sollors is inspired by Judith Stein's 1985 book *The World of Marcus Garvey*.

13. This clock-gramophone also echoes the gramophone played by the indifferent typist "with automatic hand" in *The Waste Land*'s "Fire Sermon" (l. 255), one of Wright's touchstone texts.

14. Feminist debate over this scene is joined in Joyce Ann Joyce's "Richard Wright's 'Long Black Song' " and Nagueyalti Warren's "Black Girls and Native Sons."

15. Werner Sollors, too, briefly registers the importance of "the symbol of money . . . in the 'natural' or prelapsarian state of the couple's sexual relations" ("Anthropological" 39).

6. Native Sons Divorce

1. For an illuminating consideration of the composition and culture of the party's John Reed Clubs across the United States, see Michael Denning, *The Cultural Front* (205–11).

2. Wright, de Beauvoir, and Sartre's high mutual regard is detailed in Michel Fabre's *The Unfinished Quest of Richard Wright* (320–50); Algren's protoexistentialism and later adoption by de Beauvoir and Sartre is discussed in Kenneth G. McCollum's biographical portrait "Nelson Algren" (11).

3. The first novel Wright composed, *Lawd Today*, assumed something close to its final shape in 1936 but did not reach print until 1963. The Library of America edition of Wright's *Early Works* rectifies this publication history by leading with the novel, whose techniques are touched in particular by Dreiser and Dos Passos.

4. I have not encountered treatments of Algren in the criticism on *Native Son*, though James R. Giles's *Confronting the Horror: The Novels of Nelson Algren* (1989), one of the few full-length studies of Algren, notes that *Somebody in Boots* "expresses views concerning the necessity of Marxist socioeconomic reform which are similar to the vision underlying Richard Wright's 1940 black protest novel" (38).

5. African-American Communist Benjamin Davis did worry, however, that *Native Son* "permits of the impression that had it not been for Bigger's contact with Communists, however untypical these Communists were, he would not have been forced to kill" (73).

6. The ongoing prominence of Joyce's study is attested in the James A. Miller–edited collection *Approaches to Teaching Wright's* Native Son (1997), which reports the results of a survey showing the book to be "the most often cited critical reference by both students and teachers of [Wright's novel]" (Miller, "Materials" 4).

7. For two examples of this periodization in action, see Robert Bone's *The Negro Novel in America* (1958), one of the classic histories of the African-American novel, which identifies 1940 as the year in which the "Role of the Communist Party" waned and a "Revolt against Protest" took shape (114, 153); and the best-known recent history of the genre, Bernard W. Bell's *The Afro-American Novel and Its Tradition* (1987), which declares 1939 to be the year in which most black writers "saw their hopes and their race betrayed" by Communism (153).

8. This somewhat competitive devotion to Marx and Engels' vision of the lumpenproletariat is revisited in Algren's 1965 preface to *Somebody in Boots*. There, Lee Harvey Oswald, cast as a descendant of Cass McKay, is described as follows: "Belonging neither to the bourgeoisie nor to a working class, seeking roots in revolution one week and in reaction the next, not knowing what to cling to nor what to abandon, compulsive, unreachable, dreaming of some sacrificial heroism, he murders a man he does not even hate, simply, by that act, to join the company of men at last" (9).

9. An incisive analysis of the short history of Algren criticism can be found in Carla Cappetti's *Writing Chicago* (144–55).

10. Communist-led rent strikes and antieviction demonstrations were not uncommon sights in northern ghettos during the 1930s, a state of affairs that Ellison's *Invisible Man* spoofs through the Brotherhood's headlong embrace of the narrator after his impromptu speech denouncing the eviction of an old Harlem couple.

Bibliography

"The Acid Test of White Friendship." *The Crusader* 4.5 (July 1921): 8–9.

Adorno, Theodor W. "On Lyric Poetry and Society." *Notes to Literature*. Ed. Rolf Tiedemann. Trans. Shierry Weber Nicholsen. Vol. 1. New York: Columbia University Press, 1991. 37–54.

"The African Blood Brotherhood." *The Crusader* 2.10 (June 1920): 7, 22.

"Aims of *The Crusader*." *The Crusader* 1.3 (November 1918): 1.

"Aims of *The Crusador* [*sic*]" *The Crusader* 1.1 (September 1918): 4.

Algren, Nelson. *Somebody in Boots: A Novel*. 1935. New York: Thunder's Mouth, 1987.

———. Preface. 1965. *Somebody in Boots* 5–9.

Allen, Ernest, Jr. "The New Negro: Explorations in Identity and Social Consciousness, 1910–1922." *1915, the Cultural Moment*. Ed. Adele Heller and Lois Rudnick. New Brunswick: Rutgers University Press, 1991. 48–68.

Allen, Robert G. *Horrible Prettiness: Burlesque and American Culture*. Chapel Hill: University of North Carolina Press, 1991.

Althusser, Louis. "Ideology and Ideological State Apparatuses (Notes Towards an Investigation)." *Lenin and Philosophy and Other Essays*. Trans. Ben Brewster. New York: Monthly Review, 1971. 127–86.

Anderson, Benedict. *Imagined Communities: Reflections on the Origin and Spread of Nationalism*. Rev. ed. New York: Verso, 1991.

Awkward, Michael. *Inspiriting Influences: Tradition, Revision, and Afro-American Women's Novels*. New York: Columbia University Press, 1989.

Baker, Houston A., Jr. *Modernism and the Harlem Renaissance*. Chicago: University of Chicago Press, 1987.

Baldwin, James. "Alas, Poor Richard." *Nobody Knows My Name: More Notes of a Native Son*. New York: Dial, 1961. 181–215.

———. "Everybody's Protest Novel." 1949. *Notes of a Native Son* 13–23.

———. "Many Thousands Gone." 1951. *Notes of a Native Son* 24–45.

———. *Notes of a Native Son*. 1955. Boston: Beacon, 1961.

————. *The Price of the Ticket.* New York: St. Martin's, 1985.

Baraka, Amiri. "Restaging Langston Hughes's *Scottsboro Limited.*" Interview with Vèvè Clark. *Conversations with Amiri Baraka.* Ed. Charlie Reilly. Jackson: University Press of Mississippi, 1994. 157–67.

Bates, Ruby. "Save Their Lives." *Working Woman* 5 (April 1934): 10.

Bauman, Zygmunt. "The Left as the Counter-Culture of Modernity." *Telos* 70 (winter 1986–87): 81–93.

Baxandall, Rosalyn. "The Question Seldom Asked: Women and the CPUSA." *New Studies in the Politics and Culture of U.S. Communism.* Ed. Michael E. Brown et al. 141–61.

Bell, Bernard W. *The Afro-American Novel and Its Tradition.* Amherst: University of Massachusetts Press, 1987.

————. *The Folk Roots of Contemporary Afro-American Poetry.* Detroit: Broadside, 1974.

Bender, Thomas. *Community and Social Change in America.* New Brunswick: Rutgers University Press, 1978.

Benstock, Shari. *Women of the Left Bank: Paris, 1900–1940.* Austin: University of Texas Press, 1986.

"Biggest Song Hit of the Century!" *The Crusader* 1.7 (March 1919): 22.

Billings [Otto Huiswoud]. "Report on the Negro Question." *International Press Correspondence* (English ed.) 5 January 1923: 14–16.

Bloom, James D. *Left Letters: The Culture Wars of Mike Gold and Joseph Freeman.* New York: Columbia University Press, 1992.

Bone, Robert. *The Negro Novel in America.* 1958. New Haven: Yale University Press, 1965.

————. "Richard Wright and the Chicago Renaissance." *Callaloo* 9.3 (1986): 446–68.

Borden, Anne. "Heroic 'Hussies' and 'Brilliant Queers': Genderracial Resistance in the Works of Langston Hughes." *African American Review* 28.3 (1994): 333–45.

Bourdieu, Pierre. *The Field of Cultural Production: Essays on Art and Literature.* Ed. and intro. Randal Johnson. New York: Columbia University Press, 1993.

————. "The Field of Cultural Production; or, The Economic World Reversed." 1983. Trans. Richard Nice. *The Field* 29–73.

————. "Principles for a Sociology of Literary Works." 1986. Trans. Claud Du Verlie. *The Field* 176–91.

Branch, Taylor. *Pillar of Fire: America in the King Years, 1963–65.* New York: Simon and Schuster, 1998.

Braxton, Joanne M., and Andrée Nicola McLaughlin, eds. *Wild Women in the Whirlwind: Afra-American Culture and the Contemporary Literary Renaissance.* New Brunswick: Rutgers University Press, 1990.

Bremer, Sidney H. *Urban Intersections: Meetings of Life and Literature in United States Cities.* Urbana: University of Illinois Press, 1992.

Brown, Michael E. "The History of the History of U.S. Communism." Introduction. *New Studies in the Politics and Culture of U.S. Communism.* Ed. M. Brown et al. 15–44.

Brown, Michael E., et al., eds. *New Studies in the Politics and Culture of U.S. Communism.* New York: Monthly Review, 1993.

Brown, Sterling. *The Negro in American Fiction.* 1937. *Negro Poetry and Drama and The Negro in American Fiction.*

———. *Negro Poetry and Drama.* 1937. *Negro Poetry and Drama and The Negro in American Fiction.*

———. *Negro Poetry and Drama and The Negro in American Fiction.* New York: Atheneum, 1969.

Cappetti, Carla. *Writing Chicago: Modernism, Ethnography, and the Novel.* New York: Columbia University Press, 1993.

Carby, Hazel V. "Ideologies of Black Folk: The Historical Novel of Slavery." *Slavery and the Literary Imagination.* Ed. Deborah E. McDowell and Arnold Rampersad. Baltimore: Johns Hopkins University Press, 1989. 125–43.

———. "The Politics of Fiction, Anthropology, and the Folk: Zora Neale Hurston." *New Essays on* Their Eyes Were Watching God. Ed. Michael Awkward. New York: Cambridge University Press, 1990. 71–93.

———. *Reconstructing Womanhood: The Emergence of the Afro-American Woman Novelist.* New York: Oxford University Press, 1987.

Carter, Dan T. *Scottsboro: A Tragedy of the American South.* 1969. New York: Oxford University Press, 1971.

Chauncey, George, Jr. *Gay New York: Gender, Urban Culture, and the Making of the Gay Male World, 1890–1940.* New York: Basic, 1994.

Chisholm, Anne. *Nancy Cunard.* New York: Knopf, 1979.

Christian, Barbara. "What Celie Knows That You Should Know." *Anatomy of Racism.* Ed. David Theo Goldberg. Minneapolis: University of Minnesota Press, 1990. 135–45.

"Claude McKay with The Liberator [sic]." *The Crusader* 4.2 (April 1921): 21.

Clifford, James. *The Predicament of Culture: Twentieth-Century Ethnography, Literature, and Art.* Cambridge: Harvard University Press, 1988.

Clum, John M. "Ridgely Torrence's Negro Plays: A Noble Beginning." *The South Atlantic Quarterly* 63 (1969): 96–108.

Cohen, David Steven. *Folk Legacies Revisited.* New Brunswick: Rutgers University Press, 1995.

Coiner, Constance. *Better Red: The Writing and Resistance of Tillie Olsen and Meridel Le Sueur.* New York: Oxford University Press, 1995.

Cooper, Wayne F. *Claude McKay: Rebel Sojourner in the Harlem Renaissance: A Biography.* Baton Rouge: Louisiana State University Press, 1987.

Crane, Hart. *The Bridge. The Bridge: The Complete Poems and Selected Letters and Prose of Hart Crane.* Ed. Brom Weber. Garden City, NY: Doubleday, Anchor, 1966. 43–117.

Cromartie, John, and Carol B. Stack. "Reinterpretation of Black Return and Nonreturn Migration to the South, 1975–1980." *The Geographical Review* 79.3 (July 1989): 297–310.

Crossman, Richard, ed. *The God That Failed.* New York: Harper, 1950.

Cruse, Harold. *The Crisis of the Negro Intellectual.* New York: Morrow, 1967.

Cullen, Countee. "Scottsboro, Too, Is Worth Its Song (A Poem to American Poets)." 1935. *My Soul's High Song: The Collected Writings of Countee Cullen, Voice of the*

Harlem Renaissance. Ed. Gerald Early. New York: Doubleday, Anchor, 1991. 258–59.

Cunard, Nancy. "Rape." Poem printed on verso of July 1933 request for contributions to the Scottsboro defense fund. Nancy Cunard Papers. Harry Ransom Humanities Research Center, University of Texas at Austin.

—, ed. *Negro.* 1934. New York: Negro Universities Press, 1969.

Davis, Angela Y. *Women, Race and Class.* New York: Vintage, 1983.

Davis, Benjamin, Jr. Rev. of *Native Son,* by Richard Wright. *The New York Sunday Worker* 14 April 1940, sec. 2: 4 ff. Rpt. in *Richard Wright's* Native Son*: A Critical Handbook.* Ed. Richard Abcarian. Belmont, CA: Wadsworth, 1970. 68–77.

Davis, Mike. *Prisoners of the American Dream: Politics and Economy in the History of the U.S. Working Class.* London: Verso, 1986.

Davis, Thadious M. "Race and Region." *The Columbia History of the American Novel.* Ed. Emory Elliott. New York: Columbia University Press, 1991. 407–36.

———. "Wright, Faulkner, and the South: Reconstitution and Transfiguration." *Callaloo* 9.3 (1986): 469–80.

de Beauvoir, Simone. *Force of Circumstance.* Trans. Richard Howard. New York: Putnam, 1965.

Denning, Michael. *The Cultural Front: The Laboring of Culture in the Twentieth Century.* New York: Verso, 1996.

Dietrich, Julia. *The Old Left in History and Literature.* New York: Twayne, 1996.

"A Different Meaning." *The Crusader* 1.3 (November 1918): 17.

Diner, Hasia. *In the Almost Promised Land: American Jews and Blacks, 1915–1935.* 1977. Baltimore: Johns Hopkins University Press, 1995.

Douglas, Ann. *Terrible Honesty: Mongrel Manhattan in the 1920s.* New York: Farrar, Straus, 1995.

Doyle, Laura. *Bordering on the Body: The Racial Matrix of Modern Fiction and Culture.* New York: Oxford University Press, 1994.

"Draft Manifesto: John Reed Clubs." 1932. *Communism in America: A History in Documents.* Ed. Albert Fried. New York: Columbia University Press, 1997. 176–77.

Draper, Theodore. *American Communism and Soviet Russia: The Formative Period.* 2d ed. New York: Vintage, 1986.

———. "The Life of the Party." Rev. of *When the Old Left Was Young: Student Radicals and America's First Mass Student Movement, 1929–1941,* by Robert Cohen; and *New Studies in the Politics and Culture of U.S. Communism,* ed. Michael E. Brown et al. *The New York Review of Books* 13 January 1994: 45–51.

Drew, Bettina. *Nelson Algren: A Life on the Wild Side.* Austin: University of Texas Press, 1991.

Duberman, Martin Bauml. *Paul Robeson.* New York: Knopf, 1988.

Du Bois, W. E. B. *Black Reconstruction in America.* 1935. Intro. David Levering Lewis. New York: Atheneum, 1992.

———. *The Gift of Black Folk.* 1924. Millwood, NY: Kraus-Thomson, 1975.

———. Rev. of *Nigger Heaven,* by Carl Van Vechten. 1926. *W. E. B. Du Bois: Writings.* New York: Library of America, 1986. 1216–1218.

———. Rev. of *Quicksand,* by Nella Larsen; *Home to Harlem,* by Claude McKay; and *The American Negro,* by Melville J. Herskovitz. 1928. *Book Reviews by W. E. B. Du Bois.* Ed. Herbert Aptheker. Millwood, NY: кто/Kraus-Thomson, 1977. 113–15.

———. *The Souls of Black Folk.* 1903. New York: New American Library, 1969.

duCille, Ann. *The Coupling Convention: Sex, Text, and Tradition in Black Women's Fiction.* New York: Oxford University Press, 1993.

———. "The Unbearable Darkness of Being: 'Fresh' Thoughts on Race, Sex, and the Simpsons." *Birth of a Nation'hood: Gaze, Script, and Spectacle in the O. J. Simpson Case.* Ed. Toni Morrison and Claudia Brodsky Lacour. New York: Pantheon, 1997. 293–338.

Dunning, William A. *Reconstruction, Political and Economic, 1865–1877.* New York: Harper and Bros., 1907.

Eastman, Max. Letter to Claude McKay. 12 April 1923. Lilly Library, Indiana University, Bloomington, Indiana.

———. "To Claude McKay." Spring 1923. McKay, *The Passion* 78–82.

Eliot, T. S. *The Complete Poems and Plays, 1909–1950.* New York: Harcourt Brace, 1971. 37–55.

———. *Sweeney Agonistes.* 1932. *The Complete Poems and Plays* 74–85.

———. *The Waste Land.* 1922. *The Complete Poems and Plays* 37–55.

Ellison, Ralph. *Invisible Man.* 1952. New York: Vintage, 1989.

———. "Richard Wright's Blues." 1945. *Shadow and Act* 89–104.

———. *Shadow and Act.* New York: New American Library, 1966.

———. "Twentieth-Century Fiction and the Black Mask of Humanity." 1953. *Shadow and Act* 42–60.

———. "The World and the Jug." 1963–64. *Shadow and Act* 115–47.

Evans, Mari. "I Am a Black Woman." 1970. *The Heath Anthology of American Literature.* Ed. Paul Lauter et al. 2d ed. Vol. 2. Lexington, MA: Heath, 1994. 2655.

Fabre, Michel. "From *Native Son* to *Invisible Man*: Some Notes on Ralph Ellison's Evolution in the 1950s." *Speaking for You: The Vision of Ralph Ellison.* Ed. Kimberly W. Benston. Washington, DC: Howard University Press, 1987. 199–216.

———. *The Unfinished Quest of Richard Wright.* 1973. Trans. Isabel Barzun. 2d ed. Urbana: University of Illinois Press, 1993.

———. *The World of Richard Wright.* Jackson: University Press of Mississippi, 1985.

Felski, Rita. *The Gender of Modernity.* Cambridge: Harvard University Press, 1995.

Fishkin, Shelley Fisher. "Interrogating 'Whiteness,' Complicating 'Blackness': Remapping American Culture." *American Quarterly* 47.3 (September 1995): 428–66.

Floyd, Samuel A., ed. *Black Music in the Harlem Renaissance: A Collection of Essays.* Knoxville: University of Tennessee Press, 1990.

Foley, Barbara. *Radical Representations: Politics and Form in U.S. Proletarian Fiction, 1929–1941.* Durham: Duke University Press, 1993.

———. "The Rhetoric of Anticommunism in *Invisible Man.*" *College English* 59.5 (September 1997): 530–47.

Foner, Eric. *Reconstruction: America's Unfinished Revolution, 1863–1877.* New York: Harper and Row, 1988.

Foner, Philip S., and James S. Allen, eds. *American Communism and Black Americans: A Documentary History, 1919–1929.* Philadelphia: Temple University Press, 1987.

Freeman, Joseph. *An American Testament.* New York: Farrar, Rinehart, 1936.

Freud, Sigmund. *Totem and Taboo: Some Points of Agreement Between the Mental Lives of Savages and Neurotics.* 1913. Trans. James Strachey. New York: Norton, 1950.

Furia, Philip. *The Poets of Tin Pan Alley: A History of America's Great Lyricists.* New York: Oxford University Press, 1992.

Garber, Eric. "A Spectacle in Color: The Lesbian and Gay Subculture of Jazz Age Harlem." *Hidden from History: Reclaiming the Gay and Lesbian Past.* Ed. Martin Bauml Duberman, Martha Vicinus, and George Chauncey, Jr. New York: New American Library, 1989. 318–31.

Gates, Henry Louis, Jr. *The Signifying Monkey: A Theory of Afro-American Literary Criticism.* New York: Oxford University Press, 1988.

———. "The Trope of a New Negro and the Reconstruction of the Image of the Black." *Representations* 24 (1988): 129–55.

———. "Zora Neale Hurston: 'A Negro Way of Saying.' " Afterword. Zora Neale Hurston, *Their Eyes Were Watching God.* 1937. New York: Harper Perennial, 1990. 185–95.

Gates, Henry Louis, Jr., and Nellie Y. McKay, eds. *The Norton Anthology of African American Literature.* New York: Norton, 1997.

Gayle, Addison, Jr. *The Way of the New World: The Black Novel in America.* Garden City, NY: Doubleday, Anchor, 1975.

Genet, Jean. *The Blacks: A Clown Show.* 1958. Trans. Bernard Frechtman. New York: Grove, 1960.

Genovese, Eugene D. *Roll, Jordan, Roll: The World the Slaves Made.* New York: Vintage, 1976.

Gibson, Donald B. "Wright's Invisible Native Son." 1969. *Twentieth-Century Interpretations of* Native Son. Ed. Houston A. Baker, Jr. Englewood Cliffs, NJ: Prentice-Hall, 1972. 96–108.

Giles, James R. *Confronting the Horror: The Novels of Nelson Algren.* Kent, OH: Kent State University Press, 1989.

Gilroy, Paul. *The Black Atlantic: Modernity and Double Consciousness.* Cambridge: Harvard University Press, 1993.

———. *"There Ain't No Black in the Union Jack": The Cultural Politics of Race and Nation.* 1987. Chicago: University of Chicago Press, 1991.

Gold, Mike [Michael]. "At Last, a Negro Theater?" *The New Masses* 10 March 1936: 18.

———. "Doing the Big Apple for the *Daily Worker* Drive." *Daily Worker* 20 November 1937: 7.

———. "Drunk with Sunlight." Rev. of *Banjo,* by Claude McKay. *The New Masses* July 1929: 17.

———. "Go Left, Young Writers!" 1928. *Mike Gold* 186–89.

———. "The Gun is Loaded, Dreiser!" 1935. *Mike Gold* 223–230.

———. *Hoboken Blues; or, The Black Rip Van Winkle: A Modern Negro Fantasia on* an *Old American Theme. The American Caravan: A Yearbook of American Litera-ture.* Ed. Van Wyck Brooks et al. New York: Literary Guild of America, 1927. 548–626.

———. *The Hollow Men.* New York: International Publishers, 1941.

———. Introduction. Langston Hughes, *A New Song.* New York: International Workers Order, 1938. 7–8.

———. *Jews Without Money.* New York: International Publishers, 1930.

———. Letter. *The Nation* 14 July 1926: 37.

———. *Life of John Brown.* 1923. New York: Roving Eye, 1960.

———. *Mike Gold: A Literary Anthology.* Ed. Michael Folsom. New York: International Publishers, 1972.

———. *The Mike Gold Reader.* Ed. Samuel Sillen. New York: International Publishers, 1954.

———. "Notes of the Month." *The New Masses* February 1930: 3.

———. "Proletarian Realism." 1930. *Mike Gold* 203–8.

———. "A Secret Meeting in the Pines." 1934. *The Mike Gold Reader* 95–96.

———. "Towards Proletarian Art." 1921. *Mike Gold* 62–70.

———. "The Writer in America." 1953. *The Mike Gold Reader* 181–188.

Goldstein, Malcolm. *The Political Stage: American Drama and the Theater of the Great Depression.* New York: Oxford University Press, 1974.

Goodman, James. *Stories of Scottsboro.* New York: Pantheon, 1994.

Gorman, Paul R. *Left Intellectuals and Popular Culture in Twentieth-Century America.* Chapel Hill: University of North Carolina Press, 1996.

Gornick, Vivian. *The Romance of American Communism.* New York: Basic, 1977.

Gramsci, Antonio. *Selections from the Prison Notebooks.* Ed. and trans. Quintin Hoare and Geoffrey Nowell Smith. New York: International Publishers, 1971.

Griffin, Farah Jasmine. *"Who Set You Flowin'?": The African-American Migration Narrative.* New York: Oxford University Press, 1995.

Group of Socialist Women. "The Racist Use of Rape and the Rape Charge: A Statement to the Women's Movement from a Group of Socialist Women." Louisville: Socialist Women's Caucus, 1974.

Gubar, Susan. *Racechanges: White Skin, Black Face in American Culture.* New York: Oxford University Press, 1997.

Gunning, Sandra. *Race, Rape, and Lynching: The Red Record of American Literature, 1890–1912.* New York: Oxford University Press, 1996.

Gutman, Herbert G. *The Black Family in Slavery and Freedom, 1750–1925.* New York: Vintage, 1976.

Hall, Stuart. "Gramsci's Relevance for the Study of Race and Ethnicity." 1986. *Stuart Hall: Critical Dialogues in Cultural Studies.* Ed. David Morley and Kuan-Hsing Chen. New York: Routledge, 1996. 411–40.

———. "Race, Articulation, and Societies Structured in Dominance." 1980. *Black British Cultural Studies: A Reader.* Ed. Houston A. Baker Jr., Manthia Diawara, and Ruth H. Lindeborg. Chicago: University of Chicago Press, 1996. 16–60.

Harrington, Joseph. "Why American Poetry Is Not American Literature." *American Literary History* 8.3 (1996): 496–515.

Haywood, Harry. *Black Bolshevik: Autobiography of an Afro-American Communist.* Chicago: Liberator, 1978.

Hemenway, Robert E. *Zora Neale Hurston: A Literary Biography.* Urbana: University of Illinois Press, 1977.

Henry, Charles A. "Speech." *The Crusader* 5.4 (December 1921): 32.

Hicks, Granville, et al., eds. *Proletarian Literature in the United States: An Anthology.* New York: International Publishers, 1935.

Hill, Robert A. "Racial and Radical: Cyril V. Briggs, *The Crusader* Magazine, and the African Blood Brotherhood, 1918–1922." Introduction. *The Crusader.* Ed. Robert A. Hill. Facsimile rpt. 3 vols. New York: Garland, 1987. v–lxvi.

Hochschild, Arlie Russell. *The Managed Heart: Commercialization of Human Feeling.* Berkeley: University of California Press, 1983.

Holcomb, Gary E. "Diaspora Cruises: Claude McKay and the Harlem Renaissance." Paper presented at the Future of the Harlem Renaissance Conference, Knoxville, Tennessee, March 1997.

Hoover, Marjorie L. *Meyerhold: The Art of Conscious Theater.* Amherst: University of Massachusetts Press, 1974.

Huggins, Nathan Irvin, ed. *Voices from the Harlem Renaissance.* New York: Oxford University Press, 1976.

Hughes, Langston. *The Big Sea.* New York: Knopf, 1940.

———. "Christ in Alabama." 1931. *The Collected Poems* 143.

———. *The Collected Poems of Langston Hughes.* Ed. Arnold Rampersad. Assoc. ed. David Roessel. New York: Knopf, 1994.

———. "Columbia." 1933. *The Collected Poems* 168–69.

———. *Fine Clothes to the Jew.* New York: Knopf, 1927.

———. *I Wonder as I Wander: An Autobiographical Journey.* 1956. New York: Thunder's Mouth, 1991.

———. "Justice." 1923. *The Collected Poems* 31.

———. "The Negro Mother." *The Collected Poems* 155–56.

———. "Open Letter to the South." 1932. *The Collected Poems* 160–61.

———. "Scottsboro." 1931. *The Collected Poems* 142–43.

———. *Scottsboro, Limited: A One Act Play. The New Masses* November 1931: 18–21.

———. "Southern Gentlemen, White Prostitutes, Mill-Owners, and Negroes." 1931. *Good Morning Revolution: Uncollected Writings of Social Protest by Langston Hughes.* Ed. Faith Berry. Westport, CT: Lawrence Hill, 1973. 49.

———. "The Town of Scottsboro." 1932. *The Collected Poems* 168.

———. *The Weary Blues.* New York: Knopf, 1926.

Hull, Gloria T. *Color, Sex, and Poetry: Three Women Poets of the Harlem Renaissance.* Bloomington: Indiana University Press, 1987.

Hurston, Zora Neale. *Dust Tracks on a Road.* 1942. *Folklore, Memoirs, and Other Writings* 557–808.

———. "The Fire and the Cloud." 1934. *Novels and Stories* 997–1000.

———. *Folklore, Memoirs, and Other Writings.* New York: Library of America, 1995.

———. "The Gilded Six-Bits." 1933. *Novels and Stories* 985–96.

———. *Moses, Man of the Mountain.* 1939. *Novels and Stories* 335–595.

———. *Mules and Men.* 1935. *Folklore, Memoirs, and Other Writings* 1–267.

———. *Novels and Stories.* New York: Library of America, 1995.

———. "Stories of Conflict." *Saturday Review of Literature* 2 April 1938: 32.

———. *Their Eyes Were Watching God.* 1937. *Novels and Stories* 173–333.

Hutchinson, George. *The Harlem Renaissance in Black and White.* Cambridge: Harvard University Press, Belknap, 1995.

Isserman, Maurice. "Notes from Underground." Rev. of *The Secret World of American Communism,* by Harvey Klehr, John Earl Haynes, and Fridrikh Igorevich Firsov. *The Nation* 12 June 1995: 846 ff.

———. *Which Side Were You On? The American Communist Party During the Second World War.* Middletown, CT: Wesleyan University Press, 1982.

James, C. L. R. *Beyond a Boundary.* 1963. Durham: Duke University Press, 1993.

———. "The Revolutionary Answer to the Negro Problem in the U.S.A." 1948. *The C. L. R. James Reader.* Ed. Anna Grimshaw. Cambridge: Blackwell, 1992. 182–89.

James, Winston. *Holding Aloft the Banner of Ethiopia: Caribbean Radicalism in Early Twentieth-Century America.* New York: Verso, 1998.

Johnson, Barbara. "Metaphor, Metonymy, and Voice in *Their Eyes Were Watching God.*" *A World of Difference.* Baltimore: Johns Hopkins University Press, 1984. 155–71.

Johnson, James Weldon, ed. *The Book of American Negro Poetry.* Rev. ed. 1931. New York: Harcourt Brace, 1959.

Joyce, Joyce Ann. *Richard Wright's Art of Tragedy.* Iowa City: University of Iowa Press, 1986.

———. "Richard Wright's 'Long Black Song': A Moral Dilemma." *Mississippi Quarterly* 42 (fall 1989): 379–85.

Kalaidjian, Walter. *American Culture Between the Wars: Revisionary Modernism and Postmodern Critique.* New York: Columbia University Press, 1993.

Karcher, Carolyn. *Shadow Over the Promised Land: Slavery, Race, and Violence in Melville's America.* Baton Rouge: Louisiana State University Press, 1980.

Keeran, Roger. *The Communist Party and the Auto Workers Unions.* Bloomington: Indiana University Press, 1980.

Kelley, Robin D. G. *Hammer and Hoe: Alabama Communists During the Great Depression.* Chapel Hill: University of North Carolina Press, 1990.

Kellner, Bruce, ed. *The Harlem Renaissance: A Historical Dictionary for the Era.* New York: Methuen, 1987.

Kellner, Bruce, and Priscilla Oppenheimer. "Louise [Patterson] Thompson." *The Harlem Renaissance: A Historical Dictionary for the Era.* Ed. Bruce Kellner. 353–55.

Kerlin, Robert T. *Negro Poets and Their Poems.* Washington, DC: Associated Publishers, 1923.

Klehr, Harvey, John Earl Haynes, and Kyrill M. Anderson. *The Soviet World of American Communism.* New Haven: Yale University Press, 1998.

Klehr, Harvey, John Earl Haynes, and Fridrikh Igorevich Firsov. *The Secret World of American Communism.* New Haven: Yale University Press, 1995.

Klein, Marcus. *Foreigners: The Making of American Literature, 1900–1940.* Chicago: University of Chicago Press, 1981.

Kornweibel, Theodore, Jr. *"Seeing Red": Federal Campaigns Against Black Militancy, 1919–1925.* Bloomington: Indiana University Press, 1998.

Lafargue, Paul. *The Right to Be Lazy.* Trans. Charles H. Kerr. 1898. Chicago: Solidarity, 1969.

Lemke, Sieglinde. *Primitivist Modernism: Black Culture and the Origins of Transatlantic Modernism.* New York: Oxford University Press, 1998.

Lenz, Gunter H. "Southern Exposures: The Urban Experience and the Re-Construction of Black Folk Culture and Community in the Works of Richard Wright and Zora Neale Hurston." *New York Folklore* 6.8 (summer 1981): 3–39.

LeSeur, Geta. "Claude McKay's Marxism." *The Harlem Renaissance: Revaluations.* Ed. Amritjit Singh, William S. Shriver, and Stanley Brodwin. New York: Garland, 1989. 219–31.

Lewis, David Levering. "Parallels and Divergences: Assimilationist Strategies of Afro-American and Jewish Elites from 1910 to the Early 1930s." *Bridges and Boundaries: African Americans and American Jews.* Ed. Jack Salzman. New York: Braziller, 1992. 17–35.

———. *When Harlem Was in Vogue.* 1981. Rpt. New York: Vintage, 1982.

—, ed. *The Portable Harlem Renaissance Reader.* New York: Viking, 1994.

Lewis, Sinclair. "Garland for Clowns." *Newsweek* 25 October 1937: 37.

The Liberator. "Liberator News." *The Liberator* July 1922: 27.

———. Subscription offer. *The Liberator* August 1922: 31.

———. Subscription offer. *The Liberator* May 1922: 31.

Locke, Alain. "Harlem." *Survey Graphic* (*Harlem: Mecca of the New Negro*) 6.6 (March 1925): 629–30.

———. "Negro Youth Speaks." *The New Negro* 47–53

———. "The New Negro." *The New Negro* 3–16.

———. "Resume of Talk and Discussion." *Official Proceedings of the Second National Negro Congress, October 15–17, 1937.* Philadelphia: Metropolitan Opera House, 1937. N.p.

—, ed. *The New Negro.* 1925. New York: Atheneum, 1969.

Looking for Langston. Dir. Isaac Julien. Sankofa, 1989.

Lott, Eric. "Cornel West in the Hour of Chaos: Culture and Politics in Race Matters." *Social Text* 40 (fall 1994): 39–50.

———. *Love and Theft: Blackface Minstrelsy and the American Working Class.* New York: Oxford University Press, 1993.

———. "White Like Me: Racial Cross-Dressing and the Construction of American Whiteness." *Cultures of United States Imperialism.* Ed. Amy Kaplan and Donald E. Pease. Durham: Duke University Press, 1993. 474–95.

Lyon, Janet. "Militant Discourse, Strange Bedfellows: Suffragettes and Vorticists Before the War." *Differences* 4.2 (1992): 100–133.

Lyons, Paul. *Philadelphia Communists, 1936–1956.* Philadelphia: Temple University Press, 1982.

"Make Their Cause Your Own." *The Crusader* 1.11 (July 1919): 6.

"Mamie Smith and Her Jazz Hounds." *The Crusader* 3.6 (February 1921): 6.

Marcus, Jane. "Bonding and Bondage: Nancy Cunard and the Making of the *Negro Anthology.*" *Borders, Boundaries, and Frames: Cultural Criticism and Cultural Studies.* Ed. Mae Henderson. New York: Routledge, 1995. 33–63.

Marks, Carole. *Farewell—We're Good and Gone: The Great Black Migration.* Bloomington: Indiana University Press, 1989.

Marx, Karl. *The Eighteenth Brumaire of Louis Bonaparte.* 1852. New York: International Publishers, 1987.

Marx, Karl, and Friedrich Engels. *The German Ideology.* 1845. *The Marx-Engels Reader* 146–200.

———. *Manifesto of the Communist Party.* 1848. *The Marx-Engels Reader* 469–500.

———. *The Marx-Engels Reader.* 2d ed. Ed. Robert C. Tucker. New York: Norton, 1978.

Maxwell, William J. "Black and White, Unite and Write: New Integrationist Criticism of U.S. Literary Modernism." Rev. of *The Dialect of Modernism: Race, Language, and Twentieth-Century Literature,* by Michael North; *The Harlem Renaissance in Black and White,* by George Hutchinson; and *Radical Representations: Politics and Form in U.S. Proletarian Fiction, 1929–1941,* by Barbara Foley. *the minnesota review* 47 (1996): 205–15.

———. " 'Is It True What They Say About Dixie?': Richard Wright, Zora Neale Hurston, and Rural/Urban Exchange in Modern African-American Literature." *Knowing Your Place: Rural Identity and Cultural Hierarchy.* Ed. Barbara Ching and Gerald W. Creed. New York: Routledge, 1996. 71–104.

McCollum, Kenneth G. "Nelson Algren." *Dictionary of Literary Biography.* Vol. 9. Detroit: Gale Research, 1981. 10–15.

McDowell, Deborah E. "Lines of Descent/Dissenting Lines." Introduction. Zora Neale Hurston, *Moses, Man of the Mountain.* 1939. New York: Harper Perennial, 1991. vii–xxii.

McKay, Claude. "America." *Harlem Shadows* 6.

———. "Birthright." Rev. of *Birthright,* by T. S. Stribling. 1922. *The Passion* 73–76.

———. "Enslaved." *The Liberator* July 1921: 10.

———. "Exhortation: Summer, 1919." *Harlem Shadows* 49.

———. *Harlem: Negro Metropolis.* New York: Dutton, 1940.

———. *Harlem Shadows: The Poems of Claude McKay.* Intro. Max Eastman. New York: Harcourt, Brace, 1922.

———. *Home to Harlem.* 1928. Boston: Northeastern University Press, 1987.

———. "If We Must Die." *The Liberator* 2 (July 1919): 21. Rpt. in *Harlem Shadows* 53.

———. "In Bondage." *Harlem Shadows* 28.

———. Letter to Nancy Cunard. 18 September 1932. Nancy Cunard Papers. Harry Ransom Humanities Research Center, University of Texas at Austin.

———. Letter to Max Eastman. 3 April 1923. *The Passion* 82–87.

———. Letter to Max Eastman. 19 December 1934. *The Passion* 212–14.

———. *A Long Way from Home.* 1937. New York: Arno–New York Times, 1969.

———. *The Negroes in America.* 1923. Trans. Robert J. Winter. Ed. Alan L. McLeod. Port Washington, NY: Kennikat, 1979.

———. *The Passion of Claude McKay: Selected Poetry and Prose, 1912–1948*. Ed. Wayne F. Cooper. New York: Schocken, 1973.

———. "Petrograd: May Day, 1923." *The Liberator* 6 (August 1923): 15.

———. "Report on the Negro Question." *International Press Correspondence* (English ed.) 5 January 1923: 16–17.

———. Rev. of *My Trip Abroad*, by Charlie Chaplin. *The Liberator* April 1922: 28–29.

———. "Soviet Russia and the Negro." *The Passion of Claude McKay* 95–106.

———. "The White City." *Harlem Shadows* 23.

———. "The White House." *The Liberator* May 1922: 16.

Meier, August, and Elliott Rudwick. "Attitudes of Negro Leaders Toward the American Labor Movement from the Civil War to World War I." *The Negro and the American Labor Movement*. Ed. Julius Jacobson. Garden City, NY: Doubleday, 1968. 27–48.

———. *Black History and the Historical Profession, 1915–1980*. Urbana: University of Illinois Press, 1986.

"Men of Our Times." *The Crusader* 1.7 (March 1919): 20.

Michaels, Walter Benn. *Our America: Nativism, Modernism, and Pluralism*. Durham: Duke University Press, 1995.

Miller, James A. "African-American Writing of the 1930s: A Prologue." *Radical Representations: Rereading 1930s Culture*. Ed. Bill Mullen and Sherry Linkon. 78–90.

———. "Communism." *The Oxford Companion to African American Literature*. Ed. William L. Andrews, Frances Smith Foster, and Trudier Harris. New York: Oxford University Press, 1997. 165–67.

———. "Materials." *Approaches to Teaching Wright's* Native Son 1–8.

—, ed. *Approaches to Teaching Wright's* Native Son. New York: Modern Language Association, 1997.

Moore, David Chioni. "Local Color, Global 'Color': Langston Hughes, the Black Atlantic, and Soviet Central Asia, 1932." *Research in African Literatures* 27.4 (winter 1996): 49–70.

Morrison, Toni. *Playing in the Dark: Whiteness and the Literary Imagination*. Cambridge: Harvard University Press, 1992.

Mullen, Bill. *Popular Fronts: Chicago and African-American Cultural Politics, 1935–46*. Urbana: University of Illinois Press, 1999.

Mullen, Bill, and Sherry Linkon, ed. *Radical Representations: Rereading 1930s Culture*. Urbana: University of Illinois Press, 1996.

Mumford, Kevin J. *Interzones: Black/White Sex Districts in Chicago and New York in the Early Twentieth Century*. New York: Columbia University Press, 1997.

Munck, Ronaldo. *The Difficult Dialogue: Marxism and Nationalism*. Atlantic Highlands, NJ: Zed, 1986.

Murray, Hugh T., Jr. "Changing America and the Changing Image of Scottsboro." *Phylon* 38.1 (March 1977): 82–92.

Naison, Mark. *Communists in Harlem During the Depression*. 1983. Rpt. New York: Grove, 1984.

"The Negro's Place Is With Labor." *The Crusader* 1.10 (June 1919): 7.

Nekola, Charlotte, and Paula Rabinowitz, eds. *Writing Red: An Anthology of American Women Writers, 1930–1940.* New York: Feminist Press, 1987.

Nelson, Cary. *Repression and Recovery: Modern American Poetry and the Politics of Cultural Memory.* Madison: University of Wisconsin Press, 1989.

Newitz, Annalee, and Matthew Wray. "What Is 'White Trash'?: Stereotypes and Economic Conditions of Poor Whites in the United States." *Whiteness: A Critical Reader.* Ed. Mike Hill. New York: New York University Press, 1997. 168–84.

North, Michael. *The Dialect of Modernism: Race, Language, and Twentieth-Century Literature.* New York: Oxford University Press, 1994.

"The Old Negro Goes: Let Him Go in Peace." *The Crusader* 2.2 (October 1919): 9–10.

O'Neill, Eugene. "To Michael Gold." 2 July 1926. Letter 187 of *The Selected Letters of Eugene O'Neill.* Ed. Travis Bogard and Jackson R. Bryer. New Haven: Yale University Press, 1988. 206.

Oppenheimer, Paul. *The Birth of the Modern Mind: Self, Consciousness, and the Invention of the Sonnet.* New York: Oxford University Press, 1989.

"Organized Labor and Negro Workers." *The Messenger* 2.3 (March 1920): 6.

Parker, George Wells. *The Children of the Sun.* New York: Hamitic League, 1918.

Pierpont, Claudia Roth. "A Society of One: Zora Neale Hurston, American Contrarian." *The New Yorker* 17 February 1997: 80–91.

Rabinowitz, Paula. *Labor and Desire: Women's Revolutionary Fiction in Depression America.* Chapel Hill: University of North Carolina Press, 1991.

"Race Catechism." *The Crusader* 1.1 (September 1918): 11.

"Rally to the Cause." *The Crusader* 2.2 (October 1919): 11.

Rampersad, Arnold. *The Life of Langston Hughes.* Vol. 1. *1902–1941: I, Too, Sing America.* New York: Oxford University Press, 1986.

———. "Too Honest for His Own Time." *The Richard Wright Newsletter* 2.1 (fall 1992): 1–4.

Rawick, George P. *From Sundown to Sunup: The Making of the Black Community.* Westport, CT: Greenwood, 1972.

Razaf, Andy. "Communist." *The Negro Has to Laugh and Other Poems.* N.p.

———. "Dixie Songs." *The Crusader* 1.8 (April 1919): 7.

———. "Don't Tread on Me." *The Crusader* 1.8 (April 1919): 7.

———. "Dusky Stevedore." 1928. Music by J. C. Johnson. Triangle Music Publishing.

———. "A Harlem Rhymster." *The Negro Has to Laugh and Other Poems.* N.p.

———. "Kitchen Mechanic's Parade." 1930. Music by Jimmy Johnson. Edwin H. Morris and Company, a Division of MPL Communications. Hal Leonard Publishing.

———. "Labor Lines." *The Crusader* 6.1 (January–February 1922): 10.

———. "Machinery." 1935. Music by Paul Denniker. EMI Mills Music. Warner Bros. Publications.

———. *The Negro Has to Laugh and Other Poems.* MS 35, Box 2, Vol. 1. Andy Razaf Papers. Manuscripts, Archives, and Rare Books Division. Schomburg Center for Research in Black Culture, New York Public Library, New York.

———. "The New Negro." 1919. *The Negro Has to Laugh and Other Poems.* N.p.

———. "Ole Jim Crow" 1928. Music by J. C. Johnson. Al Piantadosi Publishing.

———. "A Parting Word." *The Crusader* 1.3 (November 1918): 4.

————. *Poems for a Mixed-Up World.* Intro. Langston Hughes. MS 35. Andy Razaf Papers. Manuscripts, Archives, and Rare Books Division. Schomburg Center for Research in Black Culture, New York Public Library, New York. 1–3.

————. "A Porter's Love Song to a Chambermaid." 1930. Music by Jimmy Johnson. Edwin H. Morris and Company, a Division of MPL Communications. Hal Leonard Publishing.

————. "Ranavalona—Dead." *The Negro Has to Laugh and Other Poems.* N.p.

————. "Sambo's Syncopated Russian Dance." 1930. Music by Jimmy Johnson. Edwin H. Morris and Company, a Division of MPL Communications. Hal Leonard Publishing.

————. " 'Shuffle Along': A Rhymed Review." *The Crusader* 6.1 (January–February 1922): 17.

————. "Socialism." *The Negro Has to Laugh and Other Poems.* N.p.

————. "(What Did I Do to Be So) Black and Blue." 1929. Music by Thomas Waller and Harry Brooks. EMI Mills Music, Inc. Warner Bros. Publications.

————. "Why I Am Proud." *The Crusader* 1.2 (October 1918): 11.

Record, Wilson. *The Negro and the Communist Party.* Chapel Hill: University of North Carolina Press, 1951.

Rideout, Walter B. *The Radical Novel in the United States, 1900–1954: Some Interrelations of Literature and Society.* 1956. New York: Columbia University Press, 1992.

Robinson, Cedric J. *Black Marxism: The Making of the Black Radical Tradition.* London: Zed, 1983.

Roediger, David R. *Towards the Abolition of Whiteness: Essays on Race, Politics, and Working Class History.* New York: Verso, 1994.

————. *The Wages of Whiteness: Race and the Making of the American Working Class.* New York: Verso, 1991.

—, ed. *Black on White: Black Writers on What It Means to Be White.* New York: Schocken, 1998.

Rogin, Michael. *Blackface, White Noise: Jewish Immigrants in the Hollywood Melting Pot.* Berkeley: University of California Press, 1996.

Rosenfelt, Deborah S. "From the Thirties: Tillie Olsen and the Radical Tradition." *Feminist Studies* 7 (fall 1981): 370–406.

————. "Getting Into the Game: American Women Writers and the Radical Tradition." *Women's Studies International Forum* 9.4 (1986): 363–72.

Rubin, Gayle. "The Traffic in Women: Notes Toward a Political Economy of Sex." *Toward an Anthropology of Women.* Ed. Rayna Reiter. New York: Monthly Review, 1975. 157–210.

"Russia and Self-Determination." *The Crusader* 5.4 (December 1921): 11–12.

"The Salvation of the Negro." *The Crusader* 4.2 (April 1921): 8–9.

Salzman, Jack, and Barry Wallenstein, eds. *Years of Protest: A Collection of American Writings of the 1930s.* New York: Pegasus, 1967.

San Juan, E. Jr. "Problems in the Marxist Project of Theorizing Race." *Rethinking Marxism* 2.2 (1989): 58–80.

Sartre, Jean-Paul. Preface. Frantz Fanon, *The Wretched of the Earth.* Trans. Constance Farrington. New York: Grove, 1963. 7–31.

Schomburg, Arthur A. "The Negro Digs Up His Past." *The New Negro.* Ed. Alain Locke. 231–37.

Schroeder, Aribert. "Claude McKay and the Discourse of International Communists in His Autobiography *A Long Way from Home*." *Revue AFRAM Review* 46 (December 1997): 2–18.

Sedgwick, Eve Kosofsky. *Between Men: English Literature and Male Homosocial Desire.* New York: Columbia University Press, 1985.

Short, Bobby. *Guess Who's in Town: Bobby Short Performs the Songs of Andy Razaf.* Atlantic Records, 1987.

Singer, Barry. *Black and Blue: The Life and Lyrics of Andy Razaf.* New York: Schirmer, 1992.

Smethurst, James Edward. *The New Red Negro: The Literary Left and African American Poetry.* New York: Oxford University Press, 1999.

Smith, Virginia Whatley. "*Native Son* as Depiction of a Carceral Society." *Approaches to Teaching Wright's* Native Son. Ed. James A. Miller. 95–101.

Sollors, Werner. "Anthropological and Sociological Tendencies in American Literature of the 1930s and 1940s: Richard Wright, Zora Neale Hurston, and American Culture." *Looking Inward, Looking Outward: From the 1930s through the 1940s.* Ed. Steve Ickringill. Amsterdam: VU University Press, 1990. 22–75.

———. *Beyond Ethnicity: Consent and Descent in American Culture.* New York: Oxford University Press, 1986.

———. *Neither Black Nor White Yet Both: Thematic Explorations of Interracial Literature.* New York: Oxford University Press, 1997.

Sowinska, Suzanne. *American Women Writers and the Radical Agenda, 1925–1940.* Ann Arbor: UMI, 1992. 9230438.

———. "Writing Across the Color Line: White Women Writers and the 'Negro Question' in the Gastonia Novels." *Radical Representations: Rereading 1930s Culture.* Ed. Bill Mullen and Sherry Linkon. 120–43.

Spickard, Paul R. *Mixed Blood: Intermarriage and Ethnic Identity in Twentieth-Century America.* Madison: University of Wisconsin Press, 1989.

Stack, Carol. *Call to Home: African Americans Reclaim the Rural South.* New York: Basic, 1996.

Stalin, Joseph. "Marxism and the National Question." 1913. *Marxism and the National Question: Selected Writings and Speeches.* New York: International Publishers, 1942. 7–68.

Stearns, Marshall W. *The Story of Jazz.* New York: Oxford University Press, 1956.

Stein, Judith. *The World of Marcus Garvey: Race and Class in Modern Society.* Baton Rouge: Louisiana State University Press, 1985.

Stokes, Rose Pastor. "The Communist International and the Negro." 1923. *American Communism and Black Americans: A Documentary History, 1919–1929.* Ed. Philip S. Foner and James S. Allen. 30–32.

"A Successful Business Man." *The Crusader* 1.12 (August 1919): 27–28.

Sundquist, Eric J. *Cultural Contexts for Ralph Ellison's* Invisible Man. Boston: St. Martin's, 1995.

———. "Red, White, Black and Blue." *Transition* 6.2 (summer 1996): 94–115.

"Theses on the Negro Question of the IVth World Congress." *American Communism and Black Americans: A Documentary History, 1919–1929.* Ed. Philip S. Foner and James S. Allen. 28–30.

Thompson, E. P. *The Making of the English Working Class.* New York: Vintage, 1966.

Thompson, Louise [Patterson]. "Southern Terror." *The Crisis* 41.11 (November 1934): 327–28.

———. "With Langston Hughes in the U.S.S.R." *Freedomways* 8.2 (spring 1968): 152–58.

Tillery, Tyrone. *Claude McKay: A Black Poet's Struggle for Identity.* Amherst: University of Massachusetts Press, 1992.

Tolson, Melvin B. "Claude McKay's Art." *Poetry* 83.4 (1954): 287–90.

"2 [Two] Basket Ball Games and Dance." *The Liberator* March 1922: 3.

United States. Federal Bureau of Investigation. Claude McKay file. Assorted documents dated December 16, 1921, to May 31, 1940. 61–3497.

Vincent, Ted. *Keep Cool: The Black Activists Who Built the Jazz Age.* East Haven, CT: Pluto, 1995.

Wald, Alan M. *Writing from the Left: New Essays on Radical Culture and Politics.* New York: Verso, 1994.

Walker, Alice. "Zora Neale Hurston—A Cautionary Tale and a Partisan View." Foreword. *Zora Neale Hurston: A Literary Biography.* Ed. Robert E. Hemenway. xi–xviii.

———. *Meridian.* New York: Harcourt Brace, 1976.

Walker, Clarence. "The American Negro as Historical Outsider, 1836–1935." *Deromanticizing Black History.* Knoxville: University of Tennessee Press, 1992. 87–107.

Wall, Cheryl A. *Women of the Harlem Renaissance.* Bloomington: Indiana University Press, 1995.

Waller, Fats, and His Rhythm, "A Porter's Love Song to a Chambermaid." By Andy Razaf and Jimmy Johnson. *Breakin' the Ice: The Early Years, Part One (1934–35).* Bluebird-RCA, 1995.

Waller/Razaf: American Songbook Series. Smithsonian Collection of Recordings–Sony, 1994.

Ward, Douglas Turner. *Happy Ending and Day of Absence.* New York: Dramatists Play Service, 1966.

Warren, Nagueyalti. "Black Girls and Native Sons: Female Images in Selected Works by Richard Wright." *Richard Wright.* Ed. C. James Trotman. New York: Garland, 1988. 59–77.

Washington, Mary Helen. Foreword. Zora Neale Hurston, *Their Eyes Were Watching God.* 1937. New York: Harper Perennial, 1990. vii–xiv.

———. "Zora Neale Hurston: A Woman Half in Shadow." Introduction. *I Love Myself When I Am Laughing . . . and Then Again When I Am Looking Mean and Impressive: A Zora Neale Hurston Reader.* Ed. Alice Walker. Old Westbury, NY: Feminist Press, 1979. 7–25.

Waskow, Arthur I. *From Race Riot to Sit-In: 1919 and the 1960s: A Study in the Connections Between Conflict and Violence.* Garden City, NY: Doubleday, 1967.

Watson, Steven. *The Harlem Renaissance: Hub of African-American Culture, 1920–1930.* New York: Pantheon, 1995.

"We 'Rile' the Crackerized Department of Justice." *The Crusader* 2.9 (May 1920): 5–6.

West, Cornel. "Marxist Theory and the Specificity of Afro-American Oppression." *Marxism and the Interpretation of Culture.* Ed. Cary Nelson and Lawrence Grossberg. Urbana: University of Illinois Press, 1988. 17–26.

Wicke, Jennifer. "Modernity Must Advertise: Aura, Desire, and Decolonization in Joyce." *James Joyce Quarterly* 30.4 (summer 1993): 593–613.

Wiegman, Robyn. *American Anatomies: Theorizing Race and Gender.* Durham: Duke University Press, 1995.

Wilkerson, Margaret B. "Excavating Our History: The Importance of Biographies of Women of Color." *Black American Literature Forum* 24.1 (spring 1990): 73–84.

Williams, George Washington. *History of the Negro Race in America from 1619 to 1880.* New York: Putnam's Sons, 1882.

Willis, Susan. *Specifying: Black Women Writing the American Experience.* Madison: University of Wisconsin Press, 1987.

Wirth, Louis. "Urbanism as a Way of Life." 1938. *Louis Wirth: On Cities and Social Life.* Ed. Albert J. Reiss, Jr. Chicago: University of Chicago Press, 1964. 60–83.

Wixson, Douglas. *Worker-Writer in America: Jack Conroy and the Tradition of Midwestern Literary Radicalism, 1898–1990.* Urbana: University of Illinois Press, 1994.

Wood, Charles W. "An Open Letter from Charles W. Wood." *The Liberator* June 1922: 9.

Woodson, Carter Godwin, and Charles H. Wesley. *The Negro in Our History.* 10th ed. Washington, DC: Associated Publishers, 1962.

Wordsworth, William. "Composed Upon Westminster Bridge, September 3, 1802." *Selected Poems and Prefaces.* Ed. Jack Stillinger. Boston: Houghton Mifflin, 1965. 170.

Wright, John S. "A Scintillating Send-Off for Falling Stars: The Black Renaissance Reconsidered." *A Stronger Soul Within a Finer Frame: Portraying African-Americans in the Black Renaissance.* Minneapolis: University Art Museum, University of Minnesota at Minneapolis, 1990. 13–45.

Wright, Mother Ada. "Save Their Lives." *Working Woman* 5 (April 1934): 10.

Wright, Richard. *Black Boy (American Hunger).* 1945, 1977. *Later Works* 1–365.

———. "Between Laughter and Tears." *New Masses* 5 (October 1937): 22, 25.

———. "Blueprint for Negro Writing." *New Challenge* fall 1937: 53–65.

———. "Bright and Morning Star." 1938. *Uncle Tom's Children* 407–41.

———. *Early Works.* New York: Library of America, 1991.

———. "Fire and Cloud." 1938. *Uncle Tom's Children* 355–406.

———. "How 'Bigger' Was Born." 1940. *Early Works* 851–81.

———. Introduction. St. Clair Drake and Horace R. Cayton, *Black Metropolis: A Study of Negro Life in a Northern City.* 1945. 2 vols. New York: Harcourt Brace, 1970. xvii–xxxiv.

———. *Later Works.* New York: Library of America, 1991.

———. *Lawd Today.* 1963. *Early Works* 1–219.

———. "Long Black Song." 1938. *Uncle Tom's Children* 329–54.

———. *Native Son.* 1940. *Early Works* 443–850.

———. *Uncle Tom's Children.* 1938, 1940. *Early Works* 221–441.

"Write For Us!" *The New Masses* 4 (July 1928): 2.

Wynter, Sylvia. "Sambos and Minstrels." *Social Text* I (winter 1979): 149–156.

Young, James O. *Black Writers of the Thirties.* Baton Rouge: Louisiana State University Press, 1973.

Zinoviev, Gregory. Letter to Claude McKay. 8 May 1923. The Records of the NAACP. Group 1, Series C, Box 90. Walter White Personal Correspondence. Manuscript Division, Library of Congress, Washington, DC.

Index